MORAVIAN
DAILY
TEXTS

*Bible Texts with Hymn Verses
and Prayers for Every Day
in the Year*

2015

Two Hundred Eighty-Fifth Year

The Moravian Church in North America
1021 Center St., Bethlehem, PA 18018
459 S. Church St., Winston-Salem, NC 27101
www.moravian.org

Moravian Daily Texts 2015

Verse translation by Erdmute Frank. Compilation and copy
editing by Renee Schoeller, with assistance from Kenn Nowack
and Mike Riess.

Cover photo: Detail of the stained glass Moravian Seal
at Fairview Moravian Church, Winston-Salem, N.C.
Photo by Mike Riess, IBOC.

Book design: Sandy Fay, Laughing Horse Graphics, Inc.,
Doylestown, Pa.

Printed by McNaughton & Gunn, Inc., Saline, Mich.

Printed in the United States of America

ISBN: 978-1-933571-55-3 large print edition

INTERPROVINCIAL BOARD
OF COMMUNICATION

MIX
Paper from
responsible sources
FSC® C011935

NEW EVERY MORNING

"The steadfast love of the Lord never ceases, his mercies never come to an end; they are new every morning."
Lamentations 3:22,23

The first printed edition of the *Daily Texts* (Losungen) was published in Herrnhut, Saxony, in 1731. The title page of that edition quoted the passage from Lamentations and promised a daily message from God that would be new every morning. It was an outgrowth of a spiritual renewal of the Moravian Church (Unitas Fratrum) that dated from August 13, 1727.

In 1722 refugees from Bohemia and Moravia began arriving at the estate of Count Nicholas Ludwig von Zinzendorf (1700-1760), where he gave them a welcome and land on which to establish the settlement of Herrnhut ("Watch of the Lord").

Each day the settlers came together for morning and evening devotions, consciously placing their lives in the context of God's Word. On May 3, 1728, during the evening service, Count Zinzendorf gave the congregation a "watchword" for the next day. It was to be a "Losung" (watchword) to accompany them through the whole day.

Thereafter one or more persons of the congregation went daily to each of the 32 houses in Herrnhut to bring them the watchword for the day, and engage the families in pastoral conversations about the text.

From this oral tradition, the *Daily Texts* soon became fixed in printed form. Zinzendorf compiled 365 watchwords for the year and the first edition of the Losungen was published for 1731.

Even in the first editions there appeared the characteristic coupling of a Bible verse and hymn stanza. Zinzendorf called the hymns "collects" and considered them to be the answer of the congregation to the Word of God. The *Daily Texts* would be a great deal poorer without the mixture of God's Word and our human response.

The watchword soon became accompanied by a "doctrinal" text. The idea of an additional text grew out of a number of collections of texts from the Bible that were put together by Zinzendorf. Such additional lists (some of them for children) were used for special study within the groups in the community, and they came to be referred to as doctrinal texts.

For the *Daily Texts,* as for the whole Moravian Church, Count Zinzendorf's death (May 9, 1760), was a turning point.

His co-workers sensed the uniqueness of Zinzendorf's watchwords, textbooks, and lessons and had them published at Barby-on-the-Elbe in a four-volume collection 1762.

From then on the watchwords and doctrinal texts are distinguished by the way they are selected each year. The watchwords are chosen from various verse collections and, since 1788, they have been drawn by lot from a collection of around 2,000 suitable Old Testament texts. The doctrinal texts are not chosen by lot but are selected. The difference between the watchwords and doctrinal texts was explained in 1801 as follows: "The watchword is either a promise, an encouragement, an admonition or word of comfort; the doctrinal text contains a point of revealed doctrine."

By 1812 it was established that all watchwords would be drawn by lot from a selection of Old Testament texts, and the doctrinal texts would be selected from the New Testament. No doctrinal text is used more than once in a given year. By the end of the nineteenth century, the custom was established to relate the two texts in theme or thought.

Into all the world

Another characteristic of the *Daily Texts* that was already apparent in the early years of its publication was its worldwide distribution. Missionaries who went as "messengers" from Herrnhut after 1732 had a *Daily Texts (Losungen)* in their luggage. They felt united with their home congregation through the daily contemplation of the same Scripture passages.

The *Daily Texts* of 1739 lists a multitude of places around the globe where messengers were witnessing for the Savior. The introduction read:

"The Good Word of the Lord, 1739, From all the Prophets for His congregations, and servants at Herrnhut, Herrnhaag, Herrendijk [Holland], Pilgerruh [Denmark], Ebersdof, Jena, Amsterdam, Rotterdam, London, Oxford, Berlin, Greenland, St. Croix, St. John and St. Thomas [Virgin Islands], Berbice [Guyana], Palestine, Surinam, Savannah in Georgia, among the Moors in Carolina, with the wild Indians in Irene [an island in the Savannah River in Georgia], in Pennsylvania, among the Hottentots [South Africa], in Guinea, in Latvia, Estonia and Lithuania, Russia, on the White Sea, in Lappland, Norway, in Switzerland, [Isle of] Man, Hittland [Scotland], in prison, on pilgrimage, to Ceylon, Ethiopia, Persia, on visitation to the missionaries among the heathen, and elsewhere on land and sea."

This distribution of the Moravians into every continent in the known world seems all the more amazing when you consider that the settlement at Herrnhut was only 17 years old, and the first missionaries had gone out only seven years earlier in 1732.

Present membership of the worldwide Moravian Church is more than 1 million in 21 provinces. The *Daily Texts* has a press run of more than 1 million copies in the German language alone. This far surpasses the 25,000 members of the Moravian Church in all of Europe. Other language editions bring the total circulation of this small devotional book to over 1.5 million copies. The *Daily Texts* is now published in more than 50 languages and dialects.

The physical form of the *Daily Texts* varies considerably from country to country. Some, like this North American edition, have a separate page for the verses, hymns, and prayers of each day. Others have several days' texts printed on one page, which makes a thin, pocket-size volume. Some are beautiful examples of the printing and bookbinding arts. Others are simply photocopied and stapled together.

These external nonessentials pale beside the fact that this little book is probably the most widely read devotional guide in the world, next to the Bible. It forms an invisible bond between Christians on all continents, transcending barriers of confession, race, language, and politics. In its quiet way it performs a truly ecumenical service for the whole of Christendom.

North American editions

The printing of the *Daily Texts* in North America dates back at least to 1767, when the Losungen was printed "at Bethlehem on the Forks of the Delaware by Johan Brandmuller." The printer's imprint bears the date of 1767 as well and may have been an extra printing for the German version done at Barby-on-the-Elbe in Germany, where most of the printing was done for the Moravian Church those days.

During the crucial days of the Revolution, the German-language edition was printed in Philadelphia by Heinrich Miller, who had worked for Benjamin Franklin when he first came to America. The daily text for July 4, 1776, was from Isaiah 55:5 —"Behold, you shall call nations that you know not, and nations that knew you not shall run to you" (RSV).

English versions were printed in London as early as 1746, and the title page bears the imprint of "James Hutton near the Golden Lion in Fetter Lane." Hutton was the well-known London printer associated with the Moravian Church who was a friend of John and Charles Wesley in the formative years of their ministry.

The 1850s were crucial years for the Moravian Church in North America as the congregations established in the United States broke away from direct control from the Moravian headquarters in Europe. Both German and English editions of the Daily Texts were regularly printed in Philadelphia or Bethlehem, Pennsylvania, and in a few years the custom was established to include the statistics of the provinces and districts of the Moravian Church in North America.

The biblical texts for each day are chosen in Herrnhut, Germany, and then sent around the world to those who prepare the different language editions. Since 1959 the edition published in the United States has included a prayer for each day. For this North American edition, the hymns are chosen or written, and the prayers are written by Moravian clergy and laypersons from the United States and Canada. Each month is prepared by a different individual or couple, of a variety of ages, so that the prayers reflect the great diversity of devotion in the Moravian Church.

DAILY TOPICS FOR PRAYER

On August 27, 1727, certain members of the Moravian Church in Herrnhut, Saxony, formed a remarkable prayer union known as the "Hourly Intercession." This provided that, for every hour of the day and night, one of the volunteer intercessors would, for one hour in private, bear on his or her heart and mind the interests and hopes of the Kingdom of God in the world. This wonderful intercession continued for over 100 years.

On August 27, 1872, a Moravian Prayer union was formed in England as a form of resuscitation of the Hourly Intercession, and today its members are found in all areas of the Moravian world. You are invited to join in this prayer covenant. The following prayer suggestions may be helpful:

Sunday: The Church At Worship. For her purity and peace, unity and power. For the congregation to which we belong or with which we worship. For the ministry of the word of God. For the winning of people into fellowship with Christ. For all church schools, youth ministries, and other church groups at work.

Monday: The Church At Work. For the church in its mission next door and in other lands. For new congregations and specialized ministries. For the workers and leaders in these endeavors. For the worker volunteers to carry out the mission of the church.

Tuesday: Home and School. For households. For the Christian education of the young, and that our children may be led to give themselves to Christ. For all schools and teachers. For young people enrolled in colleges and universities. For the training of ministers in theological seminaries.

Wednesday: For Those In Need. For all in special need, whether as aged, sick, poor, or homeless. For those in prison. For all victims of famine, oppression, aggression, and war.

Thursday: Our Nation and Our World. For those who govern and for those who are governed. For the guidance of God to all who are in authority. For unity of nations and all agencies for peace. For the whole human family and equal rights for all. For the guidance and blessing of God as humanity enters the future.

Friday: Our Own Church Fellowship. For the purity, zeal, and practice of the church as a witnessing fellowship of the love of God. That the church may be a light to the world wherever its congregations are found, and that it may be active in redeeming mission in these communities.

Saturday: The Witness of Christians. That all who confess the name of Christ may grow in the grace and knowledge of Jesus Christ as Lord and Savior.

"O thou King of kings and Lord of lords, who desirest that all people should dwell together in unity, let thy will be known and done among the nations; guide their feet into the way of peace. Remember us and all humanity in thy mercy. Deliver us from the sins which give rise to war and conflict, and strengthen within our hearts the will to establish righteousness and justice in the earth. Give unto us and to all who worship thee the sincere desire to live in peaceful and loving fellowship with all people. Fix our minds and hearts upon thine eternal purposes for your children on earth."

— A Prayer for Peace

THE *DAILY TEXTS* IN FAMILY WORSHIP

Almost from the very beginning the *Daily Texts* has been used as a guide for family worship as well as for private and personal devotions. The use of the *Daily Texts* in family worship will vary depending on the time available and the age of the children. One of the values of the *Daily Texts* is that it is adaptable to numerous patterns of use.

One pattern followed by many families is to begin the meal (usually breakfast or the evening meal) with the reading of the texts of the day and the accompanying hymn stanzas. After this, the family joins in the blessing or table grace. A suitable blessing may be chosen from among the following:

Come, Lord Jesus, our Guest to be,
and bless these gifts bestowed by thee.
Bless thy dear ones everywhere,
and keep them in thy loving care.

Be present at our table, Lord;
be here and everywhere adored;
from thine all-bounteous hand our food
may we receive with gratitude.

The worship of the family can then close with a prayer offered in the leader's own words or in those of the printed prayer offered in the *Daily Texts*. As a part of free prayer by the leader or in connection with the printed prayer, use can be made from day to day of the subjects of the Daily Topics for Prayer as given in the preceding pages.

HOW TO USE THE *DAILY TEXTS*

The strength of the *Daily Texts* lies in presenting the Scripture unhindered by illustration. The texts are left to stand alone and to speak to each reader in his or her life. This also allows the *Daily Texts* to be adaptable to different patterns of devotion and study.

Contents For Each Day

90   MARCH

(1) **Tuesday, March 31 — Psalm 41**
Esther 9:18–10:3; Romans 10:14–11:6

(2) **Woe to those who go to great depths to hide their plans from the Lord, who do their work in darkness and think, "Who sees us? Who will know?" Isaiah 29:15 (NIV)**

(3)
O, send your Spirit, Lord,   502
now unto me,
that he may touch my eyes
and make me see.
Show me the truth concealed
within your word,
and in your book revealed
I see my Lord.

(4) **Take no part in the unfruitful works of darkness, but instead expose them. Everything exposed by the light becomes visible. Ephesians 5:11,13**

(3)
As you with Satan did contend,   341
and did the vict'ry win,
O give us strength in you to fight,
in you to conquer sin.

(5) O Glorious Lord, free us from the blindness to your everlasting light shining before us, and never let us hide in darkness from the wondrous love and grace that you offer to us, your children. Amen.

1. **SCRIPTURE LESSONS:** At the top of each page for ongoing study. Not related to the printed texts. Monday through Saturday are part of a plan to read through the Psalms in one year and the rest of the Bible in two. Sundays and special days are the assigned lessons for that day of the church year from the Moravian Revised Common Lectionary, also common to many denominations.

2. **WATCHWORD FOR THE DAY:** From the Old Testament, the first printed text. It is to be a "watchword" to accompany you throughout the day. Usually a promise, encouragement, admonition, or comfort.

3. **HYMN VERSES:** Broken down by meter and usually related to the watchword or theme for the day. It is a devotional response or commentary on the text. Can be used for prayers.

4. **DOCTRINAL TEXT:** From the New Testament. Usually contains some point of Christian doctrine to expand on the watchword.

5. **PRAYER:** A response to God of praise, confession, thanksgiving, or intercession in light of the texts and hymn verses.

• Every Sunday and some church holidays, the *Daily Texts* page will include the **WATCHWORD FOR THE WEEK/ HOLIDAY.** Like the daily watchword, the weekly/holiday text is to accompany the reader throughout the week or holiday and is related to the events of the church year. These differ every year based upon the lectionary cycle.

Devotions

The printed texts, hymn verses, and prayers are the heart of the devotional guide. Their purpose is to help the reader get more closely in touch with God and to meditate upon the Word of God. When reading the texts, hymns and prayers, feel the encouragement found in them. Hear any word or correction for your life; ponder the great message of faith; meditate upon the hymn verses and prayers; feel God's presence surrounding you in faith; and in silence, hear God's word speaking to you.

These texts can also be the center of a daily spiritual diary where you keep a journal of your daily meditations and their meaning in your life.

ACKNOWLEDGMENTS

Bible texts in this publication are quoted from the *New Revised Standard Version Bible*, © 1989 by the Division of Christian Education of the National Council of the Churches of Christ in the United States of America, and are used by permission. Verses marked NIV are taken from *The Holy Bible New International Version®*, NIV®, © 1973, 1978, 1984, 2011 by Biblica, Inc.® Used by permission. All rights reserved worldwide. Verses marked NASB are taken from the *New American Standard Bible®*, © 1960, 1962, 1963, 1968, 1971, 1972, 1973, 1975, 1977, 1995 by The Lockman Foundation. Used by permission. Verses marked ESV are taken from *The Holy Bible, English Standard Version,* © 2001 by Crossway. Verses marked NKJV are taken from the *New King James Version®* © 1982 by Thomas Nelson, Inc. Used by permission. All rights reserved. Verses marked GNT are taken from the *Good News Translation,* ©1992 by the American Bible Society.

Sunday readings are taken from the *Revised Common Lectionary,* © 1992 by the Consultation on Common Texts (CCT).

Unless otherwise noted, hymn stanzas found in the *Daily Texts* are taken from the *Moravian Book of Worship,* 1995. The number found to the right of each stanza designates the source of the stanza in that hymnal. If the number is preceded by a p the hymn used is from one of the liturgies and the p designates the page number. The letter b after a number denotes the Hymnal and Liturgies of the Moravian Church Unitas Fratrum, 1920. The letter r after a number denotes the Hymnal of the Moravian Church, 1969. The letter s after a number denotes a hymn or song from *Sing to the Lord A New Song, A New Moravian Songbook,* 2013. When hymns are copyrighted, information is given at the bottom of the page; we gratefully acknowledge permission to use copyrighted material.

Hymn stanzas are broken down by meter except when space would not allow.

The Scripture readings for Monday through Saturday are part of a plan to read through the Old and New Testaments in two years and the Psalms in one year.

Thursday, January 1 — Psalm 1
1 Chronicles 3; Acts 9:1–9

The Lord your God has been with you; you have lacked nothing. Deuteronomy 2:7

Jesus' name, Jesus' name,   324
source of life and happiness!
In this name true consolation
mourning sinners may possess;
here is found complete salvation.
Blessed Jesus, we your name will praise
all our days, all our days.

Be thankful. Colossians 3:15

Songs of thankfulness and praise,   313
Jesus, Lord, to you we raise,
manifested by the star
to the sages from afar;
branch of royal David's stem
in your birth at Bethlehem;
anthems be to you addressed,
God in flesh made manifest.

Lord, we give you thanks for another year's end and
for a new year's beginning. You continue to bless
us with exactly what we need, reminding us to stay
grateful. Thank you, gracious Lord. Amen.

Friday, January 2 — Psalm 2
1 Chronicles 4:1–23; Acts 9:10–22

O Lord our God—we set our hope on you. Jeremiah 14:22

> Jesus is my joy,   p197
> therefore blessed am I;
> O, his mercy is unbounded,
> all my hope on him is grounded;
> Jesus is my joy,
> therefore blessed am I.

Through Jesus Christ we have gained access by faith into this grace in which we now stand. And we rejoice in the hope of the glory of God. Romans 5:2 (NIV)

> We thank you, then, O God of heav'n,   700
> that you to us this faith have giv'n
> in Jesus Christ your Son, who is
> our only fount and source of bliss.

Heavenly Father, we put our hope and trust in you and we are thankful for all that you do. Although we are undeserving, you give us grace; help us to share that grace with those we meet today and forever. In Jesus' name. Amen.

Saturday, January 3 — Psalm 3
1 Chronicles 4:24–43; Acts 9:23–35

Turn my heart to your decrees, and not to selfish gain. Psalm 119:36

> Lord Jesus, think on me   764
> and purge away my sin;
> from selfish passions set me free
> and make me pure within.

One's life does not consist in the abundance of possessions. Luke 12:15

> Come, O Christ, and reign among us,   648
> King of love and Prince of peace;
> hush the storm of strife and passion,
> bid its cruel discords cease.
> By your patient years of toiling,
> by your silent hours of pain,
> quench our fevered thirst of pleasure;
> stem our selfish greed of gain.

Lord, we are thankful for your patience with us.
Renew us today for your service and remind us that
our possessions are not as important as you are.
We lift up our belongings, time, and talents to you,
Lord. Amen.

Second Sunday after Christmas

Watchword for the Week — In him we have redemption through his blood, the forgiveness of our trespasses, according to the riches of his grace. Ephesians 1:7

Sunday, January 4 — Jeremiah 31:7–14; Psalm 147:12–20
Ephesians 1:3–14; John 1:(1–9),10–18

I will punish you according to the fruit of your doings, says the Lord. Jeremiah 21:14

Now we bring ourselves to you;   741
cleanse us, Lord, we humbly pray;
undeserving though we be,
draw us closer ev'ry day.
Lord, our refuge, hope, and strength!
Keep, O keep us safe from harm,
shield us through our earthly life
by your everlasting arm.

Forgive us our debts, as we forgive our debtors. Matthew 6:12 (NKJV)

Pardon, Lord, and are there those   779
who my debtors are, or foes?
I, who by forgiveness live,
here their trespasses forgive.

Heavenly Father, you who are unseen are able to see all. Forgive us for forgetting that you know what we need before we can even ask. Keep our hearts open to sharing your forgiveness with the world. Thank you, Lord. Amen.

Monday, January 5 — Psalm 4
1 Chronicles 5:1–22; Acts 9:36–10:8

I give thanks to your name for your steadfast love and your faithfulness; for you have exalted your name and your word above everything. Psalm 138:2

> Hail, First and Last, the great I Am,   703
> in whom we live and move;
> increase our little spark of faith,
> and fill our hearts with love.

Our Father in heaven, hallowed be your name. Matthew 6:9

> Come now, O Lord, and teach us how to pray.   742
> Teach us to ask ourselves from day to day
> if we are yours and yours alone will be
> through earthly days and through eternity.

Precious Lord, encourage us to love and serve you as we ought, not to serve ourselves but those around us. Continue to show us your faithfulness so we, your church, can do your will. Thank you, Lord. Amen.

Epiphany of the Lord

Watchword for the Epiphany — Arise, shine; for your light has come, and the glory of the Lord has risen upon you. Isaiah 60:1

Epiphany of the Lord — Isaiah 60:1–6; Psalm 72:1–7,10–14
Ephesians 3:1–12; Matthew 2:1–12

Tuesday, January 6 — Psalm 5
1 Chronicles 5:23–6:30; Acts 10:9–23a

Out of my distress I called on the Lord; the Lord answered me and set me in a broad place. Psalm 118:5

Good news! Our Christ has come!　　　　　　　630*
Good news to all the world.
He comes to preach good news,
new life forevermore.
God's Spirit dwells in all who care,
in all who share 'til want is gone.

You are God's own people in order that you may proclaim the mighty acts of him who called you out of darkness into his marvelous light. 1 Peter 2:9

"Comfort, comfort now my people;　　　　　　　264
tell of peace!" So says our God.
Comfort those who sit in darkness
bowed beneath oppression's load.
To God's people now proclaim
that God's pardon waits for them!
Tell them that their war is over;
God will reign in peace forever!

Light of the world, thank you for responding to us in our time of need. We declare ourselves to your holy way. Help us respond to others and proclaim your amazing grace. Amen.

---

*　© 1988 by Sharon M. Benson. Used by permission.

Wednesday, January 7 — Psalm 6
1 Chronicles 6:31–81; Acts 10:23b–33

O Lord, open my lips, that my mouth may declare your praise. Psalm 51:15 (NASB)

Stand up, and bless the Lord,   531
you people of his choice!
Stand up and bless the Lord your God,
with heart and soul and voice.

Whoever speaks must do so as one speaking the very words of God; whoever serves must do so with the strength that God supplies, so that God may be glorified in all things through Jesus Christ. 1 Peter 4:11

Jesus calls us; by your mercies,   600
Savior, may we hear your call,
give our hearts to your obedience,
serve and love you best of all.

Lord, may the words on our lips declare your praise
and may the thoughts of our minds be pleasing
to you. Give us the strength we need to be your
disciples. God, we give you the glory. Amen.

Thursday, January 8 — Psalm 7:1–9
1 Chronicles 7; Acts 10:34–43

Stand up and tell them everything that I command you. Jeremiah 1:17

> O tell of his might, O sing of his grace,   566
> whose robe is the light, whose canopy space.
> His chariots of wrath the deep thunderclouds form,
> and dark is his path on the wings of the storm.

We do not proclaim ourselves; we proclaim Jesus Christ as Lord. 2 Corinthians 4:5

> You're our strength and motivation,   622*
> Christ, you send us out to serve.
> We hold back, but your salvation
> gives us energy and nerve.
> You still fill us with your Spirit;
> lift us up on eagle's wings.
> Give your call, we gladly hear it;
> in your work our spirit sings.

Gracious God, give us the strength, energy, and words we need to stand up to this world today. You are our motivation and we are prepared to answer your call. You are our only Lord and Savior. Amen.

Friday, January 9 — Psalm 7:10–17
1 Chronicles 8; Acts 10:44–11:10

Return, O faithless children, I will heal your faithlessness. "Here we come to you; for you are the Lord our God." Jeremiah 3:22

Save us from weak resignation   751
to the evils we deplore;
let the gift of your salvation
be our glory evermore.
Grant us wisdom, grant us courage
serving you whom we adore,
serving you whom we adore.

Draw near to God, and he will draw near to you. Cleanse your hands, you sinners, and purify your hearts, you double-minded. James 4:8

You are the truth; your word alone   661
true wisdom can impart;
you only can inform the mind
and purify the heart.

Lord, our God, your graciousness is constant through the ups and downs of life. You are always there to forgive us and accept us as we are. Forgive us and cleanse us, Lord, we pray. Amen.

Saturday, January 10 — Psalm 8
1 Chronicles 9:1–34; Acts 11:11–24

Hear, O Israel: The Lord is our God, the Lord alone. Deuteronomy 6:4

> God reveals his presence;   554
> let us now adore him
> and with awe appear before him.
> God is in his temple;
> all in us keep silence
> and before him bow with reverence.
> Him alone God we own;
> he's our Lord and Savior.
> Praise his name forever.

There is one God; there is also one mediator between God and humankind, Christ Jesus, himself human, who gave himself a ransom for all. 1 Timothy 2:5–6

> Slain to redeem us by his blood,   469
> to cleanse from ev'ry sinful stain,
> and make us kings and priests to God;
> "Worthy the Lamb, for he was slain!"

Almighty God, we thank you for your son, Jesus Christ, and the ransom he made for our souls. Teach us to be living sacrifices and to obey your call. Worthy is the Lamb who was slain! Amen.

First Sunday after the Epiphany

Watchword for the Week — Ascribe to the Lord the glory of his name; worship the Lord in holy splendor. Psalm 29:2

Sunday, January 11 — Genesis 1:1–15; Psalm 29
Acts 19:1–7; Mark 1:4–11

Help, O Lord, for there is no longer anyone who is godly; the faithful have disappeared from humankind. Psalm 12:1

My Lord, what you did suffer   345
was all for sinners' gain;
mine, mine was the transgression,
but yours the deadly pain.
So here I kneel, my Savior,
for I deserve your place;
look on me with your favor
and save me by your grace.

Jesus asked the twelve, "Do you also wish to go away?" Simon Peter answered him, "Lord, to whom can we go? You have the words of eternal life." John 6:67–68

O Jesus, I have promised   603
to serve you to the end;
be now and ever near me,
my master and my friend.
I shall not fear the battle
if you are by my side,
nor wander from the pathway
if you will be my guide.

Master and Friend, we promise never to turn our backs on you. We believe you are everything we need. Keep us loyal to you in everything we do. Amen.

Monday, January 12 — Psalm 9:1–10
1 Chronicles 9:35–11:3; Acts 11:25–12:5

Noah found favor in the sight of the Lord. Genesis 6:8

> The task your wisdom has assigned   638
> here let me cheerfully fulfill,
> in all my work your presence find
> and prove your good and perfect will.

We believe that we will be saved through the grace of the Lord Jesus. Acts 15:11

> For God, in grace and tenderness,   519
> regarded us in our distress;
> yea, to our aid himself he came;
> let all adore God's holy name.

Almighty God, help us to obey like Noah did. Let us not turn to our selfish ways and run ahead without your guidance. Your grace and guidance is all we need! Amen.

Tuesday, January 13 — Psalm 9:11–20
1 Chronicles 11:4–47; Acts 12:6–19

Who can hide in secret places so that I cannot see them? says the Lord. Do I not fill heaven and earth? says the Lord. Jeremiah 23:24

Move in our midst, O Spirit of God.   489
Go with us down from your holy hill.
Walk with us through the storm and the calm.
Spirit of God, now go with us still.

Live as children of light. Ephesians 5:8

We've a story to tell to the nations,   621
that shall turn their hearts to the right,
a story of truth and mercy,
a story of peace and light,
a story of peace and light.
For the darkness shall turn to dawning,
and the dawning to noon-day bright;
and Christ's great kingdom shall come on earth,
the kingdom of love and light.

Lord, we know we cannot hide from you. You are everywhere and we are grateful for that. Continue to watch over us and make us true lights to those around us. Our prayer is to spread your light and presence everywhere. Amen.

Wednesday, January 14 — Psalm 10:1–11
1 Chronicles 12; Acts 12:20–13:7

Speak, Lord, for your servant is listening.
1 Samuel 3:9

> In mercy, Lord, this grace bestow,   643
> that in your service we may do
> with gladness and a willing mind
> whatever is for us assigned.

A certain woman named Lydia, a worshiper of God, was listening to us; she was from the city of Thyatira and a dealer in purple cloth. The Lord opened her heart to listen eagerly to what was said by Paul. Acts 16:14

> Consecrate me now to thy service, Lord,   607
> by the pow'r of grace divine;
> let my soul look up with a steadfast hope
> and my will be lost in thine.
> Draw me nearer, nearer, blessed Lord,
> to the cross where thou hast died;
> draw me nearer, nearer, nearer, blessed Lord,
> to thy precious, bleeding side.

Precious Lord, forgive us for not listening to your voice when you call us to be your servants. We come to you now with willing hearts and minds! Draw us closer to those in need so we can do your will. Amen.

Thursday, January 15 — Psalm 10:12–18
1 Chronicles 13:1–14:7; Acts 13:8–20a

The days are surely coming, says the Lord, when the city shall be rebuilt for the Lord. Jeremiah 31:38

My hope is built on nothing less   771
than Jesus' blood and righteousness;
no merit of my own I claim
but wholly lean on Jesus' name.
On Christ the solid rock, I stand;
all other ground is sinking sand,
all other ground is sinking sand.

You are the light of the world. A city built on a hill cannot be hid. Matthew 5:14

O Christians, haste, your mission high fulfilling, 618
to tell to all the world that God is light,
that he who made all nations is not willing
one life should perish, lost in shades of night.
Publish glad tidings, tidings of peace,
tidings of Jesus, redemption, and release.

Light of the world, you have asked us to shine our
light on our nations and in the world. Give us the
strength and courage we need to fulfill your call.
You are our salvation, Christ our solid Rock. Amen.

Friday, January 16 — Psalm 11
1 Chronicles 14:8–15:29; Acts 13:20b–33

It was not because you were more numerous than any other people that the Lord set his heart on you and chose you—for you were the fewest of all peoples. It was because the Lord loved you. Deuteronomy 7:7-8

O seed of Israel's chosen race,   403
now ransomed from the fall,
hail him who saves you by his grace,
and crown him lord of all!
Hail him who saves you by his grace,
and crown him Lord of all!

It does not, therefore, depend on human desire or effort, but on God's mercy. Romans 9:16 (NIV)

Because the Lord our God is good,   539
his mercy is forever sure.
His truth at all times firmly stood,
and shall from age to age endure.

Heavenly Father, thank you for choosing us and saving us by your grace. What a privilege to be your chosen people! Forgive us for following our own desires and not your great will. We know that your truth is our solid foundation. Amen.

Saturday, January 17 — Psalm 12
1 Chronicles 16:1–36; Acts 13:34–47

Lift up your heads, O gates! And be lifted up, O ancient doors! that the King of glory may come in. Psalm 24:7

Within the Father's house   318
the Son has found his home,
and to his temple suddenly
the Lord of life has come.

Be like those who are waiting for their master to return from the wedding banquet, so that they may open the door for him as soon as he comes and knocks. Luke 12:36

So may I prove true,   608
devoted to you,
and cheerfully stand,
prepared to comply
with your ev'ry command.

Glorious King, we are prepared to be your faithful servants, accepting of your plan. Keep our minds set on the path you placed before us so we can be good examples. Let our actions teach others about your amazing call. Thank you, Lord. Amen.

Second Sunday after the Epiphany

Watchword for the Week — How weighty to me are your thoughts, O God! How vast is the sum of them! Psalm 139:17

Sunday, January 18 — 1 Samuel 3:1–10,(11–20); Psalm 139:1–6,13–18 1 Corinthians 6:12–20; John 1:43–51

Naked I came from my mother's womb, and naked I will depart. Job 1:21 (NIV)

Take full possession of my heart;   721
to me your lowly mind impart;
break nature's bonds, and let me see,
he whom you free indeed is free.

We brought nothing into this world, and it is certain we can carry nothing out. And having food and clothing, with these we shall be content. 1 Timothy 6:7–8 (NKJV)

We give you but your own   657
in any gifts we bring;
all that we have is yours alone,
a trust from you, our King.

Lord, we worship you through the highs and lows! When everything is a mess, we question you. Remind us today that even in those times you have a plan. You will see us through. We give ourselves to you, O Lord! Amen.

Monday, January 19 — Psalm 13
1 Chronicles 16:37–17:27; Acts 13:48–14:7

Be gracious to me, O Lord, for I am languishing; O Lord, heal me, for my soul is struck with terror. Psalm 6:2–3

How good the name of Jesus sounds   487
to all believing ears!
It soothes our sorrows, heals our wounds,
and drives away our fears.
It makes the wounded spirit whole,
and calms the troubled mind;
his manna for each hungry soul,
the lost and weary find.

Paul wrote: The Lord said to me, "My grace is sufficient for you, for my power is made perfect in weakness." 2 Corinthians 12:9 (NIV)

When the Lord appears,   594
this my spirit cheers;
when, his love to me revealing
he, the Sun of grace, with healing
in his beams appears,
this my spirit cheers.

Healing Savior, you have the power we need to stay
strong in our times of weakness! Your undeserved
grace is all we need. Help us rid our lives of
pointless treasures so we can clearly see you, our
true Savior. Amen.

Tuesday, January 20 — Psalm 14
1 Chronicles 18; Acts 14:8–20

The Lord spoke and it came to be; he commanded, and it stood firm. Psalm 33:9

> For the beauty of the earth,   538
> for the glory of the skies,
> for the love which from our birth
> over and around us lies,
> Lord of all, to you we raise
> this our hymn of grateful praise.

The centurion answered Jesus, "Only speak the word, and my servant will be healed." Matthew 8:8

> Just as I am; thou wilt receive,   762
> wilt welcome, pardon, cleanse, relieve;
> because thy promise I believe,
> O Lamb of God, I come, I come!

Creator of everything, we give you thanks. We are blessed by your creation and your healing every day. Thank you for believing in us, broken though we are. Remind us that we are still another part of your wonderful creation. Amen.

Wednesday, January 21 — Psalm 15
1 Chronicles 19,20; Acts 14:21–15:5

In your hand are power and might, so that no one is able to withstand you. 2 Chronicles 20:6

Sing praise to God who reigns above,   537
the God of all creation,
the God of pow'r, the God of love,
the God of our salvation.
My soul with comfort rich he fills,
and ev'ry grief he gently stills:
to God all praise and glory!

Christ says, "All authority in heaven and on earth has been given to me. Go therefore and make disciples of all nations." Matthew 28:18–19

In loving service may our lives be spent,   587
in other's gladness finding sweet content,
striving to show God's fellowship to all.
To show God's loving work—the servant's call.
In loving service may our lives be spent.

Maker of heaven and earth, your power and love is remarkable! We know there are people who still need to hear your word. Inspire us to make disciples for you. Let us share that our Lamb has conquered, and invite others to come and follow him! Amen.

Thursday, January 22 — Psalm 16:1–6
1 Chronicles 21:1–26; Acts 15:6–18

The Lord your God is bringing you into a good land, a land with flowing streams, with springs and underground waters welling up in valleys and hills. Deuteronomy 8:7

> This is my Father's world: 456
> he shines in all that's fair;
> in rustling grass I hear him pass—
> he speaks to me ev'rywhere.
> This is my Father's world:
> why should my heart be sad?
> The Lord is King, let heaven ring!
> God reigns; let earth be glad.

John, the seer, wrote: Then the angel showed me the river of the water of life, bright as crystal, flowing from the throne of God and of the Lamb through the middle of the street of the city. On either side of the river is the tree of life with its twelve kinds of fruit, producing its fruit each month; and the leaves of the tree are for the healing of the nations. Revelation 22:1–2

> This is my Father's world,   456
> and to my list'ning ears
> all nature sings and round me rings
> the music of the spheres.
> This is my Father's world;
> I rest me in the thought
> of rocks and trees, of skies and seas—
> his hand the wonders wrought.

Gracious Ruler, we cannot thank you enough for your leading and guiding. You always show us the way! We know the promises you have in store for us; we pray that this world would see those promises as well, through us. Amen.

Friday, January 23 — Psalm 16:7–11
1 Chronicles 21:27–22:19; Acts 15:19–31

Do not be exceedingly angry, O Lord, and do not remember iniquity forever. Now consider we are all your people. Isaiah 64:9

> 'Twas grace that taught my heart to fear   783
> and grace my fears relieved;
> how precious did that grace appear
> the hour I first believed.

Christ came and proclaimed peace to you who were far off and peace to those who were near. Ephesians 2:17

> People and realms of ev'ry tongue   404
> dwell on his love with sweetest song,
> and infant voices shall proclaim
> their early blessings on his name.

Merciful God, we are grateful for your forgiveness! Thank you for showing us your grace and promise for a bright future. We are all united by your Spirit; help us to reach out to those near and far. Amen.

Saturday, January 24 — Psalm 17:1–7
1 Chronicles 23; Acts 15:32–16:3

I will sing to the Lord, for he has triumphed gloriously. Exodus 15:1

> Come now, almighty King,   555
> help us your name to sing,
> help us to praise.
> Father all glorious,
> ever victorious,
> come and reign over us,
> Ancient of Days.

If the Son makes you free, you will be free indeed. John 8:36

> Green pastures are before me   732
> which yet I have not seen;
> bright skies will soon be o'er me
> where darkest clouds have been.
> My hope I cannot measure,
> my path to life is free,
> my Savior has my treasure,
> and he will walk with me.

Victorious Lord, you continue to protect and reign over us. Thank you for sending your Son to set us free from all sin and oppression. Let us never forget that you are always beside us. Amen.

Third Sunday after the Epiphany

Watchword for the Week — Trust in him at all times; pour out your heart before him; God is a refuge for us. Psalm 62:8

Sunday, January 25 — Jonah 3:1–5,10; Psalm 62:5–12
1 Corinthians 7:29–31; Mark 1:14–20

Take care, or you will be seduced into turning away, serving other gods and worshiping them. Deuteronomy 11:16

Be thou my vision, O Lord of my heart;   719
naught be all else to me save that thou art—
thou my best thought, by day or by night,
waking or sleeping, thy presence my light.

Do not store up for yourselves treasures on earth, where moth and rust consume and where thieves break in and steal; but store up for yourselves treasures in heaven, where neither moth nor rust consumes and where thieves do not break in and steal. For where your treasure is, there your heart will be also. Matthew 6:19–21

Grant by guidance from above   586
that obedience, faith, and love
show our hearts to you are giv'n,
that our treasure is in heav'n.

Lord, you are our strength when we feel tempted by the world around us. Keep us accountable to ourselves and to those you put in our lives. We know we don't need worldly possessions and that you, our True Treasure, await us in heaven! Amen.

Monday, January 26 — Psalm 17:8–15
1 Chronicles 24; Acts 16:4–15

Lord, who would not fear you, O King of the nations? For that is your due. Jeremiah 10:7

> Let the earth now praise the Lord,   261
> who has truly kept his word
> and at last to us did send
> Christ, the sinner's help and friend.

We must obey God rather than human beings! Acts 5:29 (NIV)

> His righteous government and power   320
> shall over all extend;
> on judgment and on justice based,
> his reign shall have no end.

King of all nations we offer our praises to you! We apologize for idolizing people and things other than you. May we turn back toward you and always faithfully follow you. Amen.

Tuesday, January 27 — Psalm 18:1–6
1 Chronicles 25; Acts 16:16–29

Bring me out of prison, so that I may give thanks to your name. Psalm 142:7

Long my imprisoned spirit lay   773
fast bound in sin and nature's night.
Your sunrise turned that night to day;
I woke—the dungeon flamed with light!
My chains fell off, your voice I knew;
was freed, I rose, and followed you.
My chains fell off, your voice I knew;
was freed, I rose, and followed you.

Where the Spirit of the Lord is, there is freedom. 2 Corinthians 3:17

Praise to the Spirit, comforter of Israel,   383
sent from the Father and the Son to bless us!
Praise to the Father, Son, and Holy Spirit!
Praise to the triune God!

Heavenly Father, our true Refuge, guide us through these coming days. Renew us with your Spirit so we can share your freedom with the world! We praise you, Triune God! Amen.

Wednesday, January 28 — Psalm 18:7–15
1 Chronicles 26; Acts 16:30–17:3

The fear of the Lord is hatred of evil. Proverbs 8:13

Stand up, stand up for Jesus,   752
stand in his strength alone;
the arm of flesh will fail you,
you dare not trust your own.
Put on the gospel armor,
each piece put on with prayer;
where duty calls, or danger,
be ever faithful there.

Consider yourselves to be dead to sin, but alive to God in Christ Jesus. Romans 6:11 (NASB)

Far as east from west is distant,   458
God has put away our sin;
like the pity of a father
has the Lord's compassion been.

Lord, why do we make excuses for our sins when you have redeemed us with the cross? You died to give us your grace and a new life! We must truly believe that sin has no power over us! Thank you, gracious Lord! Amen.

Thursday, January 29 — Psalm 18:16–24
1 Chronicles 27; Acts 17:4–15

**Even though I walk through the darkest valley,
I fear no evil; for you are with me; your rod and
your staff—they comfort me. Psalm 23:4**

> Savior, you came to give   380
> those who in darkness live
> healing and sight,
> health to the sick in mind,
> sight to the inward blind:
> now to all humankind
> let there be light!

**We are hard pressed on every side, but not
crushed; perplexed, but not in despair; persecuted,
but not abandoned; struck down, but not
destroyed. 2 Corinthians 4:8–9 (NIV)**

> Have we trials and temptations?   743
> Is there trouble anywhere?
> We should never be discouraged;
> take it to the Lord in prayer!
> Can we find a friend so faithful
> who will all our sorrows share?
> Jesus knows our ev'ry weakness;
> take it to the Lord in prayer!

Heavenly Shepherd, we give you thanks for
protecting us every day. Forgive us for not bringing
our cares, temptations, and fears to you more often.
In our times of trial, let us focus our faith on you.
Amen.

Friday, January 30 — Psalm 18:25–29
1 Chronicles 28,29; Acts 17:16–28

Daniel went home to his upstairs room where the windows opened toward Jerusalem. Three times a day he got down on his knees and prayed, giving thanks to his God. Daniel 6:10 (NIV)

> Upon your precepts and your ways   510
> my heart will meditate with awe;
> your word shall be my chief delight,
> and I will not forget your law.

Rejoice in hope, be patient in suffering, persevere in prayer. Romans 12:12

> Give thanks in hope, rejoice, repent,   451*
> and practice all you prayed;
> true thanks can never be content
> to foul the world God made.
> Lord, teach us all an attitude
> that thanks you all our days,
> a love that shows our gratitude
> through deeds that live our praise.

Dear Lord, we thank you for the gift of prayer. You have all the answers! Let us always remember to give you the praise you deserve even in our times of pain. We can get through all things with you by our side. Amen.

* ©1990 by David G. Mehrtens

Saturday, January 31 — Psalm 18:30–36
2 Chronicles 1,2; Acts 17:29–18:7

Yet it was I who taught Ephraim to walk, I took them up in my arms; but they did not know that I healed them. Hosea 11:3

> O God, our help in ages past, 461
> our hope for years to come,
> remain our guard while life shall last,
> and our eternal home.

If we are faithless, he remains faithful—for he cannot deny himself. 2 Timothy 2:13

> Faithful soul, pray, always pray, 729
> and still in God confide;
> he your stumbling steps shall stay,
> and shall not let you slide;
> safe from known or secret foes,
> free from sin and Satan's hold,
> when the flesh, earth, hell oppose,
> he'll keep you in his fold.

Faithful Lord, let us never forget all you have done for us! Continue to be our Guide and Sustainer. Throughout the rest of this year may we strive to be as faithful as you are! Amen.

Fourth Sunday after the Epiphany

Watchword for the Week — The fear of the Lord is the beginning
of wisdom; all those who practice it have a good understanding.
Psalm 111:10

Sunday, February 1 — Deuteronomy 18:15–20; Psalm 111
1 Corinthians 8:1–13; Mark 1:21–28

See, the Lord God comes with might, and his arm rules for him. Isaiah 40:10

God is our strength and song,   531
and his salvation ours;
then be his love in Christ proclaimed
with all our ransomed pow'rs.

Who will not fear you, Lord, and bring glory to your name? For you alone are holy. All nations will come and worship before you. Revelation 15:4 (NIV)

Christ, to you, with God the Father   483
and the Spirit, there shall be
hymn and chant and high thanksgiving
and the shout of jubilee:
honor, glory, and dominion
and eternal victory
evermore and evermore!

Heavenly Father, you are our strength. Without you
we are helpless. You negotiate for us in our trials,
showing us the way and giving us peace. We praise
you with great thanks, God, for your mercy and
grace. Amen.

Monday, February 2 — Psalm 18:37–45
2 Chronicles 3:1–5:1; Acts 18:8–21

I keep my eyes always on the Lord. Psalm 16:8 (NIV)

> Lift your eyes and see the light;　　　789
> Zion's city is in sight!
> There our endless home shall be;
> there our Lord we soon shall see.

Let us run with perseverance the race that is set before us, looking to Jesus the pioneer and perfecter of our faith. Hebrews 12:1–2

> May I run the race before me,　　　585
> strong and brave to face the foe,
> looking only unto Jesus
> as I onward go.

Great Pioneer and Perfecter, help us to keep our eyes on the prize of your love and grace. You make this race worth running; guide us as we reach for you. Amen.

Tuesday, February 3 — Psalm 18:46–50
2 Chronicles 5:2–6:23; Acts 18:22–19:5

The spirit of the Lord shall rest on him, the spirit of wisdom and understanding, the spirit of counsel and might, the spirit of knowledge and the fear of the Lord. Isaiah 11:2

> Strike from our feet the fetters that bind. 489
> Lift from our lives the weight of our wrong.
> Teach us to love with heart, soul, and mind.
> Spirit of God, your love makes us strong.

And when Jesus had been baptized, just as he came up from the water, suddenly the heavens were opened to him and he saw the Spirit of God descending like a dove and alighting on him. Matthew 3:16

> Crown him the Lord of life, 405
> who triumphed o'er the grave,
> and rose victorious in the strife
> for those he came to save.
> His glories now we sing,
> who died and rose on high,
> who died, eternal life to bring
> and lives that death may die.

You are the one true God. Take away all of our doubts and shower us with the knowledge of your presence. Lord, overwhelm us with your awesomeness and keep us close all of our days. May we never cease to revel in your glory. Amen.

Wednesday, February 4 — Psalm 19:1–6
2 Chronicles 6:24–7:22; Acts 19:6–20

I will set my eyes upon them for good. I will build them up, and not tear them down; I will plant them, and not pluck them up. Jeremiah 24:6

> Around Christ's table we commune   439
> in fellowship supreme;
> inspired by Christ, through word and tune,
> of things divine we dream.
> Forth from this sacred place we go
> with challenge in each soul
> to love, to lift, to build, to grow.
> God's kingdom is our goal.

Therefore, there is now no condemnation for those who are in Christ Jesus. Romans 8:1 (NIV)

> No condemnation now I dread,   773
> for Christ, and all in him, is mine!
> Alive in him, my living Head,
> and clothed in righteousness divine,
> bold I approach the eternal throne
> and claim the crown, through Christ, my own.

Heavenly Builder, you have created a foundation of love and a garden of life. You give us the strength to grow and thrive, to do your will and seek your kingdom. May we never stop reaching. Amen.

Thursday, February 5 — Psalm 19:7–14
2 Chronicles 8:1–9:12; Acts 19:21–31

Be merciful to me, O God, be merciful to me, for in you my soul takes refuge. Psalm 57:1

> Jesus, refuge of the weary, 331
> blessed Redeemer, whom we love,
> Fountain in life's desert dreary,
> Savior from the world above:
> often have your eyes, offended,
> gazed upon the sinner's fall;
> yet upon the cross extended,
> you have borne the pain of all.

If you, then, though you are evil, know how to give good gifts to your children, how much more will your Father in heaven give good gifts to those who ask him! Matthew 7:11 (NIV)

> Praise God, who gives our daily bread 816
> and has again our table spread.
> May he with all his gifts impart
> his crowning gift, a thankful heart.

Great Creator, we are your chosen. How did this come to be? Your blessings are immeasurable; let us build your kingdom here to bring you the glory that is rightfully yours. Remind us that we are not our own, but yours. Amen.

Friday, February 6 — Psalm 20
2 Chronicles 9:13–10:19; Acts 19:32–20:3

I know, my God, that you search the heart, and take pleasure in uprightness. 1 Chronicles 29:17

Rejoice, the Lord is King! 372
Your Lord and King adore.
Rejoice, give thanks and sing
and triumph evermore.
Lift up your heart, lift up your voice
rejoice, again I say, rejoice!

Blessed are the pure in heart, for they will see God. Matthew 5:8

Rejoice in glorious hope; 372
for Christ, the Judge, shall come
to gather all his saints
to their eternal home.
We soon shall hear the archangel's voice;
the trump of God shall sound, rejoice!

Loving God, we are a heart-led people. In your name, we seek to end heartbreak and suffering and live lives of hope, love, compassion, and caring. Help keep our hearts true to your calling. In this we pray. Amen.

Saturday, February 7 — Psalm 21
2 Chronicles 11:1–12:12; Acts 20:4–16

The precepts of the Lord are right, rejoicing the heart. Psalm 19:8

O may I never do my will,　　　　　　　733
but yours, and only yours, fulfill;
let all my time and all my ways
be spent and ended to your praise.

Let the word of Christ dwell in you richly; teach and admonish one another in all wisdom. Colossians 3:16

O teach me, Lord, that I may teach　　　646
the precious truths which you impart.
And wing my words that they may reach
the hidden depths of many a heart.

Holy Spirit, dwell in us and make us whole. Make us teachers of your word, comforters to those who struggle, and friends to those who do not know you. May we always strive to make this world reflect the love of its Creator. Amen.

Fifth Sunday after the Epiphany

Watchword for the Week — Great is our Lord, and abundant in power; his understanding is beyond measure. Psalm 147:5

Sunday, February 8 — Isaiah 40:21–31; Psalm 147:1–11,20c
1 Corinthians 9:16–23; Mark 1:29–39

Truly, the fear of the Lord, that is wisdom; and to depart from evil is understanding. Job 28:28

Breath of God, O life-giving Spirit,   499*
yours the truth that we seek this day.
Yours the wisdom, yours the understanding,
yours the guidance on life's dark way.
Source of courage when hearts are weary,
source of strength for the day's long journey,
Spirit God, our hope and our faith,
breathe now within us your holy breath.

The wisdom from above is first pure, then peaceable, gentle, willing to yield, full of mercy and good fruits, without a trace of partiality or hypocrisy. James 3:17

I bind unto myself today   p237
the power of God to hold and lead,
his eye to watch, his might to stay,
his ear to hearken to my need,
the wisdom of my God to teach,
his hand to guide, his shield to ward;
the word of God to give me speech,
his heavenly host to be my guard.

Eternal God, grant to us the wisdom to understand those with whom we disagree. May your gentle hand guide us to peace, mercy, compassion, and love in this ever-needful world. Amen.

* © 1989 by Kieran Sawyer

Monday, February 9 — Psalm 22:1–8
2 Chronicles 12:13–13:22; Acts 20:17–31

Give me, O God, the pledge you demand. Who else will put up security for me? Job 17:3 (NIV)

My Shepherd will supply my need;   730
the Lord God is his name.
In pastures fresh he makes me feed,
beside the living stream.
He brings my wand'ring spirit back
when I forsake his ways,
and leads me for his mercy's sake
in paths of truth and grace.

Who is the one who condemns? Christ Jesus is He who died, yes, rather who was raised, who is at the right hand of God, who also intercedes for us. Romans 8:34 (NASB)

Who can condemn, since Christ was dead,   364
and ever lives to God?
Now our whole debt is fully paid;
he saves us by his blood.
The ransomed hosts in earth and heav'n
through countless choirs proclaim,
"He has redeemed us; praise be giv'n
to God and to the Lamb."

Savior, help us to understand the magnitude of the sacrifice that you made and your love for us. God, you are great. Sinless and pure, you paid our debt. We bow before you in absolute awe and sing praise to you forevermore. Amen.

Tuesday, February 10 — Psalm 22:9–21
2 Chronicles 14,15; Acts 20:32–21:4

I know that the Lord maintains the cause of the needy, and executes justice for the poor. Psalm 140:12

> He comes with rescue speedy   263
> to those who suffer wrong,
> to help the poor and needy,
> and bid the weak be strong,
> to give them songs for sighing,
> their darkness turn to light,
> whose souls, condemned and dying,
> were precious in his sight.

Has not God chosen the poor in the world to be rich in faith and to be heirs of the kingdom that he has promised to those who love him? James 2:5

> Vainly we offer each ample oblation,   317
> vainly with gifts would his favor secure;
> richer by far is the heart's adoration,
> dearer to God are the prayers of the poor.

Lord, your love of all, especially the poor in both treasure and spirit, provides the shining example upon which we must build our lives. Help us to follow your example, bringing comfort and justice to those who need it most. Amen.

Wednesday, February 11 — Psalm 22:22–28
2 Chronicles 16,17; Acts 21:5–16

Those who sow with tears will reap with songs of joy. Those who go out weeping, carrying seed to sow, will return with songs of joy, carrying sheaves with them. Psalm 126:5–6 (NIV)

Revive your work; amid the years   399
our members still employ
on needy souls to sow in tears,
with hope to reap in joy.
Though wide the fields, the lab'rers few,
if you our failing faith renew,
though weak, we as your servants, Lord,
may still fulfill your word.

Let us not lose heart in doing good, for in due time we will reap if we do not grow weary. Galatians 6:9 (NASB)

Blessings abound where'er he reigns,   404
the pris'ners leap to lose their chains,
the weary find eternal rest,
and all who suffer want are blessed.

Peaceful Savior, our strength is in you. You deliver us from the difficult times in our lives and you give us peace through hope for what is still to come. May our struggles always find us in your care. In Jesus' name. Amen.

Thursday, February 12 — Psalm 22:29–31
2 Chronicles 18; Acts 21:17–30

Know that the Lord is God. Psalm 100:3

> You are the way, the truth, the life;   661
> grant to us that way to know;
> that truth to keep, that life to win,
> whose joys eternal flow.

The Son of God has come and has given us understanding so that we may know him who is true. 1 John 5:20

> You are the living truth;   486*
> all wisdom dwells in you,
> the course of ev'ry skill,
> the one eternal true!
> O great I Am! in you we rest,
> sure answer to our ev'ry quest.

Great Truth, we never see you directly but we know you are there. Deep down, we feel your power and presence. Help us to share that understanding with those for whom the trials of the world cause their faith in you to falter. Amen.

Friday, February 13 — Psalm 23
2 Chronicles 19:1–20:19; Acts 21:31–22:2

Let the heavens be glad, and let the earth rejoice, and let them say among the nations, "The Lord is king!" 1 Chronicles 16:31

Christ, whose glory fills the skies,   475
Christ, the true and only light,
Sun of righteousness, arise,
triumph o'er the shades of night;
dayspring from on high, be near;
daystar, in my heart appear.

For Yours is the kingdom and the power and the glory forever. Matthew 6:13 (NKJV)

We praise you, Jesus, Redeemer;   p103
we adore you forever.
We praise you, Spirit of power;
we adore you forever.

We rejoice in your kingdom, your power, and your glory, great God and Father. Everything we have is yours. The wind and the rain are under your command and bend to your will. May we also do your will in love as you taught us. Amen.

Saturday, February 14 — Psalm 24
2 Chronicles 20:20–21:17; Acts 22:3–16

**The Lord stirred up the spirit of all the people;
and they came and worked on the house of the
Lord of hosts, their God. Haggai 1:14**

> God, grant me strength to do   615
> with ready heart and willing,
> whatever you command,
> my calling here fulfilling;
> and do it when I ought,
> with zeal and joyfulness;
> and bless the work I've wrought,
> for you must give success.

**Live your life in a manner worthy of the gospel
of Christ, so that you are standing firm in one
spirit, striving side by side with one mind for the
faith of the gospel. Philippians 1:27**

> As you, Lord, have lived for others,   648
> so may we for others live;
> freely have your gifts been granted;
> freely may your servants give.
> Yours the gold and yours the silver,
> yours the wealth of land and sea;
> we but stewards of your bounty
> held in solemn trust will be.

Gracious Redeemer, we long to feel that stirring
of the Spirit that drives us to be your presence in
the world. Help us to quiet our minds and open
our souls to listen for your voice, encouraging and
strengthening us to make your word known. Amen.

Last Sunday after the Epiphany
Transfiguration of our Lord

Watchword for the Week — For we do not proclaim ourselves; we proclaim Jesus Christ as Lord and ourselves as servants for Jesus' sake. 2 Corinthians 4:5

Sunday, February 15 — 2 Kings 2:1–12; Psalm 50:1–6
2 Corinthians 4:3–6; Mark 9:2–9

You must follow exactly the path that the Lord your God has commanded you, so that you may live. Deuteronomy 5:33

> Jesus calls us; o'er the tumult   600
> of our life's wild, restless sea,
> day by day his voice is sounding,
> saying, "Christian, follow me."

Jesus said, "Everyone then who hears these words of mine and acts on them will be like a wise man who built his house on rock." Matthew 7:24

> Grant that we may love you truly;   p67
> Lord, our thoughts and actions sway,
> and to ev'ry heart more fully
> your atoning pow'r display.

Creator, ignite a fire of passion within your people.
Let your strength carry us to action on your behalf.
Lead us to forge straight paths for the afflicted
and lost so they may be found in your open arms.
Amen.

Monday, February 16 — Psalm 25:1–7
2 Chronicles 21:18–23:21; Acts 22:17–29

As a shepherd looks after his scattered flock when he is with them, so will I look after my sheep. Ezekiel 34:12 (NIV)

Since we, though unworthy,   746
through electing grace,
'mid your ransomed people
have obtained a place,
Lord, may we be faithful
to our cov'nant found,
to you, as our shepherd,
and your flock fast bound.

Be merciful to those who doubt. Jude 22 (NIV)

Amazing grace, how can it be   77s*
that God to us is true,
that we are precious in God's sight,
despite the things we do?
Creator, former, shaper,
making real what we have known,
that God's love is dependable
and names us as God's own.

Glorious Shepherd, we often struggle with our doubts and stray from your presence. But then we see you in the smile of a friend, hear you in the whisper of the breeze, feel you in the warmth of the sun, and return to the fold. Keep us close. Amen.

*   © 2007 by Judith M. Ganz

Tuesday, February 17 — Psalm 25:8–22
2 Chronicles 24:1–25:4; Acts 22:30–23:11

The Lord was with Joseph; and whatever he did, the Lord made it prosper. Genesis 39:23

The Lord is never far away,   537
but through all grief distressing,
an everpresent help and stay,
our peace, and joy, and blessing.
As with a mother's tender hand,
he leads his own, his chosen band.
To God all praise and glory!

You were called for the very purpose that you might inherit a blessing. 1 Peter 3:9 (NASB)

Come, Almighty to deliver,   474
let us all your life receive;
suddenly return, and never,
nevermore your temple leave.
You we would be always blessing,
serve you as your hosts above,
pray, and praise you without ceasing,
glory in your perfect love.

Lord, we are so blessed. Your hand guides us and provides for us always. Let us bless those around us as you have called us to do, guiding and providing with your word as our foundation. Amen.

Ash Wednesday

Wednesday, February 18 — Psalm 26
2 Chronicles 25:5–26:15; Acts 23:12–24

Ash Wednesday — Joel 2:1–2,12–17; Psalm 51:1–17
2 Corinthians 5:20b–6:10; Matthew 6:1–6,16–21

Who dares despise the day of small things, will rejoice when they see the chosen capstone. Zechariah 4:10 (NIV)

"'Til he come!" O let the words   413
linger on the trembling chords;
let the "little while" between
in their golden light be seen;
let us think how heav'n and home
lie beyond that "'Til he come!"

As they were gathering in Galilee, Jesus said to his disciples, "The Son of Man is going to be betrayed into human hands, and they will kill him, and on the third day he will be raised." Matthew 17:22–23

How great the love of Jesus Christ,   24s*
for showing us the way.
He taught us to be faithful servants
each and ev'ry day.
By his example we must share
his everlasting love.
As his disciples, we receive
his blessing from above.

As we prepare for the solemn time of Lent, help us grow closer to you. Teach us about the life of your Son so that we may better understand the sacrifice he made for us. We look toward Easter with anticipation and hope. Amen.

*   © 2009 by Zachariah D. Bailey

Thursday, February 19 — Psalm 27:1–6
2 Chronicles 26:16–28:8; Acts 23:25–24:3

Boaz said to Ruth, "May you have a full reward from the Lord, under whose wings you have come for refuge!" Ruth 2:12

Other refuge have I none;   724
hangs my helpless soul on thee;
leave, ah, leave me not alone,
still support and comfort me.
All my trust on thee is stayed,
all my help from thee I bring;
cover my defenseless head
with the shadow of thy wing.

You are no longer strangers and aliens, but you are citizens with the saints and also members of the household of God. Ephesians 2:19

Join we all with one accord;   525
praise we all our common Lord;
for we all have heard his voice,
all have made his will our choice.
Join we with the saints of old,
no more strangers in the fold,
one the Shepherd who us sought,
one the flock his blood has bought.

We are all your people, Lord. Make our hearts rejoice in the triumphs of our brothers and sisters worldwide. Give us compassion for those whom we have not yet had the chance to meet. Let us no longer see barriers and divisions, but join together in community. Amen.

Friday, February 20 — Psalm 27:7–14
2 Chronicles 28:9–29:19; Acts 24:4–16

Praise him, sun and moon; praise him, all you shining stars! For he commanded, and they were created. Psalm 148:3,5

> Praise the Lord! You heav'ns, adore him,   454
> praise him, angels in the height;
> sun and moon, rejoice before him;
> praise him, all you stars and light.
> Praise the Lord! For he has spoken;
> worlds his mighty voice obeyed;
> laws which never shall be broken
> for their guidance he has made.

Great and marvelous are your deeds, Lord God Almighty. Revelation 15:3 (NIV)

> Joyful, joyful, we adore you,   544
> God of glory, Lord of love;
> hearts unfold like flow'rs before you,
> op'ning to the sun above.
> Melt the clouds of sin and sadness;
> drive the dark of doubt away;
> giver of immortal gladness,
> fill us with the light of day!

Almighty One, you shine on us through your sun, your moon, your stars. Day or night, we need only look to the heavens to feel your presence and know that you are there for us. May your light shine on everyone. Amen.

Saturday, February 21 — Psalm 28
2 Chronicles 29:20–30:27; Acts 24:17–27

Who am I, O Lord God, and what is my house, that you have brought me thus far? 2 Samuel 7:18

God has given, he has taken,   667
but his children ne'er forsaken;
his the loving purpose solely
to preserve them pure and holy.

God called us with a holy calling, not according to our works but according to his own purpose and grace. 2 Timothy 1:9

Today we all are called to be   696*
disciples of the Lord,
to help to set the captive free,
make plowshare out of sword,
to feed the hungry, quench their thirst,
make love and peace our fast,
to serve the poor and homeless first,
our ease and comfort last.

Wise Comforter, sometimes we feel small. We lose
our way and we question our purpose. Remind
us today that you have a plan for each of us.
Remind us that we are valuable and full of purpose,
beautifully and wonderfully made. May we glorify
you. Amen.

* © 1989 by H. Kenn Carmichael

First Sunday in Lent

Watchword for the Week — Good and upright is the Lord; therefore he instructs sinners in the way. Psalm 25:8

Sunday, February 22 — Genesis 9:8–17; Psalm 25:1–10
1 Peter 3:18–22; Mark 1:9–15

Remember the Lord in a distant land, and let Jerusalem come into your mind. Jeremiah 51:50

> Remember thee, and all thy pains,   422
> and all thy love to me?
> Yea, while a breath, a pulse remains
> will I remember thee.

We are always confident; even though we know that while we are at home in the body we are away from the Lord—for we walk by faith, not by sight. 2 Corinthians 5:6–7

> We walk by faith and not by sight;   713
> no gracious words we hear from Christ,
> who spoke as none e'er spoke;
> but we believe him near.

As we travel life's highways, we know you travel with us. No matter where we roam, there is always a home with you. Guide our path and light our way, we pray. Amen.

Monday, February 23 — Psalm 29
2 Chronicles 31; Acts 25:1–15

**Because you obey the voice of the Lord your God:
Blessed shall you be in the city, and blessed shall
you be in the country. Deuteronomy 28:2–3 (NKJV)**

> They who Jesus' followers are   672
> and enjoy his faithful care,
> by a mutual, hearty love
> their belief in Jesus prove.

**Jesus said to his disciples: Blessed are your
eyes, for they see, and your ears, for they hear.
Matthew 13:16**

> In all the world around me   792
> I see his loving care,
> and though my heart grows weary,
> I never will despair;
> I know that he is leading
> through all the stormy blast,
> the day of his appearing
> will come at last.
> He lives, he lives,
> Christ Jesus lives today!
> He walks with me and talks with me
> along life's narrow way.
> He lives, he lives,
> salvation to impart!
> You ask me how I know he lives?
> He lives within my heart.

No matter where we go, Lord, you go with us. In
each breath we take there is the Holy Spirit filling
us to excess with love, mercy, and grace. May each
breath that leaves us gift others with the same
blessings. Amen.

Tuesday, February 24 — Psalm 30:1–5
2 Chronicles 32; Acts 25:16–26:1

You shall know that I am the Lord, when I deal with you for my name's sake, not according to your evil ways or corrupt deeds. Ezekiel 20:44

> From all that dwell below the skies 551
> let the Creator's praise arise;
> let the Redeemer's name be sung
> through every land, by every tongue.

Your sins are forgiven on account of his name. 1 John 2:12

> You o'ercame the foe 542*
> so that we might go
> on to heaven, cleansed, forgiven.
> You o'ercame the foe.

Forgiving Father, you know our sins. You see our need for love, hope, and forgiveness. Despite our sometimes-troubled days, we know deep down that you are there for us and we ask you to forgive us our trespasses. In your name we pray. Amen.

* © 1991 by Albert H. Frank

Wednesday, February 25 — Psalm 30:6–12
2 Chronicles 33:1–34:7; Acts 26:2–14

Woe to him who piles up stolen goods and makes himself wealthy by extortion! How long must this go on? Habakkuk 2:6 (NIV)

> Take my wealth, all I possess,   647
> make me rich in faithfulness.
> Take my mind that I may use
> ev'ry pow'r as you should choose.

Paul wrote: Aspire to live quietly, to mind your own affairs, and to work with your hands. 1 Thessalonians 4:11

> Lord, as you have lived for others,   p41
> so may we for others live;
> freely have your gifts been granted;
> freely may your servants give.
> Yours the gold and yours the silver,
> yours the wealth of land and sea,
> we but stewards of your bounty
> sharing all by your decree.

Lord Jesus, you lead us by example against a life of excess. Make us comfortable with less in a society that says "more." Let us live our lives with the goal of praising you, not of being praised for what we have. Remind us whose we are. Amen.

Thursday, February 26 — Psalm 31:1–5
2 Chronicles 34:8–33; Acts 26:15–27

Restore me, and I will return, because you are the Lord my God. Jeremiah 31:18 (NIV)

From your house when I return,   553
may my heart within me burn,
and at evening let me say,
"I have walked with God today."

The other criminal who was hanged there, said, "Jesus, remember me when you come into your kingdom." Luke 23:42

Christ came from heaven's throne   482
salvation to bestow,
but people scorned and none
the longed-for Christ would know.
But O my friend, my friend indeed,
who at my need his life did spend.

O Wondrous Restorer, as we remain faithful to you, remember us in times of trial and despair. Refresh our lives and faith with your Spirit. May we do all we can to be welcomed into your kingdom. Amen.

Friday, February 27 — Psalm 31:6–9
2 Chronicles 35; Acts 26:28–27:8

Good and upright is the Lord; therefore he instructs sinners in the way. Psalm 25:8

Teach us to use our lives   801*
with purpose and with power
for visions of a better world
and for decision's hour;
to choose the way of life,
reject the way of death,
until the radiant force of God
fills mind and strength and breath.

Welcome those who are weak in faith, but not for the purpose of quarreling over opinions. Romans 14:1

Come, you thirsty, come and welcome,   765
God's free bounty glorify;
true belief and true repentance,
ev'ry grace that brings you nigh.
I will arise and go to Jesus;
he will embrace me in his arms;
in the arms of my dear Savior,
O there are ten thousand charms.

Let us take the time to listen, Lord, when you are calling. You are not always direct in your speaking to us. Let us be ready to meet you in the places and times of your choosing. Make us instruments of your peace and love. Amen.

Saturday, February 28 — Psalm 31:10–20
2 Chronicles 36; Acts 27:9–20

I delight to do your will, O my God; your law is within my heart. Psalm 40:8

O teach us all your perfect will   734
to understand and fulfill:
when human insight fails, give light;
this will direct our steps aright.

In fact, this is love for God: to keep his commands. And his commands are not burdensome. 1 John 5:3 (NIV)

Who in Christ find greatest treasure   717
and upon his grace depend;
who but want to do his pleasure,
just fulfilling his commands;
who to Jesus humbly cleaving
pay obedience to his word,
who in closest union living
with our Saviour, Head, and Lord.

Heavenly Father, we have learned your commands
from pastors, teachers, and friends. May our love
for you be evident in how we live our lives and obey
your laws. Guide us to follow our hearts to you.
Amen.

Second Sunday in Lent
March 1, 1457:
Beginning of the Unity of the Brethren in Bohemia

Watchword for the Week — God says, "I will establish my covenant between me and you, and your offspring after you throughout their generations." Genesis 17:7

Sunday, March 1 — Genesis 17:1–7,15–16; Psalm 22:23–31 Romans 4:13–25; Mark 8:31–38

Your steadfast love, O Lord, extends to the heavens, your faithfulness to the clouds. Psalm 36:5

> O, to grace how great a debtor   782
> daily I'm constrained to be!
> Let that grace, Lord, like a fetter,
> bind my wand'ring heart to thee.
> Prone to wander, Lord, I feel it,
> prone to leave the God I love,
> here's my heart, O take and seal it;
> seal it for thy courts above.

Who will separate us from the love of Christ? Romans 8:35

> Witness here to all around you   515
> of your Savior's dying love;
> tell them how he sought and found you,
> gave you grace from heav'n above.

Dearest Lord, never let us be separated from you or our brothers and sisters in Christ. Help us to share your many blessings and boundless comfort with those whom we encounter today. Amen.

Monday, March 2 — Psalm 31:21–24
Ezra 1,2; Acts 27:21–38

**Hezekiah received the letter and read it; then he
went up to the house of the Lord and spread it
before the Lord. 2 Kings 19:14**

Bring justice to our land,   681*
that all may dwell secure,
and finely build for days to come
foundations that endure.

**Do not worry about anything, but in everything
by prayer and supplication with thanksgiving
let your requests be made known to God.
Philippians 4:6**

Peace, perfect peace, our future all unknown?   710
Jesus we know, and he is on the throne.

Loving Father, we come to you today with many
questions. Guide us in our journey as we pray for
the purpose that you have placed into our hearts,
our minds, and our hands. Amen.

*   © by Emmanuel College, Toronto. Used by permission.

Tuesday, March 3 — Psalm 32
Ezra 3; Acts 27:39–28:6

The earth is full of the steadfast love of the Lord. Psalm 33:5

We covenant in church and home   p121
this peace to show each other,
to represent your steadfast love
as sister and as brother.
O, may we through each other know
your grace which fails us never,
and find at last our true abode
within your house forever. Amen.

Every good thing given and every perfect gift is from above, coming down from the Father of lights. James 1:17 (NASB)

We thank you, our Creator,   453
for all things bright and good,
the seedtime and the harvest,
our life, our health, our food;
accept the gifts we offer
for all your love imparts,
and what you most would treasure—
our humble, thankful hearts.
All good gifts around us
are sent from heav'n above;
then thank the Lord, O thank the Lord
for all his love.

We thank you today, Lord, for all your gracious gifts given to us upon this earth. We look forward to the day when, joyfully, we may join with you in our eternal home. Amen.

Wednesday, March 4 — Psalm 33:1–5
Ezra 4; Acts 28:7–16

O Lord, be gracious to me; heal me, for I have sinned against you. Psalm 41:4

> Praise, my soul, the King of heaven,   529
> to his feet your tribute bring.
> Ransomed, healed, restored, forgiven,
> evermore his praises sing.
> Alleluia! Alleluia!
> Praise the everlasting King!

The prayer of faith will save the sick, and the Lord will raise them up; and anyone who has committed sins will be forgiven. James 5:15

> Great and even greater,   778
> are your mercies here,
> true and everlasting
> are the glories there,
> where no pain or sorrow,
> toil or care is known,
> where the angel legions
> circle 'round your throne.

Precious Savior and Lord, bind up our wounds today, both physical and spiritual, and allow us to see your grace that renews our imperfect lives. Bless and comfort us, and have mercy upon us. Amen.

Thursday, March 5 — Psalm 33:6–11
Ezra 5:1–6:12; Acts 28:17–31

Lord, let your compassion come to me, that I may live. Psalm 119:77 (NIV)

> O let me feel you near me;   603
> the world is ever near:
> I see the sights that dazzle,
> the tempting sounds I hear.
> My foes are ever near me,
> around me and within;
> but, Jesus, draw still nearer
> and shield my soul from sin!

The king said to his servants, "Therefore go into the highways, and as many as you find, invite to the wedding." So those servants went out into the highways and gathered together all whom they found, both bad and good. And the wedding hall was filled with guests. Matthew 22:9–10 (NKJV)

> Eternal thanks, O God,   p214
> the source of our salvation;
> to you our hearts are led
> through your blessed invitation.
> Your children now are we,
> and may we yours remain.
> In grateful hymns we praise
> the Christ, the Lamb once slain.

Draw us nearer to you today, Lord. As we encounter temptations, let your guiding hand take hold of ours and lead each of us down the path of your choosing and not our own. Amen.

Friday, March 6 — Psalm 33:12–22
Ezra 6:13–7:28; Romans 1:1–12

The Lord is your praise; he is your God. Deuteronomy 10:21

Praise to the Lord! 530
  O, let all that is in me adore him!
All that has life and breath,
  come now with praises before him!
Let the amen
sound from his people again.
Gladly forever adore him!

We boast in God through our Lord Jesus Christ, through whom we have now received reconciliation. Romans 5:11

By faith your word has made us bold p228
to seize the gift of love retold;
all that you are we here receive,
and all we are to you we give.

Lord Jesus Christ, as we come to you today in prayer and praise, we recognize you as our Creator, Defender, and Sustainer. Let us always remember what you suffered for the forgiveness of our sins. Amen.

Saturday, March 7 — Psalm 34:1–7
Ezra 8:1–20; Romans 1:13–25

The Lord says, "See, I am sending an angel ahead of you to guard you along the way and to bring you to the place I have prepared." Exodus 23:20 (NIV)

For the Lord our God shall come   450
and shall take his harvest home,
he himself in that great day
all offense shall take away,
give his angels charge at last
in the fire the weeds to cast,
but the fruitful ears to store
in his garner evermore.

Are not all angels spirits in the divine service, sent to serve for the sake of those who are to inherit salvation? Therefore we must pay greater attention to what we have heard, so that we do not drift away from it. Hebrews 1:14–2:1

Visit, then, this soul of mine,   475
pierce the gloom of sin and grief;
fill me, radiancy divine;
scatter all my unbelief;
more and more yourself display,
shining to the perfect day!

Beautiful Savior, you do shine brighter and purer than all the angels in the sky. Help us to offer our glory, honor, praise, and adoration to you today, tomorrow, and evermore. Amen.

Third Sunday in Lent

Watchword for the Week — For the message about the cross is foolishness to those who are perishing, but to us who are being saved it is the power of God. 1 Corinthians 1:18

Sunday, March 8 — Exodus 20:1–17; Psalm 19
1 Corinthians 1:18–25; John 2:13–22

You, O Lord, have made me glad by your work; at the works of your hands I sing for joy. Psalm 92:4

> Then with delight may I employ 638
> all that your bounteous grace has giv'n,
> and run my earthly course with joy,
> and closely walk with you to heav'n.

Jesus put his hands on her, and immediately she straightened up and praised God. Luke 13:13 (NIV)

> Praise to the Savior for his deep compassion, 383
> graciously caring for his chosen people;
> young men and women, aging folk and children,
> praise to the Savior!

Compassionate Father, as we come before you this Sabbath day, let us be ever mindful of your helpful and healing hands that protect us and hold us close to you always. Thanks be to God! Amen.

Monday, March 9 — Psalm 34:8–18
Ezra 8:21–10:6; Romans 1:26–2:4

The war horse is a vain hope for victory, and by its great might it cannot save. Truly the eye of the Lord is on those who fear him, on those who hope in his steadfast love. Psalm 33:17–18

> O Jesus, my Lord,   608
> forever adored,
> my portion, my all,
> at your holy feet
> humbly pleading I fall.

We boast in Christ Jesus and have no confidence in the flesh. Philippians 3:3

> On him we'll venture all we have,   479
> our lives, our all, to him we owe.
> None else is able us to save,
> naught but the Savior will we know;
> this we subscribe with heart and hand,
> resolved through grace thereby to stand.

Blessed Shepherd, our hope rests in you. Loving Savior, defend us from temptations today and keep our eyes and hearts focused on the unending grace and love that you supply to us, your erring servants. Amen.

Tuesday, March 10 — Psalm 34:19–22
Ezra 10:7–44; Romans 2:5–16

You are my help and my deliverer; do not delay, O my God. Psalm 40:17

I need thee ev'ry hour;   740
stay thou nearby;
temptations lose their pow'r
when thou art nigh.
I need thee, O I need thee,
ev'ry hour I need thee!
O bless me now, my Savior—
I come to thee!

Hope does not put us to shame. Romans 5:5 (ESV)*

Sing, pray, and keep his ways unswerving,   712
offer your service faithfully,
and trust his word; though undeserving,
you'll find his promise true to be.
God never will forsake in need
the soul that trusts in him indeed.

Our spirits depend on you, dear God. You are the Deliverer, Redeemer, and Provider of all great gifts which we gladly accept. We rejoice this day and always. Bless your holy name. Amen.

Wednesday, March 11 — Psalm 35:1–10
Nehemiah 1:1–2:10; Romans 2:17–3:2

I will seek the lost, and I will bring back the strayed, and I will bind up the injured, and I will strengthen the weak. Ezekiel 34:16

We are yours; in love befriend us,   731
be the guardian of our way;
keep your flock, from sin defend us,
seek us when we go astray.
Blessed Jesus, blessed Jesus,
hear your children when we pray.
Blessed Jesus, blessed Jesus,
hear your children when we pray.

When the goodness and loving-kindness of God our Savior appeared, he saved us, not because of any works of righteousness that we had done, but according to his mercy. Titus 3:4–5

Cure your children's warring madness,   751
bend our pride to your control;
shame our wanton, selfish gladness,
rich in things and poor in soul.
Grant us wisdom, grant us courage,
lest we miss your kingdom's goal,
lest we miss your kingdom's goal.

God of grace and God of glory, thank you for guiding us, your wandering flock. We strive to stay near you and to follow you, our loving Shepherd. Help us to respond to your tender mercies and share them with others. Grant to us your peace. Amen.

Thursday, March 12 — Psalm 35:11–18
Nehemiah 2:11–3:32; Romans 3:3–18

Lord, there is no one like you to help the powerless against the mighty. 2 Chronicles 14:11 (NIV)

> He left his Father's throne above—   773
> so free, so infinite his grace—
> emptied himself of all but love,
> and bled for Adam's helpless race!
> What mercy this, immense and free,
> for, O my God, it found out me!
> What mercy this, immense and free,
> for, O my God, it found out me!

Christ says, "In this world you will have trouble. But take heart! I have overcome the world." John 16:33 (NIV)

> "Fear not, I am with you; O be not dismayed,   709
> for I am your God and will still give you aid;
> I'll strengthen you, help you, and cause you to stand
> upheld by my righteous, omnipotent hand.

Bless us now and forever, victorious Lord and Savior, with your triumph over the grave and the forgiveness of our sin, which only you have the power to provide to us, your children. Amen.

Friday, March 13 — Psalm 35:19–28
Nehemiah 4; Romans 3:19–31

Moses said, "If now I have found favor in your sight, O Lord, I pray, let the Lord go with us." Exodus 34:9 (NASB)

The Lord bless and keep you in his favor   446
as his chosen, cherished heir;
the Lord make his face shine on you ever
and enfold you in his care.
The Lord lift his countenance upon you
may where'er you go his Spirit lead you,
and his peace on you bestow;
Amen, amen, be it so.

Jesus says, "Where two or three are gathered in my name, I am there among them." Matthew 18:20

One member may not know another here,   516
and yet their fellowship is true and near;
one is their Savior, and their Father one;
one Spirit rules them, and among them none
lives to one's self.

Come, Lord Jesus, and be with us today. Dwell with us in our homes, at school, at work, and everywhere we find ourselves. We pray that we may worship and serve you in our communities and honor you in all our actions. Amen.

Saturday, March 14 — Psalm 36
Nehemiah 5:1–6:14; Romans 4:1–12

The Lord takes pleasure in those who fear him, in those who hope in his steadfast love. Psalm 147:11

Still will I wait, O Lord, on you,   721
'til in your light I see anew;
'til you in my behalf appear,
to banish ev'ry doubt and fear.

Paul wrote: I want to know Christ and the power of his resurrection and the sharing of his sufferings. Philippians 3:10

Lord, for all that bought our pardon,   334
for the sorrows deep and sore,
for the anguish in the garden,
we will thank you evermore,
thank you for the groaning, sighing,
for the vict'ry of your dying,
for that last triumphant cry,
praise you evermore on high.

Dearest Lord, let us never forget your life, sufferings, death, and resurrection that offer us the unending grace we receive in this world. Continue to give us the comfort of one day sharing that grace with you in heaven. Amen.

Fourth Sunday in Lent

Watchword for the Week — By grace you have been saved through faith, and this is not your own doing; it is the gift of God. Ephesians 2:8

Sunday, March 15 — Numbers 21:4–9; Psalm 107:1–3,17–22 Ephesians 2:1–10; John 3:14–21

From the rising of the sun to its setting the name of the Lord is to be praised. Psalm 113:3

Minds to think and hearts to love—   649
God's good gifts to me and you;
minds and hearts he gave to us
to help each other the whole day through.

May the God of patience and comfort grant you to be like-minded toward one another, according to Christ Jesus, that you may with one mind and one mouth glorify the God and Father of our Lord Jesus Christ. Romans 15:5–6 (NKJV)

We covenant with hand and heart   p209
to follow Christ our Lord;
with world, and sin, and self to part,
and to obey his word;
to love each other heartily,
in truth and with sincerity,
and under cross, reproach, and shame,
to glorify his name.

Loving Creator, we sing your praise this day with all our brothers and sisters, united together in spirit to proclaim the love of God for all. All praise and thanksgiving be yours. Amen.

Monday, March 16 — Psalm 37:1–6
Nehemiah 6:15–7:73a; Romans 4:13–25

Obey me, and I will be your God and you will be my people. Jeremiah 7:23 (NIV)

> Having turned from other ways, 614
> now your name alone to bear,
> your dear voice alone obey
> is my daily, hourly prayer.
> Looking up to heav'n I see
> no one else my joy can be.

Jesus answered, "Those who love me will keep my word, and my Father will love them, and we will come to them and make our home with them." John 14:23

> All glory, worship, thanks, and praise, 280
> that you have come in these our days!
> O heav'nly guest, expected long,
> we hail you with a joyful song.

Most holy Lord and God, help us to keep your word in our lives, and to be willing, obedient, and caring examples of your divine love for all people. Amen.

Tuesday, March 17 — Psalm 37:7–15
Nehemiah 7:73b–8:18; Romans 5:1–11

The ways of the Lord are right, and the upright walk in them, but transgressors stumble in them. Hosea 14:9

> We'll bring him hearts that love him,   658
> we'll bring him thankful praise,
> and souls forever striving
> to follow in his ways:
> and these shall be the treasures
> we offer to the King,
> and these are gifts that even
> our grateful hearts may bring.

Jesus said, "Not everyone who says to me, 'Lord, Lord,' will enter the kingdom of heaven, but only the one who does the will of my Father in heaven." Matthew 7:21

> To you our vows with sweet accord,   677
> head of your church, we pay;
> we and our house will serve you, Lord;
> your word we will obey.
> Grant us and all our children grace
> in word and deed your name to praise,
> and in each family, your will
> and purpose to fulfill.

Christ our Savior, help us to follow your path, to take up your cross, and to lift it up high for others to see. You suffered for us so that we could receive the blessing of everlasting life in you, our heavenly Host. Amen.

Wednesday, March 18 — Psalm 37:16–22
Nehemiah 9:1–10:27; Romans 5:12–6:4

My soul clings to you; your right hand upholds me. Psalm 63:8

You make us rejoice in serving,　　　　　　622*
giving strength where we had none;
certain tasks had seemed unnerving,
but you've proven you're the one
who gives gifts of love and power,
confidence and self-control.
Fill us now, this very hour;
help us reach your kingdom's goal.

Paul wrote: I know whom I have believed, and am convinced that he is able to guard what I have entrusted to him. 2 Timothy 1:12 (NIV)

Blessed be the day when I must roam　　　　794
far from my country, friends, and home,
an exile, poor and mean;
my fathers' God will be my Guide,
will angel guards for me provide,
my soul, my soul in danger screen.

Blessed Provider, you send us out, armed with your word and protected by your mercy. Let us seek to do your will and strive to be blessings to others as we move through your world this day. Amen.

* © 1993 by Darryl Bell

Thursday, March 19 — Psalm 37:23–26
Nehemiah 10:28–11:36; Romans 6:5–16

You turn things upside down! Shall the potter be regarded as the clay? Shall the thing made say of its maker, "He did not make me"; or the thing formed say of the one who formed it, "He has no understanding"? Isaiah 29:16

> His sov'reign pow'r without our aid   455
> formed us of clay and gave us breath;
> and when like wand'ring sheep we strayed,
> he saved us from the pow'r of death.

Who indeed are you, a human being, to argue with God? Romans 9:20

> Let all mortal flesh keep silence,   271
> and with fear and trembling stand,
> ponder nothing earthly minded,
> for with blessing in his hand
> Christ our God to earth descended
> our full homage to demand.

Our Father, we come before you this day on bended knee asking for your strength and forgiveness to reign over us in all we do. Hear us as we pray. Amen.

Friday, March 20 — Psalm 37:27–33
Nehemiah 12:1–43; Romans 6:17–7:6

Therefore I will allot him a portion with the great, and he shall divide the spoil with the strong; because he poured out himself to death, and was numbered with the transgressors. Isaiah 53:12

Jesus! Heav'nly hosts adore you,   330
seated at your Father's side.
Crucified this world once saw you;
now in glory you abide.
There for sinners you are pleading,
and our place you now prepare,
ever for us interceding,
'til in glory we appear.

When God had disarmed the rulers and authorities, He made a public display of them, having triumphed over them through Christ. Colossians 2:15 (NASB)

Our God rules on high, almighty to save;   565
and still he is nigh, his presence we have;
the great congregation his triumph shall sing,
ascribing salvation to Jesus, our King.

Almighty God, let us magnify your name in our labor and in our rest. We will praise you and know you are present with us this day and every day, Father, Son, and Holy Ghost. Amen.

Saturday, March 21 — Psalm 37:34–40
Nehemiah 12:44–13:14; Romans 7:7–20

The Israelites cried to the Lord, saying, "We have sinned against you, because we have abandoned our God." Judges 10:10

> This holy word exposes sin,   509
> convinces us that we're unclean,
> points out the wretched, ruined state
> of humankind, both small and great.

If we confess our sins, he who is faithful and just will forgive us our sins and cleanse us from all unrighteousness. 1 John 1:9

> Those who then are loyal   270
> find a welcome royal.
> Come then, O Lord Jesus,
> from our sins release us;
> let us here confess you
> 'til in heav'n we bless you.

Heavenly Father, we come before you with contrite hearts this day confessing our many sinful and selfish acts. Help us to better follow the example you set for us to make us free from sin. Amen.

Fifth Sunday in Lent

Watchword for the Week — Create in me a clean heart, O God, and put a new and right spirit within me. Psalm 51:10

Sunday, March 22 — Jeremiah 31:31–34; Psalm 51:1–12
Hebrews 5:5–10; John 12:20–33

Many peoples shall come and say, "Come, let us go up to the mountain of the Lord, to the house of the God of Jacob; that he may teach us his ways and that we may walk in his paths." Isaiah 2:3

Wherever he may guide me,   732
no want shall turn me back;
my Shepherd is beside me,
and nothing can I lack.
His wisdom ever waking,
his sight is never dim,
he knows the way he's taking,
and I will walk with him.

People will come from east and west and north and south, and will take their places at the feast in the kingdom of God. Luke 13:29 (NIV)

Lord Jesus Christ, we humbly pray: p228
O, keep us steadfast 'til that day
when each will be your welcomed guest
in heaven's high and holy feast.

This is the day that the Lord has made; let us be glad and rejoice in it before our God. Let us worship and bow down before him! Amen.

Monday, March 23 — Psalm 38:1–8
Nehemiah 13:15–31; Romans 7:21–8:8

Both we and our ancestors have sinned; we have committed iniquity, have done wickedly. Psalm 106:6

> Savior, now with contrite hearts   741
> we approach your throne of love,
> asking pardon for our sins,
> peace and comfort from above.
> You once suffered on the cross
> to atone for sinners' guilt;
> may we never, Lord, forget
> that for us your blood was spilled.

Jesus said, "I have come to call not the righteous but sinners." Mark 2:17

> Christ bids each afflicted soul   416
> "Come that I may soothe your grief.
> No one who is strong and whole
> needs a doctor for relief;
> therefore have no fear, draw nigh,
> that your want I may supply."

Lord Jesus, have mercy on us sinners. You, and only you, are the source of our comfort and protection. Redeem us, your people, and lead us not into temptation. Amen.

Tuesday, March 24 — Psalm 38:9–16
Esther 1; Romans 8:9–19

The Lord God took the man and put him in the garden of Eden to till it and keep it. Genesis 2:15

May we in service to our God   696*
act out the living word,
and walk the road the saints have trod
'til all have seen and heard.
As stewards of the earth may we
give thanks in one accord
to God who calls us all to be
disciples of the Lord.

It is required of stewards that they be found trustworthy. 1 Corinthians 4:2

Riches I heed not nor man's empty praise,   719
thou mine inheritance now and always;
thou and thou only first in my heart,
high King of heaven, my treasure thou art.

Lord our God, all good gifts are given to us through your word and grace. Let us never forget our duty to be stewards of all that you have given and to share it for your glory. Amen.

Wednesday, March 25 — Psalm 38:17–22
Esther 2:1–18; Romans 8:20–33

Then Jacob woke from his sleep and said, "How awesome is this place! This is none other than the house of God, and this is the gate of heaven." Genesis 28:17

> Fling wide the portals of your heart;   p51
> make it a temple set apart
> from earthly use for heav'n's employ,
> adorned with prayer and love and joy.

From the cloud a voice said, "This is my Son, the Beloved; with him I am well pleased; listen to him!" When the disciples heard this, they fell to the ground and were overcome by fear. But Jesus came and touched them, saying, "Get up and do not be afraid." Matthew 17:5–7

> When the Lord appears,   594
> this my spirit cheers;
> when, his love to me revealing
> he, the Sun of grace, with healing
> in his beams appears,
> this my spirit cheers.

Most kind and heavenly Father, we thank you this day for the blessings of heaven and the assurance of your calling to us. If we follow you we need not fear in anything that we do. All praise to you, our God. Amen.

Thursday, March 26 — Psalm 39:1–6
Esther 2:19–3:15; Romans 8:34–9:7

I have put my words in your mouth, and hidden you in the shadow of my hand. Isaiah 51:16

> The ground of my profession 769
> is Jesus and his blood;
> he gives me the possession
> of everlasting good.
> To me his Holy Spirit
> speaks many a precious word
> of rest to one who's seeking
> a refuge in the Lord.

Do not be afraid, but speak and do not be silent; for I am with you. Acts 18:9–10

> On this, our festive day, 633
> your people here adore you;
> we come to sing and pray
> and lay our gifts before you.
> Your hand has helped us on
> through ev'ry passing year;
> now, Father, Spirit, Son,
> our grateful praises hear!

Prince of Peace, your protective spirit watches over us in all our comings and goings. Never let us be silent in offering our joy and hope in a life with you, in this world or the next. Amen.

Friday, March 27 — Psalm 39:7–13
Esther 4,5; Romans 9:8–21

**The people came to Moses and said, "We have
sinned by speaking against the Lord and against
you; pray to the Lord to take away the serpents
from us." So Moses prayed for the people.
Numbers 21:7**

O Lord of all the living,   763*
both banished and restored,
compassionate, forgiving
and ever caring Lord,
grant now that my transgressing,
my faithlessness may cease.
Stretch out your hand in blessing,
in pardon and in peace.

**If anyone does sin, we have an advocate with the
Father, Jesus Christ the righteous. 1 John 2:1**

No prayer is made by us alone,   749
the Holy Spirit pleads,
and Jesus, on the eternal throne,
for sinners intercedes.

Compassionate Lord, we offer our thanks to you
for your power of forgiveness and the grace which
meets our needs. Help us to be witnesses for your
kingdom in all the places you would have us go. Be
with us all. Amen.

Saturday, March 28 — Psalm 40:1–8
Esther 6,7; Romans 9:22–33

I waited patiently for the Lord; he inclined to me and heard my cry. Psalm 40:1

> If you but trust in God to guide you   712
> and place your confidence in him,
> you'll find him always there beside you
> to give you hope and strength within;
> for those who trust God's changeless love
> build on the rock that will not move.

On God we have set our hope that he will rescue us again. 2 Corinthians 1:10

> When the sacred vow is made,   426
> when the hands are on them laid,
> come in this most solemn hour
> with your strength'ning gift of pow'r.
> Give them light, your truth to see;
> give them life, your own to be;
> daily pow'r to conquer sin;
> patient faith, the crown to win.

Hear our prayers, O Lord; incline your ear to us this day and let us prepare ourselves to listen for your leading. Grant to us your peace. Amen.

Palm Sunday

Watchword for the Week — Jesus said, "you will see the Son of Man seated at the right hand of the Power, and coming with the clouds of heaven." Mark 14:62

Sunday, March 29 — Isaiah 50:4–9a; Psalm 31:9–16 Philippians 2:5–11; Mark 11:1–11

I made the earth, and created humankind upon it. Isaiah 45:12

> Life-giving Creator of both great and small;   457
> of all life the maker, the true life of all;
> we blossom, then wither like leaves on the tree,
> but you live forever who was and will be.

For us there is one God, the Father, from whom are all things and for whom we exist. 1 Corinthians 8:6

> O Lord, in whom we all are one,   399
> if faithful found and true,
> your will on earth by each be done
> as each in heav'n would do.
> To you ourselves first would give;
> live to your glory while we live,
> from step to step on you rely,
> then in your service die.

Dearest Jesus, blessed are they who come in the name of the Lord. Let us humble ourselves before you and be always mindful of what you suffered, with great love, for us sinners. Hosanna in the highest. Amen.

Monday, March 30 — Psalm 40:9–17
Esther 8:1–9:17; Romans 10:1–13

Look down from your holy habitation, from heaven, and bless your people Israel. Deuteronomy 26:15

> We are God's house of living stones,   512
> built for his own habitation;
> he fills our hearts, his humble thrones,
> granting us life and salvation.
> Yet to this place, an earthly frame,
> we come with thanks to praise his name;
> God grants his people true blessing.

Praise be to the Lord, the God of Israel, because he has come to his people and redeemed them. Luke 1:68 (NIV)

> "Hosanna in the highest!"   p51
> That ancient song we sing,
> for Christ is our Redeemer,
> the Lord of heav'n our King.
> O may we ever praise him
> with heart and life and voice,
> and in his blissful presence
> eternally rejoice.

King of Kings, your love for us can never be repaid.
Let us praise your name and try to live the life
that you offer us through the merits of your life,
sufferings, death, and resurrection. Amen.

Tuesday, March 31 — Psalm 41
Esther 9:18–10:3; Romans 10:14–11:6

Woe to those who go to great depths to hide their plans from the Lord, who do their work in darkness and think, "Who sees us? Who will know?" Isaiah 29:15 (NIV)

O, send your Spirit, Lord,   502
now unto me,
that he may touch my eyes
and make me see.
Show me the truth concealed
within your word,
and in your book revealed
I see my Lord.

Take no part in the unfruitful works of darkness, but instead expose them. Everything exposed by the light becomes visible. Ephesians 5:11,13

As you with Satan did contend,   341
and did the vict'ry win,
O give us strength in you to fight,
in you to conquer sin.

O Glorious Lord, free us from the blindness to your everlasting light shining before us, and never let us hide in darkness from the wondrous love and grace that you offer to us, your children. Amen.

Wednesday, April 1 — Psalm 42
Job 1,2; Romans 11:7–18

Extol the Lord our God; worship at his footstool. Holy is he! Psalm 99:5

O worship the King, all glorious above,   566
O gratefully sing his power and his love;
our shield and defender, the ancient of days,
pavilioned in splendor, and girded with praise.

Hallelujah! Salvation and glory and power belong to our God. Revelation 19:1 (NIV)

O may your love be ever dwelling   340
within my heart alone enthroned,
all other love but yours expelling,
that love which for my sins atoned;
now Jesus, only, be my treasure,
my joy, my crown while life shall last;
none else on earth shall yield me pleasure,
none else in heav'n, when earth is past.

God of life and salvation, make your home in our hearts. Lead us to walk in your ways that we might become a people of peace. Amen.

Maundy Thursday

Watchword for Maundy Thursday — He has gained renown by his wonderful deeds; the Lord is gracious and merciful. Psalm 111:4

Thursday, April 2 — Psalm 43
Job 3,4; Romans 11:19–32

Comfort, O comfort my people, says your God. Isaiah 40:1

> Come, holy Comforter,   555
> your sacred witness bear
> in this glad hour.
> Your grace to us impart,
> now rule in ev'ry heart,
> never from us depart,
> Spirit of pow'r!

Come; for everything is ready now. Luke 14:17

> To your temple, Lord, I come,   553
> for it is my worship home.
> This earth has no better place,
> here I see my Savior's face.

Lead us, O God, to live by the gentle whispers of your Holy Spirit. And as you relieve the heaviness that we so often carry, give us the strength to become helping hands and listening ears. In your name we pray. Amen.

Good Friday

Watchword for Good Friday — For God so loved the world that he gave his only Son, so that everyone who believes in him may not perish but may have eternal life. John 3:16

Friday, April 3 — Psalm 44:1–8
Job 5,6; Romans 11:33–12:8

Do not delay me, since the Lord has made my journey successful. Genesis 24:56

> I fear no foe with you at hand to bless,　　　　807
> though ills have weight, and tears their bitterness.
> Where is death's sting? Where, grave, your victory?
> I triumph still, if you abide with me.

Those who passed by derided him, shaking their heads and saying, "You who would destroy the temple and build it in three days, save yourself! If you are the Son of God, come down from the cross." Matthew 27:39–40

> May our hearts incline to you　　　　352
> as we keep your cross in view,
> cheer our souls, our hope renew:
> hear us, holy Jesus.

God of the cross, you are with us in every moment of our lives. As we journey though seasons of grief, we believe that you are weeping with us. We cling to the promise of new life through Jesus Christ our Lord. Amen.

Great Sabbath

Saturday, April 4 — Psalm 44:9–16
Job 7; Romans 12:9–21

You are a people holy to the Lord your God; it is you the Lord has chosen out of all the peoples on earth to be his people, his treasured possession. Deuteronomy 14:2

> We may not know, we cannot tell   353
> what pains he had to bear;
> but we believe it was for us
> he hung and suffered there.

Jesus said, "The Father himself loves you, because you have loved me and have believed that I came from God. I came from the Father and have come into the world; again, I am leaving the world and am going to the Father." John 16:27–28

> Most loving Jesus, only child   776*
> of God your bloodshed reconciled
> our fallen world to God above:
> we praise and bless you for this love.

Most holy Lord and God, you have chosen us to be a people who are known by our love for one another. As we seek to follow the example of Jesus, teach us the way of reconciliation and peace. Amen.

* © 1994 by Madeleine Forell Marshall

Easter Sunday

Watchword for the Week — But in fact Christ has been raised from the dead, the first fruits of those who have died. 1 Corinthians 15:20

Sunday, April 5 — Acts 10:34–43; Psalm 118:1–2,14–24
1 Corinthians 15:1–11; Mark 16:1–8

This people I have formed for myself; they shall declare my praise. Isaiah 43:21 (NKJV)

Praise the Lord, praise the Lord!   528
He with you deals bounteously.
Highly favored church of Jesus,
he chose you through mercy free
to show forth his matchless praises
and rich fruit, blessed for the Master's use,
to produce, to produce.

Jesus rejoiced in the Holy Spirit and said, "I thank you, Father, Lord of heaven and earth, because you have hidden these things from the wise and the intelligent and have revealed them to infants; yes, Father, for such was your gracious will." Luke 10:21

Gracious Father, bless this congregation   444
as the purchase of your Son;
for his sake behold us with compassion,
and us all your children own;
Jesus, grant to us your peace and favor;
Holy Spirit, dwell with us forever,
and to us Christ's love explain;
hear us, Lord our God! Amen.

God of our resurrection hope, we give thanks for the living presence of Jesus and for the power of the Holy Spirit that makes us one. Reveal yourself to us this day, as we together seek to discern your will and discover you in unexpected places. Amen.

Easter Monday

Monday, April 6 — Psalm 44:17–26
Job 8; Romans 13

A thousand years in your sight are like yesterday when it is past, or like a watch in the night. Psalm 90:4

Crown him the Lord of years,   405
the risen Lord sublime,
Creator of the rolling spheres,
the Master of all time.
All hail, Redeemer, hail!
For you have died for me;
your praise and glory shall not fail
throughout eternity.

Christ says, "I am the first and the last, and the living one. I was dead, and see, I am alive forever and ever; and I have the keys of Death and of Hades." Revelation 1:17–18

Amen, yea, my lasting praises,   808
Jesus, unto you are giv'n,
that a place by you prepared
is for me secured in heav'n;
blessed my case, O truly blessed,
when to heav'nly glory raised,
I from pain and sorrow free
in your presence safe shall be.

Risen Christ, we believe that you are near to us by the power of the Holy Spirit. Make us to trust in your promises to us—that no matter where we find ourselves, no matter where we've been, you will lead us into the future. Amen.

Tuesday, April 7 — Psalm 45:1–9
Job 9; Romans 14:1–12

The snares of death encompassed me; I suffered distress and anguish. Then I called on the name of the Lord: "O Lord, I pray, save my life!" Psalm 116:3–4

> Lord Jesus, think on me,   764
> by anxious thoughts oppressed;
> let me your loving servant be
> and taste your promised rest.

Thanks be to God, who gives us the victory through our Lord Jesus Christ. 1 Corinthians 15:57

> Am I of my salvation   795
> assured through thy great love?
> May I on each occasion
> to thee more faithful prove.
> Hast thou my sins forgiven?
> Then, leaving things behind,
> may I press on to heaven
> and bear the prize in mind.

Your grace is sufficient, O Christ. It is enough to satisfy our restless hearts and anxious fears. It is enough to push through all the remnants of shame and self-hate. It is enough to break down the walls of unforgiveness and prejudice. Thanks be to God. Amen.

Wednesday, April 8 — Psalm 45:10–17
Job 10; Romans 14:13–15:2

Children, who do not know this law, must hear it and learn to fear the Lord their God as long as they live. Deuteronomy 31:13 (NIV)

> Our children, Lord, in faith and prayer,   409
> we baptize in your name.
> Let them your cov'nant mercies share
> as we our faith proclaim.

Jesus said, "Let the little children come to me, and do not hinder them, for the kingdom of God belongs to such as these." Luke 18:16 (NIV)

> Jesus loves me! This I know,   726
> for the Bible tells me so.
> Little ones to him belong;
> they are weak but he is strong.
> Yes, Jesus loves me,
> yes, Jesus loves me,
> yes Jesus loves me,
> the Bible tells me so.

God of all things great and small, lead us to be examples to one another. May we demonstrate the love of Jesus in all that we say and do. Amen.

Thursday, April 9 — Psalm 46
Job 11:1–12:12; Romans 15:3–16

Let your steadfast love come to me, O Lord, your salvation according to your promise. Psalm 119:41

> All people of each time and place   p134
> receive the promise of God's grace.
> O praise God! Alleluia!
> And all who have not heard God's voice,
> we now invite you, "Come! Rejoice!"
> O praise God! Alleluia!
> O praise God! Alleluia! Alleluia!

May our Lord Jesus Christ himself and God our Father, who loved us and through grace gave us eternal comfort and good hope, comfort your hearts and strengthen them in every good work and word. 2 Thessalonians 2:16–17

> With your presence, Lord, our Head and Savior,   447
> bless us all, we humbly pray;
> our dear heavenly Father's love and favor
> be our comfort every day.
> May God's Spirit now in each proceeding
> favor us with his most gracious leading;
> thus shall we be truly blessed
> both in labor and in rest.

O most beloved Friend, you are ever near to us.
May we encounter you this day in the faces of those around us. Amen.

Friday, April 10 — Psalm 47
Job 12:13–13:19; Romans 15:17–29

When you return to the Lord your God, then the Lord your God will restore you from captivity, and have compassion on you. Deuteronomy 30:2,3 (NASB)

> Come, you weary, heavy laden,   765
> lost and ruined by the fall;
> if you tarry 'til you're better,
> you will never come at all.
> I will arise and go to Jesus;
> he will embrace me in his arms;
> in the arms of my dear Savior,
> O there are ten thousand charms.

You have been set free from sin and have become slaves to righteousness. Romans 6:18 (NIV)

> Just as I am; thy love unknown   762
> has broken every barrier down;
> now to be thine, yea, thine alone,
> O Lamb of God, I come, I come!

O Lamb of God, your compassion is everlasting. Your affection is forever, and for this we give you thanks. May we journey this day in faith, believing that we are truly free indeed. Amen.

Saturday, April 11 — Psalm 48
Job 13:20–14:22; Romans 15:30–16:7

When the ways of people please the Lord, he causes even their enemies to be at peace with them. Proverbs 16:7

O that Jesus' love and merit   589
filled our hearts both night and day!
May the leading of his spirit
all our thoughts and actions sway!
Then should we be ever ready
cheerfully to testify
how our spirit, soul, and body
do in God our Savior joy.

The God of peace be with all of you. Romans 15:33

I've got peace like a river,   592
I've got peace like a river,
I've got peace like a river in my soul,
I've got peace like a river,
I've got peace like a river,
I've got peace like a river in my soul.

Your peace, O God, is an abundant stream. It fills
us to overflowing. Teach us to share your peace
with everyone. May we never be so afraid that we
keep your abundance to ourselves. Amen.

Second Sunday of Easter

Watchword for the Week — If we walk in the light as God is in the light, we have fellowship with one another, and the blood of Jesus his Son cleanses us from all sin. 1 John 1:7

Sunday, April 12 — Acts 4:32–35; Psalm 133
1 John 1:1–2:2; John 20:19–31

The Lord said to Abram, "I will bless you and you will be a blessing." Genesis 12:2

"I'll bless you, and you shall be set for a blessing!" 616
Thus said God, the Lord, to his servant of old;
O may we, in grace and in number increasing,
through work show our faith and in service be bold;
upon your truth founded, we shall not move,
let us ever follow, and fearless prove;
so shall we in doctrine, in word and behavior,
to ev'ryone witness that Christ is our Savior.

You are the salt of the earth. Matthew 5:13

Take my life that it may be   610
all your purpose, Lord, for me.
Take my moments and my days;
let them sing your ceaseless praise,
let them sing your ceaseless praise.

God of every blessing, fashion us according to your purposes so that we might be witnesses for you and instruments of your faithfulness. May the living Jesus be revealed in us this day. Amen.

Monday, April 13 — Psalm 49:1–12
Job 15,16; Romans 16:8–20

You shall not cheat one another, but you shall fear your God. Leviticus 25:17

> Grant by guidance from above 586
> that obedience, faith, and love
> show our hearts to you are giv'n,
> that our treasure is in heaven.

Do nothing out of selfish ambition or vain conceit. Rather, in humility value others above yourselves. Philippians 2:3 (NIV)

> May the mind of Christ my Savior 585
> live in me from day to day,
> by his love and pow'r controlling
> all I do and say.

God of love, you set an example for us in Jesus Christ. We are humbled to know that you have chosen us to be your disciples. We are encouraged to know that you will guide us as we follow after you. Amen.

Tuesday, April 14 — Psalm 49:13–20
Job 17,18; Romans 16:21–1 Corinthians 1:1–9

You have taken up my cause, O Lord, you have redeemed my life. Lamentations 3:58

Dear Lord, from whom we all derive   831
our life, our gifts, our pow'r to give:
now may we ever with you live. Amen.

We have this hope as an anchor for the soul, firm and secure. Hebrews 6:19 (NIV)

Nay, too closely am I bound   p215
unto him by hope forever;
faith's strong hand the rock has found,
grasped it and will leave it never;
not the ban of death can part
from the Lord the trusting heart.

God of hope, you are our Refuge and Strength, a very present help in times of need. May we rest in the truth of your promises to us, believing that we are called according to your purposes. Amen.

Wednesday, April 15 — Psalm 50:1–6
Job 19; 1 Corinthians 1:10–20

**Hear, O kings; give ear, O princes; to the Lord
I will sing, I will make melody to the Lord, the
God of Israel. Judges 5:3**

> Praise we now the God of nations   637*
> who through Israel long ago
> called a people in Christ Jesus,
> led them on through joy and woe.
> Alleluia! Christians faithful,
> let our tributes overflow.

**About midnight Paul and Silas were praying and
singing hymns to God, and the prisoners were
listening to them. Acts 16:25**

> Praise we all our God eternal   637*
> who created land and sea
> bringing forth the human story,
> life and love that's true and free.
> Alleluia! Through this journey
> let our lives inspired be.

God of stories and songs, may our lives resound
like music in the ears of your people. And as we
share in the journey of faith together, let us make
memories in your name and for your glory. Amen.

* © 1992 by Willard R. Harstine

Thursday, April 16 — Psalm 50:7–15
Job 20; 1 Corinthians 1:21–2:2

The Lord is in the right, for I have rebelled against his word. Lamentations 1:18

> How shall the young direct their way?   510
> What light shall be their perfect guide?
> Your word, O Lord, will safely lead
> if in its wisdom they confide.

I will get up and go to my father, and I will say to him, "Father, I have sinned against heaven and before you." Luke 15:18

> Sincerely I have sought you, Lord,   510
> O let me not from you depart;
> to know your will and keep from sin,
> your word I cherish in my heart.

God of life—reveal to us the truth of who we are:
the daughters and sons of a living Creator. Amen.

Friday, April 17 — Psalm 50:16–23
Job 21; 1 Corinthians 2:3–16

The Lord judges the peoples. Psalm 7:8

Holy, holy, holy Lord God Almighty!   381
All thy works shall praise thy name
   in earth and sky and sea.
Holy, holy, holy, merciful and mighty!

There is one lawgiver and judge who is able to save and to destroy. So who, then, are you to judge your neighbor? James 4:12

His righteous government and power   320
shall over all extend;
on judgment and on justice based,
his reign shall have no end.

God of grace, you invite us to share your good news with everyone. May we overcome all our fears and prejudices by the power of the Holy Spirit—with us and in us. Amen.

Saturday, April 18 — Psalm 51:1–6
Job 22,23; 1 Corinthians 3:1–11

**The Lord said to Moses, "Now go, and I will be
with your mouth and teach you what you are to
speak." Exodus 4:12**

> Keep me from saying words   615
> that later need recalling;
> guard me, lest idle speech
> may from my lips be falling;
> but when, within my place,
> I must and ought to speak,
> then to my words give grace,
> lest I offend the weak.

**When the Advocate comes, whom I will send to
you from the Father—the Spirit of truth who goes
out from the Father—he will testify about me.
And you also must testify. John 15:26–27 (NIV)**

> Touch now our hands to lead us aright.   489
> Guide us forever, show us your way.
> Transform our darkness into your light.
> Spirit of God, still lead us today.

Spirit of the living God, enter into the silence of our
hearts, and speak. Amen.

Third Sunday of Easter

Watchword for the Week — See what love the Father has given us, that we should be called children of God; and that is what we are. 1 John 3:1

Sunday, April 19 — Acts 3:12–19; Psalm 4
1 John 3:1–7; Luke 24:36b–48

His dominion shall be from sea to sea, and to the ends of the earth. Zechariah 9:10

Holy God, we praise your name;   386
Lord of all, we bow before you.
Saints on earth your rule acclaim;
all in heaven above adore you.
Infinite your vast domain;
everlasting is your reign.

God gave Christ Jesus the name that is above every name, so that at the name of Jesus every knee should bend, in heaven and on earth and under the earth. Philippians 2:9–10

How good the name of Jesus sounds   487
to all believing ears!
It soothes our sorrows, heals our wounds,
and drives away our fears.
It makes the wounded spirit whole,
and calms the troubled mind;
his manna for each hungry soul,
the lost and weary find.

Gentle Jesus, come alive in us this day, and strengthen us as you make beauty from our weakness. Amen.

Monday, April 20 — Psalm 51:7–12
Job 24; 1 Corinthians 3:12–23

I thank you that you have answered me and have become my salvation. Psalm 118:21

Praise the Lord, God our salvation,   298
praise him who retrieved our loss;
sing, with awe and love's sensation,
hallelujah, God with us.

Everyone who asks receives, and everyone who searches finds, and for everyone who knocks, the door will be opened. Matthew 7:8

Only be still and wait his pleasure   712
in cheerful hope with heart content.
He fills your needs to fullest measure
with what discerning love has sent;
doubt not our inmost wants are known
to him who chose us for his own.

Blessed Jesus, you are the source of our life and our
faith. As we wait for your direction, may we find
comfort in your sustaining hand. Amen.

Tuesday, April 21 — Psalm 51:13–19
Job 25–27; 1 Corinthians 4:1–15

Job answered the Lord: "See, I am of small account; what shall I answer you? I lay my hand on my mouth." Job 40:3–4

He only is the Maker   453
of all things near and far;
he paints the wayside flower,
he lights the evening star;
the winds and waves obey him,
by him the birds are fed;
much more to us, his children,
he gives our daily bread.
All good gifts around us
are sent from heav'n above;
then thank the Lord, O thank the Lord
for all his love.

Lord, teach us to pray. Luke 11:1

Prayer is the burden of a sigh,   749
the falling of a tear,
the upward glancing of an eye,
when none but God is near.

Lord, teach us to pray—to listen, to give thanks,
and to place our trust in you. May your will be done
in us this day. Amen

Wednesday, April 22 — Psalm 52
Job 28; 1 Corinthians 4:16–5:8

Moses stretched out his hand over the sea. The Lord drove the sea back by a strong east wind. Exodus 14:21

Hear then, dear Lord Jesus,   746
hear our earnest prayer,
grant your loving mercy,
keep us in your care.
All that is displeasing
unto you, forgive;
more to your name's glory
may we henceforth live.

For freedom Christ has set us free. Galatians 5:1

'Twas grace that taught my heart to fear   783
and grace my fears relieved;
how precious did that grace appear
the hour I first believed.

Faithful God, we give thanks for your unfailing
grace and for your nearness to us even when we
have lost our way. Show us the road that leads
to life. Give us the strength to follow after you, in
Jesus' name. Amen.

Thursday, April 23 — Psalm 53
Job 29; 1 Corinthians 5:9–6:8

Your days of mourning shall be ended.
Isaiah 60:20

My lasting joy and comfort here   768
is Jesus' death and blood;
I with this passport can appear
before the throne of God.
Admitted to the realms above,
I then shall see the Christ I love,
where countless pardoned sinners meet
adoring at his feet.

Keep yourselves in God's love as you wait for the mercy of our Lord Jesus Christ to bring you to eternal life. Jude 21 (NIV)

Come then, come, O flock of Jesus,   673
covenant with him anew;
unto him, who conquered for us,
pledge we love and service true;
and should our love's union holy
firmly linked no more remain,
wait ye at his footstool lowly,
'til he draw it close again.

O Lamb of God, you take away the sin of the world.
Make beauty of our broken hearts. We put our trust
in you alone. Amen.

Friday, April 24 — Psalm 54
Job 30; 1 Corinthians 6:9–20

The eyes of the Lord range throughout the entire earth, to strengthen those whose heart is true to him. 2 Chronicles 16:9

> Faith finds in Christ our ev'ry need   700
> to save or strengthen us indeed;
> we now receive the grace sent down,
> which makes us share his cross and crown.

Christ says, "I know your works, your toil and your patient endurance." Revelation 2:2

> He gives me for my tears   329r
> his oil of gladness;
> delivers, heals, and cheers,
> dispels my sadness;
> he makes sin's power to cease,
> his grace restrains me,
> and with his word of peace
> he still sustains me.

Emmanuel—God with us—you are never far away. Guide us by your tender hand. May we feel the embrace of your gentle care. Amen.

Saturday, April 25 — Psalm 55:1–8
Job 31; 1 Corinthians 7:1–16

The Lord our God is righteous in everything he does. Daniel 9:14 (NIV)

> May your church, arrayed in the glorious dress p205
> of the Lord and Savior's spotless righteousness,
> be both now and ever by your blood kept clean,
> and in all its members may your grace be seen.

The landowner said, "Friend, I am doing you no wrong; am I not allowed to do what I choose with what belongs to me? Or are you envious because I am generous?" Matthew 20:13,15

> In all things our Father, Lord and Savior,   397*
> teaches us the law of love;
> then let love determine our behavior,
> for 'tis God's command to all;
> may this motto live in all God's children
> as we strive to follow love's direction;
> may God bless us as we show
> charity in all we do.

God of love, your generosity astounds us. Teach us
to live, that we might demonstrate your endless
compassion and boundless grace. Amen.

* © 1993 by E. Artis Weber. Used by permission.

Fourth Sunday of Easter

Watchword for the Week — Jesus says, "I am the good shepherd. The good shepherd lays down his life for the sheep." John 10:11

Sunday, April 26 — Acts 4:5–12; Psalm 23
1 John 3:16–24; John 10:11–18

The Lord our God is merciful and forgiving. Daniel 9:9 (NIV)

Much forgiven, may I learn   779
love for hatred to return;
then my heart assured shall be
you, my God, have pardoned me.

One man's act of righteousness leads to justification and life for all. Romans 5:18

Whoe'er would spend   593
    their days in lasting pleasure
must come to Christ and join his flock with speed;
here is a feast prepared, rich beyond measure,
the world meanwhile on empty husks must feed.
Those souls may share in ev'ry good
whose Shepherd does possess the treasuries of God.

God of mercy, fashion our hearts after you, that we may see the world through the eyes of your everlasting love. Amen.

Monday, April 27 — Psalm 55:9–15
Job 32,33; 1 Corinthians 7:17–24

Now set your mind and heart to seek the Lord your God. 1 Chronicles 22:19

Near the cross! O Lamb of God,   313r
bring its scenes before me;
help me walk from day to day
with its shadow o'er me.
In the cross, in the cross
be my glory ever,
'til my raptured soul shall find
rest beyond the river.

Paul wrote: I do not consider that I have made it my own; but this one thing I do: forgetting what lies behind and straining forward to what lies ahead, I press on toward the goal for the prize of the heavenly call of God in Christ Jesus. Philippians 3:13–14

Near the cross I'll watch and wait,   313r
hoping, trusting ever,
'til I reach the golden strand
just beyond the river.
In the cross, in the cross
be my glory ever,
'til my raptured soul shall find
rest beyond the river.

God of all strength, renew us in the assurance
of your promises to us. And when we grow
discouraged from stumbling, enable us—by faith—
to begin again... and again... and again, in your
name. Amen.

Tuesday, April 28 — Psalm 55:16–19
Job 34:1–28; 1 Corinthians 7:25–40

I believe that I shall see the goodness of the Lord in the land of the living. Psalm 27:13

Sing hallelujah, praise the Lord!   543
Sing with a cheerful voice;
exalt our God with one accord,
and in his name rejoice.
Ne'er cease to sing, O ransomed host,
praise Father, Son, and Holy Ghost,
until in realms of endless light
your praises shall unite.

Jesus prayed: Father, I desire that those also, whom you have given me, may be with me where I am, to see my glory. John 17:24

But not for us alone this news   543
was brought by Christ our Lord.
'Twas meant for all the world to hear
and thus with one accord
with all God's children everywhere
his name and sign with pride we bear.
To us, to us, this task is giv'n:
to spread God's word. Amen.

Spirit of life, come alive in us and reveal the beauty of your creation. Guide your church into the future as you lead us out into your world. Amen.

Wednesday, April 29 — Psalm 55:20–23
Job 34:29–35:16; 1 Corinthians 8

You, O God, have tested us; you have tried us as silver is tried. Psalm 66:10

When peace, like a river, attendeth my way,   754
when sorrows like sea billows roll;
whatever my lot, you have taught me to say,
it is well, it is well with my soul.
It is well with my soul,
it is well, it is well with my soul.

Blessed is anyone who endures temptation. Such a one has stood the test and will receive the crown of life that the Lord has promised to those who love him. James 1:12

Take up your cross, and follow Christ,   758
nor think 'til death to lay it down;
for only those who bear the cross
may hope to wear the glorious crown.

Lead us, O Lord, as we follow after you. Carry us, as we carry one another, in Jesus' name. Amen.

Thursday, April 30 — Psalm 56:1–8
Job 36:1–26; 1 Corinthians 9:1–12a

Happy are those who make the Lord their trust. Psalm 40:4

My faith looks trustingly   705
to Christ of Calvary,
my Savior true!
Lord, hear me while I pray,
take all my guilt away,
strengthen in ev'ry way
my love for you!

Do not throw away your confidence; it will be richly rewarded. Hebrews 10:35 (NIV)

Help me to bear your easy yoke,   638
in ev'ry moment watch and pray,
and still to things eternal look
and hasten to that glorious day.

God of the cross, God of the empty tomb, God of
everywhere in between—no matter where we find
ourselves, you are there, ushering in newness of life,
both now and forevermore. Amen.

Friday, May 1 — Psalm 56:9–13
Job 36:27–37:24; 1 Corinthians 9:12b–27

**You have burdened me with your sins; you
have wearied me with your iniquities. I, I am
he who blots out your transgressions for my
own sake, and I will not remember your sins.
Isaiah 43:24–25**

> For God so loved us, he sent the Savior: 775
> for God so loved us, and loves me too.
> Love so unending! I'll sing your praises,
> God loves his children, loves even me.

**And you who were once estranged and hostile
in mind, doing evil deeds, Christ has now
reconciled in his fleshly body through death.
Colossians 1:21–22**

> Maker of all things, Lord our God,   p73
> now veiled in feeble flesh and blood,
> to reconcile and set us free
> from endless woe and misery;
> what heights, what depths, of love divine
> in your blessed incarnation shine!
> Let heav'n and earth unite their praise,
> to magnify your boundless grace.

Almighty God, we are so grateful for our Savior,
Jesus Christ, whom you promised to us. Help us to
adore him and to proclaim his word everywhere we
are. Amen.

Saturday, May 2 — Psalm 57:1–6
Job 38; 1 Corinthians 10:1–10

Then all flesh shall know that I am the Lord your Savior, and your Redeemer. Isaiah 49:26

You only are true life— 486*
to know you is to live
the more abundant life
that earth can never give.
O risen Lord! we live in you:
in us each day your life renew!

The Son of Man came not to be served but to serve, and to give his life a ransom for many. Matthew 20:28

Servant of God, well done! 811
Rest from your loved employ;
the battle fought, the victory won,
enter your Master's joy.

Dear Lord, make us servants of your peace. May we be faithful to you in our work in this world, preaching your word of grace. In the name of our Savior, Jesus Christ. Amen.

Fifth Sunday of Easter

Watchword for the Week — Jesus says, "Abide in me as I abide in you. Just as the branch cannot bear fruit by itself unless it abides in the vine, neither can you unless you abide in me." John 15:4

Sunday, May 3 — Acts 8:26–40; Psalm 22:25–31
1 John 4:7–21; John 15:1–8

Whoever is kind to the needy honors God.
Proverbs 14:31 (NIV)

Alleluia, alleluia!   798*
As we walk along beside you,
and we hear you speak of mercy,
then it seems our hearts are burning,
for we find you in the sharing of the word.

If a brother or sister is naked and lacks daily food, and one of you says to them, "Go in peace; keep warm and eat your fill," and yet you do not supply their bodily needs, what is the good of that? So faith by itself, if it has no works, is dead. James 2:15–17

'Tis a pleasant thing to see   670
brothers in the Lord agree,
sisters of a God of love
live as they shall live above,
acting each a Christian part,
one in word and one in heart.

O loving Creator, we recognize that you are our Provider. We give thanks to you every day. Let us share your blessings with others in need, in the name of Jesus. Amen.

Monday, May 4 — Psalm 57:7–11
Job 39; 1 Corinthians 10:11–22

You have set my feet in a broad place. Psalm 31:8

Enrich me always with your love;   733
my kind protector ever prove;
Lord, put your seal upon my heart,
that I from you may not depart.

May you have the power to comprehend, with all the saints, what is the breadth and length and height and depth, and to know the love of Christ that surpasses knowledge. Ephesians 3:18–19

O love, how deep, how broad, how high,   485
beyond all thought and fantasy,
that God, the son of God, should take
our mortal form for mortals' sake.

Thank you, God, for your boundless and infinite love for us. We want to serve you only. Lead us to recognize you through our Savior Jesus Christ. Amen.

Tuesday, May 5 — Psalm 58
Job 40; 1 Corinthians 10:23–11:2

You shall eat in plenty and be satisfied, and praise the name of the Lord your God. Joel 2:26

Lord, be ever my protector;   568
with me stay, all the day,
ever my director.
Holy, holy, holy giver
of all good life and food,
reign adored forever.

God has not left himself without a witness in doing good—giving you rains from heaven and fruitful seasons, and filling you with food and your hearts with joy. Acts 14:17

Guide me, O my great Redeemer,   790
pilgrim through this barren land.
I am weak, but you are mighty;
hold me with your pow'rful hand.
Bread of heaven, bread of heaven,
feed me now and evermore,
feed me now and evermore.

Eternal God, you are the Provider. You give us your grace through Jesus Christ and you always provide us with abundant fruits of the land to feed us. We give you thanks for all of these gifts. Amen.

Wednesday, May 6 — Psalm 59:1–9
Job 41; 1 Corinthians 11:3–16

If my father and mother forsake me, the Lord will take me up. Psalm 27:10

How good, Lord, to be here!   326
Your glory fills the night;
Your face and garments, like the sun,
shine with unborrowed light.

Christ says, "I am with you always, to the end of the age." Matthew 28:20

O wondrous sight! O vision fair   327
of glory that the church shall share,
which Christ upon the mountain shows,
where brighter than the sun he glows!

We worship you, dear Lord, with a spirit of thanksgiving for your presence with us. May you be with us always. Give us hope and love so that we can share it with others, just as you shared it with us. In the name of Jesus we pray. Amen.

Thursday, May 7 — Psalm 59:10–17
Job 42; 1 Corinthians 11:17–30

I walk before the Lord in the land of the living. Psalm 116:9

Green pastures are before me   732
which yet I have not seen;
bright skies will soon be o'er me
where darkest clouds have been.
My hope I cannot measure,
my path to life is free,
my Savior has my treasure,
and he will walk with me.

The gift of God is eternal life in Christ Jesus our Lord. Romans 6:23 (NIV)

Savior of the nations, come!   265
Virgin's son make here your home.
Marvel now, both heav'n and earth,
that the Lord chose such a birth.

Heavenly Father, we surrender to your presence
so that we can reach eternal life with you. We
praise you not because of the things you provide us
with, but simply because you are God. Be with us
through this whole journey until we get to spend
eternity with you. Amen.

Friday, May 8 — Psalm 60
Proverbs 1:1–2:8; 1 Corinthians 11:31–12:11

Lift up your voice like a trumpet! Announce to my people their rebellion. Isaiah 58:1

> Lord God, with shame I now confess   p32
> I've turned away from you;
> forgive me all my sin today,
> my heart and soul renew.

Do not be deceived; God is not mocked, for you reap whatever you sow. Galatians 6:7

> O bless his holy name,   452
> and joyful thanks proclaim
> through all the earth;
> be grateful and receive
> God's blessing; and believe;
> his love does not deceive.
> Now share your mirth!

We cannot deceive you, Lord. We can only surrender our lives to you so that you can use us to fulfill your will. Let us be the instruments through which you make beautiful music. We belong to you. Amen.

Saturday, May 9 — Psalm 61
Proverbs 2:9–3:20; 1 Corinthians 12:12–26

The Lord said, "Whom did you dread and fear so that you lied, and did not remember me?" Isaiah 57:11

For thinking you too far from us,   738*
for fearing you too close to us,
forgive us now, good Lord.
You dwell in high and holy place,
and yet touch all things with your grace.
Through all our lives be now adored.

Peter remembered what Jesus had said: "Before the cock crows, you will deny me three times." And he went out and wept bitterly. Matthew 26:75

Father, now your sinful child   779
through your love is reconciled.
By your pard'ning grace I live;
daily still I cry, forgive.

O Lord, you remember us every single moment of our lives, yet we continually fail you, only remembering you in our times of need or crisis. Please help us to be more like you so that we won't fail you as much as we do today. Amen.

Sixth Sunday of Easter

Watchword for the Week — Make a joyful noise to the Lord, all the earth; break forth into joyous song and sing praises. Psalm 98:4

Sunday, May 10 — Acts 10:44–48; Psalm 98
1 John 5:1–6; John 15:9–17

They shall know that I, the Lord their God, am with them, and that they, the house of Israel, are my people, says the Lord God. Ezekiel 34:30

Jesus, life of all the world,   363*
source and sum of all creation,
Son of God and Son of man,
only hope of our salvation,
Living Word for all our need,
life you give is life indeed.

You know the message God sent to the people of Israel, announcing the good news of peace through Jesus Christ, who is Lord of all. Acts 10:36 (NIV)

Christ the Lord is ris'n again,   360
Christ has broken ev'ry chain!
Hark, angelic voices cry,
Singing evermore on high:
Alleluia!

Father, you are everything. You are love, peace, and salvation. Shine upon us and give us peace everywhere we go, as we struggle to do anything without you. Have mercy upon us and help us find peace in you, our Savior. Amen.

Monday, May 11 — Psalm 62
Proverbs 3:21–4:27; 1 Corinthians 12:27–13:7

Speak tenderly to Jerusalem, and proclaim to her that her hard service has been completed, that her sin has been paid for. Isaiah 40:2 (NIV)

> Praise the Lord! You heav'ns adore him,   454
> praise him, angels in the height;
> sun and moon, rejoice before him;
> praise him, all you stars and light.
> Praise the Lord! For he has spoken;
> worlds his mighty voice obeyed;
> laws which never shall be broken
> for their guidance he has made.

God says, "At an acceptable time I have listened to you, and on a day of salvation I have helped you." See, now is the acceptable time; see, now is the day of salvation! 2 Corinthians 6:2

> Let earth's wide circle round   552
> in joyful notes resound:
> may Jesus Christ be praised!
> Let air and sea and sky
> from depth to height reply:
> may Jesus Christ be praised!

Father, only you know the exact time for your second coming. Only you know when it is that you will give us salvation from the disasters of this world. Prepare us, so that whenever it is that you come, we will be ready to go with you. Amen.

Tuesday, May 12 — Psalm 63
Proverbs 5; 1 Corinthians 13:8–14:5

Gideon answered the angel of the Lord, "If the Lord is with us, why then has all this happened to us?" Judges 6:13

> O God of ev'ry nation,   683*
> of ev'ry race and land,
> Redeem your whole creation
> with your almighty hand;
> where hate and fear divide us,
> and bitter threats are hurled,
> in love and mercy guide us,
> and heal our strife-torn world.

What we see now is like a dim image in a mirror; then we shall see face-to-face. What I know now is only partial; then it will be complete—as complete as God's knowledge of me. 1 Corinthians 13:12 (GNT)**

> In heav'n above, in heav'n above,   810
> where God our Father dwells:
> how boundless there the blessedness!
> No tongue its greatness tells.
> There face to face and full and free,
> the ever-living God we see,
> our God, the Lord of hosts!

God, we usually think that we have to see something to believe it. You call us to do the opposite with your kingdom; we have to believe in order to see. Allow us to become closer with your word so that we may believe and never doubt. Amen.

Wednesday, May 13 — Psalm 64
Proverbs 6; 1 Corinthians 14:6–19

The Lord says, "I will give you as a light to the nations, that my salvation may reach to the end of the earth." Isaiah 49:6

O word of God incarnate,   505
O wisdom from on high,
O truth unchanged, unchanging,
O light of our dark sky:
we praise you for the radiance
that from the scripture's page,
A lantern to our footsteps,
shines on from age to age.

Jesus said, "You will be my witnesses in Jerusalem, in all Judea and Samaria, and to the ends of the earth." Acts 1:8

O could we but love that Savior,   589
who loves us so ardently,
as we ought, our souls would ever
full of joy and comfort be;
if we, by his love incited,
could ourselves and all forget,
then, with Jesus Christ united,
we should heav'n anticipate.

Almighty God, let us be lamps in the middle of dark shadows. Help us to spread the light that you have given us to those around us who carry darkness on their shoulders. You are with us. Amen.

Ascension Day

Watchword for the Ascension — Christ says, "I, when I am lifted up from the earth, will draw all people to myself." John 12:32

Thursday, May 14 — Psalm 65:1–8
Proverbs 7; 1 Corinthians 14:20–35

Ascension of the Lord — Acts 1:1–11; Psalm 47
Ephesians 1:15–23; Luke 24:44–53

The Lord shall arbitrate for many peoples; they shall beat their swords into ploughshares, and their spears into pruning-hooks. Isaiah 2:4

> Blessed are they who show their mercy   595
> to the guilty and the poor,
> for to them, set free from judgment,
> shall be opened heaven's door.
> Blessed, the sincere and truthful
> from the lie's deception free,
> for the God of truth and beauty
> they in joy will surely see.

By the tender mercy of our God, the dawn from on high will break upon us, to give light to those who sit in darkness and in the shadow of death, to guide our feet into the way of peace. Luke 1:78–79

> Hail the day that sees him rise, alleluia!   371
> To his throne above the skies! Alleluia!
> Christ, awhile to mortals giv'n, alleluia!
> Reascends his native heav'n. Alleluia!

Father, you spoke unto us, saying that you are the only way to heaven. We reach for your hand to guide us until you call us home. We trust in the perfect timing of your plan for us. Amen.

Friday, May 15 — Psalm 65:9–13
Proverbs 8:1–9:6; 1 Corinthians 14:36–15:2

The Lord said, "Oh, that their hearts would be inclined to fear me and keep all my commands always, so that it might go well with them and their children forever!" Deuteronomy 5:29 (NIV)

> Glory to God whose witness train,   p106
> those heroes bold in faith,
> could smile on poverty and pain,
> and triumph e'en in death.

It is good for the heart to be strengthened by grace. Hebrews 13:9 (NASB)

> God whom we serve, our God can save,   p106
> can damp the scorching flame,
> can build an ark, can smooth the wave,
> for such as love his name.

Dear Heavenly Father, you are so good. We do not have words enough to thank you for your word and your promises to us, your grateful servants. Grant us today your wisdom, mercy, grace, and love. In the name of Jesus. Amen.

Saturday, May 16 — Psalm 66:1–7
Proverbs 9:7–10:32; 1 Corinthians 15:3–16

Only fear the Lord, and serve him faithfully with all your heart; for consider what great things he has done for you. 1 Samuel 12:24

> There is a balm in Gilead   500
> to make the wounded whole,
> there is a balm in Gilead
> to heal the sinsick soul.
> If you cannot preach like Peter,
> if you cannot pray like Paul,
> you can tell the love of Jesus,
> and say, "He died for all."

Jesus Christ gave himself for us that he might redeem us from all iniquity and purify for himself a people of his own who are zealous for good deeds. Titus 2:14

> God, whose almighty word   380
> chaos and darkness heard,
> and took their flight:
> hear us, we humbly pray.
> And where the gospel day
> sheds not its glorious ray,
> let there be light!

Merciful Lord, we seek to bring witness to the world. May we spread and proclaim your word with freedom and power. In the name of Jesus, we pray. Amen.

Ascension Sunday
Seventh Sunday of Easter

Watchword for the Week — Jesus says, "Sanctify them in the truth; your word is truth." John 17:17

Sunday, May 17 — Acts 1:15–17, 21–26; Psalm 1
1 John 5:9–13; John 17:6–19

Moses said to the Lord, "Now if I have found favor in your sight, show me your ways, so that I may know you." Exodus 33:13

Follow with rev'rent steps the great example   p151
of him whose holy work was doing good;
so shall the wide earth seem our Father's temple,
each loving life a psalm of gratitude.

The shepherd calls his own sheep by name and leads them out. He goes ahead of them, and the sheep follow him because they know his voice. John 10:3,4

I am Jesus' little lamb;   723
ever glad at heart I am;
for my Shepherd gently guides me,
knows my need and well provides me,
loves me ev'ry day the same,
even calls me by my name.

Dear Jesus, our Shepherd, while we make special time to worship you every Sunday, let us not forget you on other days. May we this day be blessed as we receive your word of hope. With gratitude we pray because you gave us eternal life. Amen.

Monday, May 18 — Psalm 66:8–15
Proverbs 11; 1 Corinthians 15:17–28

A broken and contrite heart, O God, you will not despise. Psalm 51:17

How shall I meet my Savior?   269
How shall I truly welcome thee?
What manner of behavior
is by thy love required of me?
I wait for thy salvation;
grant me, O Lord, thy Spirit's light;
and may my preparation
be well accepted in thy sight.

The Pharisees said to Jesus' disciples, "Why does your teacher eat with tax collectors and sinners?" Matthew 9:11

Holy Trinity, we confess with joy   p197
that our life and whole salvation
flow from Christ's blessed incarnation
and his death for us on the shameful cross.

Dear merciful God, help your servants to be more
compassionate and loving to others as you are with
us. May your love show through us to our neighbors
in all of our words and actions. In the name of our
Savior, Jesus Christ. Amen.

Tuesday, May 19 — Psalm 66:16–20
Proverbs 12; 1 Corinthians 15:29–41

The Lord said to Moses, "I will raise up for them a prophet like you from among their own people; I will put my words in the mouth of the prophet." Deuteronomy 18:18

> Lord, speak to me that I may speak   646
> in living echoes of your tone.
> As you have sought, so let me seek
> your erring children lost and lone.

In the past God spoke to our ancestors through the prophets at many times and in various ways, but in these last days he has spoken to us by his Son. Hebrews 1:1–2 (NIV)

> You speak, and it is done;   312
> obedient to your word,
> the water redd'ning into wine
> proclaims the present Lord.
> O, may this grace be ours:
> in you always to live
> and drink of those refreshing streams
> which you alone can give.

Almighty God, thank you for creating us in your image and for your service to us. We are instruments in your hands, listening for your voice. Prepare our hearts and make us willing to work at your call. Amen.

Wednesday, May 20 — Psalm 67
Proverbs 13; 1 Corinthians 15:42–58

You are the trust of all the ends of the earth and of the farthest sea. Psalm 65:6 (NASB)

> What God's almighty pow'r had made　　　537
> in mercy he is keeping;
> by morning glow or evening shade
> his eye is never sleeping.
> And where he rules in kingly might,
> there all is just and all is right:
> to God all praise and glory!

Do not move from the hope held out in the gospel. This is the gospel that you heard and that has been proclaimed to every creature under heaven. Colossians 1:23 (NIV)

> God sent his Son, they called him Jesus,　　　706
> he came to love, heal, and forgive;
> he lived and died to buy my pardon,
> an empty grave is there to prove my Savior lives.
> Because he lives I can face tomorrow,
> because he lives all fear is gone;
> because I know he holds the future,
> and life is worth the living just because he lives.

Heavenly and merciful Father, help your children be more prepared in faith and in actions according to your word. Lead our steps each day to go wherever you may take us. In the name of your son Jesus we pray. Amen.

Thursday, May 21 — Psalm 68:1–6
Proverbs 14; 1 Corinthians 16:1–11

I will counsel you with my eye upon you.
Psalm 32:8

If dangers gather round,   615
still keep me calm and fearless;
help me to bear the cross
when life is bleak and cheerless,
to overcome my foes
with words and actions kind;
O God, your will disclose,
your counsel let me find.

Mary sat at the Lord's feet and listened to what he was saying. Luke 10:39

O let me hear you speaking   603
in accents clear and still,
above the storms of passion,
the murmurs of self-will.
O speak to reassure me,
to hasten or control;
and speak to make me listen,
O guardian of my soul.

Loving Creator, we give thanks for your unconditional love and salvation. Though we may continually fail, you are our Guide and Rescue. Forgive us and transform us, that we may recognize you every day of our lives in this world. Amen.

Friday, May 22 — Psalm 68:7–18
Proverbs 15; 1 Corinthians 16:12–24

You shall rejoice in the Lord; in the Holy One of Israel you shall glory. Isaiah 41:16

To God all glory, praise, and love   548
be now ever giv'n
by saints below and saints above,
the church in earth and heav'n.

Paul wrote: Rejoice in the Lord. To write the same things to you is not troublesome to me, and for you it is a safeguard. Philippians 3:1

Lord Jesus, you are worthy   774*
for all on earth to praise;
our hymns in glad thanksgiving
in gratitude we raise,
For all you did on Calv'ry
when suffr'ing on the tree—
the world from sin's dominion
most wondrously set free.

O God, let your children in your church rejoice in you always. Let us be grateful for the many provisions you give us, especially our brothers and sisters in Christ. Make us a strong community, supporting one another in love. Amen.

*   © 1989 by Albert H. Frank

Saturday, May 23 — Psalm 68:19–27
Proverbs 16; 2 Corinthians 1:1–11

**Do not let those who wait for you be put to
shame; let them be ashamed who are wantonly
treacherous. Psalm 25:3**

> Abide with me; fast falls the even tide;   807
> the darkness deepens; Lord, with me abide.
> When other helpers fail and comforts flee,
> help of the helpless, O abide with me.

**You greatly rejoice with joy inexpressible and full
of glory, obtaining as the outcome of your faith
the salvation of your souls. 1 Peter 1:8–9 (NASB)**

> Make my calling and election,   808
> Jesus ev'ry day more sure;
> keep me under your direction,
> 'til I, through almighty pow'r,
> unto endless glory raised
> in your mansions shall be placed.
> When in you I end my race,
> weeping shall forever cease.

Dear Lord, may we proclaim your good news
around the world: news of freedom, righteousness,
mercy, and love for all. Let our joyful shouts be
heard throughout the earth. In the name of our
Savior Jesus Christ, we pray. Amen.

Day of Pentecost

Watchword for the Week — O Lord, how manifold are your works! In wisdom you have made them all. Psalm 104:24

Sunday, May 24 — Acts 2:1–21; Psalm 104:24–34,35b
Romans 8:22–27; John 15:26–27,16:4b–15

Wait for the Lord; be strong, and let your heart take courage; wait for the Lord! Psalm 27:14

O give me Samuel's heart! 609
A lowly heart that waits
where in thy house thou art,
or watches at thy gates
by day and night, a heart that still
moves at the breathing of thy will.

When the Spirit of truth comes, he will guide you into all the truth. John 16:13

O Spirit, our Lord God, 376
in this appointed hour,
as on the day of Pentecost,
descend with all your pow'r.

Heavenly Father, may we, your children, meet today once more to adore and worship you with pure hearts and thanksgiving. Bless our congregations in the world. Give us courage to serve you faithfully. In the name of your Son, Jesus Christ, we pray. Amen.

Monday, May 25 — Psalm 68:28–35
Proverbs 17; 2 Corinthians 1:12–22

On that day the root of Jesse shall stand as a signal to the peoples. Isaiah 11:10

Before the Lord's eternal throne,   455
you nations, bow with sacred joy;
know that the Lord is God alone;
he can create, and he destroy.

Simeon said, "My eyes have seen your salvation, which you have prepared in the presence of all peoples, a light for revelation to the Gentiles and for glory to your people Israel." Luke 2:30–32

Come, you sinners, poor and needy,   765
weak and wounded, sick and sore,
Jesus, Son of God, will save you,
full of pity, love, and pow'r.
I will arise and go to Jesus;
he will embrace me in his arms;
in the arms of my dear Savior,
O there are ten thousand charms.

Merciful Savior, we are your disciples today. May
we work in your kingdom and spread your word
through the power of the Holy Spirit. We work to
increase the number of believers throughout the
world, so that all may know their Creator. Amen.

Tuesday, May 26 — Psalm 69:1–12
Proverbs 18; 2 Corinthians 1:23–2:13

See, the Lord's hand is not too short to save, nor his ear too dull to hear. Rather, your iniquities have been barriers between you and your God. Isaiah 59:1–2

> O bless the Lord, my soul!   546
> His grace to all proclaim!
> And all that is within me join
> to bless his holy name.

Just as you once presented your members as slaves to impurity and to greater and greater iniquity, so now present your members as slaves to righteousness for sanctification. Romans 6:19

> "Comfort, comfort now my people;   264
> tell of peace!" So says our God.
> Comfort those who sit in darkness
> bowed beneath oppression's load.
> To God's people now proclaim
> that God's pardon waits for them!
> Tell them that their war is over;
> God will reign in peace forever!

Sovereign Lord, the world is shrouded in darkness. Many schools and homes do not pray anymore. We are dependent on material things instead of spiritual things, and we forget that you are our Creator and Sustainer. Forgive us and plant your peace in our hearts. Amen.

Wednesday, May 27 — Psalm 69:13–21
Proverbs 19; 2 Corinthians 2:14–3:11

Render true judgments, show kindness and mercy to one another. Zechariah 7:9

> Holy, holy, holy Lord God Almighty!   381
> Early in the morning our song shall rise to thee;
> holy, holy, holy, merciful and mighty!
> God in three persons, blessed Trinity!

Blessed are the merciful, for they will receive mercy. Matthew 5:7

> In mercy Lord, this grace bestow,   643
> that in your service we may do
> with gladness and a willing mind
> whatever is for us assigned.

Holy Spirit, we pray for all who are in need, all who are suffering, and all who do not know about you. Many wait for your grace and mercy; do not forget them. In the name of Jesus we pray. Amen.

Thursday, May 28 — Psalm 69:22–29
Proverbs 20; 2 Corinthians 3:12–4:6

Surely goodness and mercy shall follow me all the days of my life, and I shall dwell in the house of the Lord my whole life long. Psalm 23:6

> Teach me your patience; share with me   735
> a closer, dearer company.
> In work that keeps faith sweet and strong,
> in trust that triumphs over wrong,
> in hope that sends a shining ray
> far down the future's broad'ning way,
> in peace that only you can give;
> with you, O Master, let me live.

God who did not withhold his own Son, but gave him up for all of us, will he not with him also give us everything else? Romans 8:32

> Gather together, sing as one,   536*
> raising up a joyful song
> high and loud, into the air,
> broadcast praises ev'rywhere.
> Deep in our heart we tend the flame,
> and as your servant we remain.
> By this, we will our voice unite,
> bringing glory day and night.

Our lovely God, your mercy surpasses all understanding. It is only because of your mercy that we live. We do not deserve such love, but you give it to us anyway. Thank you for sending your Son to die for us, that we may be released from sin. Amen.

* © 1991 by Beth E. Hanson

Friday, May 29 — Psalm 69:30–36
Proverbs 21; 2 Corinthians 4:7–18

Holy, holy, holy is the Lord of hosts; the whole earth is full of his glory. Isaiah 6:3

Holy, holy, holy! All the saints adore thee,   381
casting down their golden crowns
  around the glassy sea;
cherubim and seraphim falling down before thee,
God everlasting through eternity.

From him and through him and to him are all things. To him be the glory forever. Romans 11:36

When morning gilds the skies,   552
my heart awaking cries:
may Jesus Christ be praised!
In all my work and prayer
I ask his loving care:
may Jesus Christ be praised!

Eternal God, we stand protected by your presence
and your strength. Continue being our armor and
giving us heavenly direction. We trust and depend
on you. We are not alone. You promise to be with us
always. In the name of our Savior we pray. Amen.

Saturday, May 30 — Psalm 70
Proverbs 22; 2 Corinthians 5:1–15

I will bring health and healing to it; I will heal my people and will let them enjoy abundant peace and security. Jeremiah 33:6 (NIV)

The Lord has promised good to me,   783
his word my hope secures;
he will my shield and portion be
as long as life endures.

Jesus went throughout Galilee, teaching in their synagogues and proclaiming the good news of the kingdom and curing every disease and every sickness among the people. Matthew 4:23

Treasure too you have entrusted,   652*
gain through pow'rs your grace conferred,
ours to use for home and kindred,
and to spread the gospel word.
Open wide our hands in sharing,
as we heed Christ's ageless call,
healing, teaching, and reclaiming,
serving you by loving all.

Dear Lord, make us your servants to minister to the sick and helpless. Help us to aid in healing, transforming souls, reconciling, and empowering lives. You are faithful and your love endures forever. Jesus Christ is alive and through his Holy Spirit we can serve you until you return! Amen.

Trinity Sunday

Watchword for the Week — Holy, holy, holy is the Lord of hosts; the whole earth is full of his glory. Isaiah 6:3

Sunday, May 31 — Isaiah 6:1–8; Psalm 29
Romans 8:12–17; John 3:1–17

The Lord is my strength. Habakkuk 3:19

> Take up your cross, let not its weight   758
> fill your weak spirit with alarm;
> his strength shall bear your spirit up,
> and brace your heart, and nerve your arm.

So we do not lose heart. Even though our outer nature is wasting away, our inner nature is being renewed day by day. 2 Corinthians 4:16

> All praise to you, my God, this night   569
> for all the blessing of the light.
> Keep me, O keep me, King of kings,
> beneath the shelter of your wings.

Gracious heavenly Father, we are yours alone. You have created each one of us and brought us together in love. Hold us up with your strong hands when our own strength fades. Lead us out into the world to proclaim your goodness to all. Amen.

Monday, June 1 — Psalm 71:1–8
Proverbs 23; 2 Corinthians 5:16–6:2

Let the unrighteous forsake their thoughts; let them return to the Lord, that he may have mercy on them. Isaiah 55:7

Bless the Lord, O my soul!   534*
All within me bless God's name!
Bless the Lord, who was, and is,
and shall ever be the same!
As a parent's love is endless,
so God's mercy follows us;
for the Lord who frames our being
well recalls that we are dust!

Therefore rid yourselves of all sordidness and rank growth of wickedness, and welcome with meekness the implanted word that has the power to save your souls. James 1:21

Plenteous grace with thee is found,   724
grace to cover all my sin;
let the healing streams abound;
make and keep me pure within.
Thou of life the fountain art,
freely let me take of thee;
spring thou up within my heart,
rise to all eternity.

Merciful God, as we go out into the world there are times when we follow a path leading away from you. Please forgive us our mistakes and guide us as we find our way back to you. Amen.

Tuesday, June 2 — Psalm 71:9–18a
Proverbs 24; 2 Corinthians 6:3–18

Would that all the Lord's people were prophets, and that the Lord would put his spirit on them! Numbers 11:29

> Kindle our hearts to burn with your flame.   489
> Raise up your banners high in this hour.
> Stir us to build new worlds in your name.
> Spirit of God, O send us your pow'r!

Pursue love and strive for the spiritual gifts, and especially that you may prophesy. Those who prophesy speak to other people for their building up and encouragement and consolation. 1 Corinthians 14:1–3

> Endow us richly with your gifts and grace   377
> to fit us for the duties of our place;
> so open now our lips, our hearts so raise,
> that both our hearts and lips may give you praise.

Ever knowing God, help us to discern and own the gifts you have given us so that we may share your word and help others understand what it means to be your children. Amen.

Wednesday, June 3 — Psalm 71:18b–24
Proverbs 25; 2 Corinthians 7:1–13a

You have given human beings dominion over the works of your hands; you have put all things under their feet. Psalm 8:6

This is our Father's world: 456
O let us not forget
that though the wrong is often strong,
God is the ruler yet.
He trusts us with his world,
to keep it clean and fair—
all earth and trees, all skies and seas,
all creatures ev'rywhere.

Blessed are the gentle, for they shall inherit the earth. Matthew 5:5 (NASB)

Blessed are the strong but gentle,   595
trained to serve a higher will,
wise to know th'eternal purpose
which their Father shall fulfill.
Blessed are they who with true passion
strive to make the right prevail,
for the earth is God's possession
and his purpose will not fail.

Creator God, forgive us when we get wrapped up in our lives and forget that you made us caretakers of the earth and all creatures. Open our hearts so that we are moved to help those without a voice. Amen.

Thursday, June 4 — Psalm 72:1–11
Proverbs 26; 2 Corinthians 7:13b–8:9

You shall be far from oppression, for you shall not fear; and from terror, for it shall not come near you. Isaiah 54:14

> "Fear not, I am with you; O be not dismayed,   709
> for I am your God and will still give you aid;
> I'll strengthen you, help you and cause you to stand
> upheld by my righteous, omnipotent hand."

His disciples came to Jesus and awoke him, saying, "Lord, save us! We are perishing!" But he said to them, "Why are you fearful, O you of little faith?" Then he arose and rebuked the winds and the sea, and there was a great calm. Matthew 8:25–26 (NKJV)

> Unseal our lips to sing your praise   561
> in endless hymns through all our days;
> increase our faith and light our minds;
> and set us free from doubt that blinds.

Many injustices take place every day in this world. God, make us strong in faith so that we can battle our fears and never doubt that you are always present to help us in our times of need. Amen.

Friday, June 5 — Psalm 72:12–20
Proverbs 27; 2 Corinthians 8:10–21

As a deer longs for flowing streams, so my soul longs for you, O God. Psalm 42:1

Sing, pray, and keep his ways unswerving,   712
offer your service faithfully,
and trust his word; though undeserving,
you'll find his promise true to be.
God never will forsake in need
the soul that trusts in him indeed.

Jesus said in a loud voice, "Let anyone who is thirsty come to me and drink." John 7:37 (NIV)

The springs of salvation from Christ,   616
     the Rock, bursting
and flowing throughout all the world's wilderness
bring life and salvation to those who are thirsting
to drink from this spring of salvation by grace;
as streams through the desert refresh the ground
and make land once barren with green abound,
the pow'r of his Spirit, our cold hearts o'erflowing,
renews us for service with lives bright and glowing.

O Great Conductor, drinking from the living water makes our souls sing! May those around us hear the music of our hearts and join your ensemble. Amen.

Saturday, June 6 — Psalm 73:1–12
Proverbs 28; 2 Corinthians 8:22–9:9

Do not withhold good from those to whom it is due, when it is in your power to do it. Proverbs 3:27

With praise and thanksgiving   p136*
to God ever living,
the tasks of our ev'ryday life we will face.
Our faith ever sharing,
in love ever caring,
embracing God's children of each tribe and race.
God's grace did invite us,
God's love shall unite us
to work for the kingdom and answer its call.
The seed of Christ's teaching,
receptive souls reaching,
shall blossom in action for God and for all.

John the Baptist said, "Whoever has two coats must share with anyone who has none; and whoever has food must do likewise." Luke 3:11

Lord, as you have lived for others,   p41
so may we for others live;
freely have your gifts been granted;
freely may your servants give.
Yours the gold and yours the silver,
yours the wealth of land and sea,
we but stewards of your bounty
sharing all by your decree.

Loving Father, many of our neighbors find
themselves in need. Help us to show your love for
all by accepting them as they are in addition to
sharing your word and our resources. Amen.

Second Sunday after Pentecost

Watchword for the Week — Lord, hear my voice! Let your ears be attentive to the voice of my supplications! Psalm 130:2

Sunday, June 7 — Genesis 3:8–15; Psalm 130
2 Corinthians 4:13–5:1; Mark 3:20–35

The Lord grants peace within your borders. Psalm 147:14

Peace be to this congregation,   556
peace to ev'ry soul therein;
peace, which flows from Christ's salvation,
peace, the seal of cancelled sin,
peace that speaks its heav'nly Giver,
peace, to earthly minds unknown,
peace divine that lasts forever
here erect its glorious throne.

Let us then pursue what makes for peace and for mutual edification. Romans 14:19

May the God of hope go with us ev'ry day,   708
filling all our lives with love and joy and peace.
May the God of justice speed us on our way,
bringing light and hope to ev'ry land and race.
Praying, let us work for peace,
singing, share our joy with all.
Working for a world that's new,
faithful when we hear Christ's call.

We live in a time of hatred, war, famine, poverty, and despair. Thank you, God, for providing us with hope that one day the world will be at peace. Until then, help us to be strong in faith and love. Amen.

Monday, June 8 — Psalm 73:13–20
Proverbs 29; 2 Corinthians 9:10–10:6

A son honors his father. If then I am a father, where is the honor due me? says the Lord. Malachi 1:6

Worship, honor, glory, blessing, 454
Lord, we offer as our gift;
young and old, your praise expressing,
our glad songs to you we lift.
All the saints in heav'n adore you;
we would join their glad acclaim;
as your angels serve before you,
so on earth we praise your name.

Every tongue should confess that Jesus Christ is Lord, to the glory of God the Father. Philippians 2:11

All glory, honor, thanks, and praise 518*
to Christ our Lord and Savior,
that still his church in these our days
may know his boundless favor:
for brothers and sisters united by love
stand firm o'er the earth far extended,
as countless more legions in heaven above
extol how his grace them attended

Heavenly Father, you deserve all the glory, endless praise, and adoration for your infinite love for us. There is nothing to despair knowing you are there to walk with and carry us through all of life's challenges. We are ever grateful. Amen.

* © 1982 by C. Daniel Crews

Tuesday, June 9 — Psalm 73:21–28
Proverbs 30; 2 Corinthians 10:7–18

Although these nations do give heed to soothsayers and diviners, as for you, the Lord your God does not permit you to do so. Deuteronomy 18:14

> Take us under your protection,   716
> grant us to obey your voice,
> simply follow your direction,
> to your will resign our choice.

You have one instructor, the Messiah. Matthew 23:10

> How great the bliss to be a sheep of Jesus,   593
> and to be guided by his shepherd staff!
> Earth's greatest honors, howsoe'er they please us,
> compared to this are vain and empty chaff.
> Yea, what this world can never give,
> may, through the Shepherd's grace,
>   each needy sheep receive.

You are the Alpha and the Omega, the Beginning and the End. No one but you knows what the future holds. We pray for patience and guidance as we wait for you to reveal your plan. Amen.

Wednesday, June 10 — Psalm 74:1–9
Proverbs 31; 2 Corinthians 11:1–11

My iniquities have overtaken me, until I cannot see; O Lord, make haste to help me. Psalm 40:12,13

> As you with Satan did contend,   341
> and did the vict'ry win,
> O give us strength in you to fight,
> in you to conquer sin.

Jesus said, "Come to me, all you that are weary and are carrying heavy burdens, and I will give you rest." Matthew 11:28

> Whatever God ordains is right,   718*
> and he will not deceive us.
> He leads us in the way of light
> and will not ever leave us.
> In him we rest, who makes the best
> of all the stumbling turns we take
> and loves us for his mercy's sake.

Dear Friend, you more than anyone know we are wearied by many burdens. It is not easy to bear the weight alone; thank you for making our load lighter. Help us to remember you are always present in our lives. Amen.

* © 1978 by Lutheran Book of Worship. Reprinted by permission of Augsburg Fortress.

Thursday, June 11 — Psalm 74:10–17
Ecclesiastes 1:1–3:8; 2 Corinthians 11:12–15

God says, "Call on me in the day of trouble; I will deliver you, and you shall glorify me." Psalm 50:15

> "When through the deep waters I call you to go,   709
> the rivers of sorrow shall not overflow;
> for I will be with you in trouble to bless,
> and sanctify to you your deepest distress.

Cast all your anxiety on him, because he cares for you. 1 Peter 5:7

> Thou, Lord, wilt not forsake me,   795
> though I am oft to blame;
> as thy reward, O take me
> anew, just as I am;
> grant me henceforth, dear Savior,
> through all my pilgrim years
> to look to thee and never
> give way to anxious fears.

Comforter, as we travel through the waters of fear and anxiety, we are not afraid. We know you are there to guide us. Amen.

Friday, June 12 — Psalm 74:18–23
Ecclesiastes 3:9–5:20; 2 Corinthians 11:16–33

Whoever loves money never has enough; whoever loves wealth is never satisfied with their income. Ecclesiastes 5:10 (NIV)

Come, O Christ, and reign among us,   648
King of love and Prince of peace;
hush the storm of strife and passion,
bid its cruel discords cease.
By your patient years of toiling,
by your silent hours of pain,
quench our fevered thirst of pleasure;
stem our selfish greed of gain.

Keep your lives free from the love of money, and be content with what you have; for he (the Lord) has said, "I will never leave you or forsake you." Hebrews 13:5

Lord, I would clasp thy hand in mine,   787
nor ever murmur nor repine,
content, whatever lot I see,
since 'tis my God that leadeth me.
He leadeth me, he leadeth me;
By his own hand he leadeth me,
his faithful foll'wer I would be,
for by his hand he leadeth me.

Lord, we are richer with you in our lives than we could ever be without. May we follow your path of righteousness and renounce greed while growing in our love of Christ. Amen.

Saturday, June 13 — Psalm 75
Ecclesiastes 6:1–7:14; 2 Corinthians 12:1–13

O Lord my God, I cried to you for help, and you have healed me. Psalm 30:2

> Rejoice, rejoice, O Christian,   792
> lift up your voice and sing
> eternal hallelujahs
> to Jesus Christ the King!
> The hope of all who seek him,
> the help of all who find,
> none other is so loving,
> so good and kind.
> He lives, he lives,
> Christ Jesus lives today!
> He walks with me and talks with me
> along life's narrow way.
> He lives, he lives,
> salvation to impart!
> You ask me how I know he lives?
> He lives within my heart.

Pray for one another, so that you may be healed. James 5:16

> Heal division; love renew;   521*
> help us all to turn to you.
> Mighty Shepherd, gather near
> all your sheep oppressed by fear:
> have mercy, Lord.

O great Physician, we turn to you in prayer for our physical and spiritual wounds. Bless and comfort us as we heal and teach us to pray for the healing of others. Amen.

* © 1994 by C. Daniel Crews

Third Sunday after Pentecost

Watchword for the Week — It is good to give thanks to the Lord, to sing praises to your name, O Most High. Psalm 92:1

Sunday, June 14 — Ezekiel 17:22–24; Psalm 92:1–4,12–15
2 Corinthians 5:6–10,14–17; Mark 4:26–34

God, your steadfast love is better than life. Psalm 63:3

And when from death I'm free,   328
   I'll sing on, I'll sing on,
and when from death I'm free, I'll sing on!
And when from death I'm free,
   I'll sing God's love for me,
and through eternity I'll sing on, I'll sing on;
and through eternity I'll sing on!

Paul wrote: I am convinced that neither death, nor life, nor angels, nor rulers, nor things present, nor things to come, nor powers, nor height, nor depth, nor anything else in all creation, will be able to separate us from the love of God in Christ Jesus our Lord. Romans 8:38–39

And can it be that I should gain   773
an int'rest in the Savior's blood?
Died he for me, who caused his pain—
for me, who caused his bitter death?

Loving Savior, you are so amazing! The depth of your eternal love for us was demonstrated on the cross. That you died so we may live is the greatest gift of all. In your name we pray. Amen.

Monday, June 15 — Psalm 76
Ecclesiastes 7:15–9:18; 2 Corinthians 12:14–13:4

The Lord God will take away the disgrace of his people from all the earth. Isaiah 25:8

> But, O my Jesus, you did me   602
> upon the cross embrace;
> for me you bore the nails and spear
> and manifold disgrace.

God chose what is low and despised in the world, things that are not, to reduce to nothing things that are. 1 Corinthians 1:28

> Forbid it, Lord, that I should boast,   350
> save in the death of Christ, my God;
> all the vain things that charm me most,
> I sacrifice them to his blood.

Gracious God, so many people don't know of you or your sacrifice for us. We pray that you infuse us with the courage to share your word with everyone we meet so that they can also bask in your eternal love. Amen.

Tuesday, June 16 — Psalm 77:1–9
Ecclesiastes 10:1–12:14; 2 Corinthians 13:5–13

Behold, children are a gift of the Lord.
Psalm 127:3 (NASB)

> Gracious Savior, gentle Shepherd,   660
> children all are dear to you;
> may your loving arms enfold them
> in your care their whole life through;
> fondly tend and safely keep them
> in your mercy strong and true.

Jesus said, "Yes; have you never read, 'Out of the mouths of infants and nursing babies you have prepared praise for yourself'?" Matthew 21:16

> All glory, laud, and honor   342
> to you, Redeemer, King,
> to whom the lips of children
> made sweet hosannas ring.
> You are the King of Israel
> and David's royal Son,
> now in the Lord's name coming,
> the King and Blessed One.

Father, you have called the youngest of us to do your work. Help us to understand that our children and young people are an integral part of your kingdom. May we teach them to be still and listen for your voice. Amen.

Wednesday, June 17 — Psalm 77:10–15
Song of Solomon 1:1–2:7; Galatians 1:1–12

The Lord our God protected us along all the way that we went. Joshua 24:17

Jesus, still lead on   799
'til our rest be won;
heav'nly leader, still direct us,
still support, console, protect us,
'til we safely stand
in the promised land.

Now to him who is able to keep you from falling, and to make you stand without blemish in the presence of his glory with rejoicing, to the only God our Savior, through Jesus Christ our Lord, be glory. Jude 24–25

Those who are by Christ directed,   717
trusting the Good Shepherd's care,
from all harm will be protected,
and no danger need to fear.

Good Shepherd, we pray that you continue to protect and guide us all the days of our lives. Amen.

Thursday, June 18 — Psalm 77:16–20
Song of Solomon 2:8–4:16; Galatians 1:13–24

**A glad heart makes a cheerful countenance,
but by sorrow of heart the spirit is broken.
Proverbs 15:13**

> Good news! Our Christ has come!   630*
> He heals the sad of heart.
> He sets the pris'ners free
> and helps the blind to see.
> God's Spirit works through all who love,
> through all who touch the lives of these.

**Out of the abundance of the heart the mouth
speaks. A good man out of the good treasure
of his heart brings forth good things.
Matthew 12:34–35 (NKJV)**

> Blessed are the pure in heart,   584
> for they shall see their God.
> The secret of the Lord is theirs;
> their soul is Christ's abode.

Lord, when we are hurt, heal our hearts. Help us
to share our sorrow with you and to forgive in love
as you do. When we do this, the full expression of
love becomes evident and you will be able to work
through us. In your name we pray. Amen.

* © 1988 by Sharon M. Benson. Used by permission.

Friday, June 19 — Psalm 78:1–8
Song of Solomon 5,6; Galatians 2:1–14

He makes me lie down in green pastures; he leads me beside still waters; he restores my soul. Psalm 23:2–3

> My Shepherd will supply my need;   730
> the Lord God is his name.
> In pastures fresh he makes me feed,
> beside the living stream.
> He brings my wand'ring spirit back
> when I forsake his ways,
> and leads me for his mercy's sake
> in paths of truth and grace.

Jesus said, "My sheep hear my voice. I know them, and they follow me. I give them eternal life." John 10:27–28

> Should not I for gladness leap,   662
> led by Jesus as his sheep?
> For when these blessed days are over
> to the arms of my dear Savior
> I shall be conveyed to rest.
> Amen, yea, my lot is blessed.

Savior, we are blessed to have you as our Shepherd!
You find us when we stray and return us to the fold.
It is unimaginable to not have you in our lives.
May you continue to guide us the rest of our days.
Amen.

Saturday, June 20 — Psalm 78:9–16
Song of Solomon 7,8; Galatians 2:15–3:5

Upon him was the punishment that made us whole. Isaiah 53:5

> How strange is this great paradox to ponder: 351
> the shepherd dies for sheep who love to wander;
> the master pays the debt his servants owe him,
> who would not know him.

Christ himself bore our sins in his own body on the tree, that we, having died to sins, might live for righteousness. 1 Peter 2:24 (NKJV)

> What language shall I borrow   345
> to thank you, dearest friend,
> for this, your dying sorrow,
> your mercy without end?
> Lord, make me yours forever,
> a loyal servant true,
> and let me never, never
> outlive my love for you.

Eternal Savior, thank you for your sacrifice. We are able to live because you died for our sins. May we continue to follow the path of righteousness so that we refrain from going astray. Amen.

Fourth Sunday after Pentecost

Watchword for the Week — O give thanks to the Lord, for he is good; for his steadfast love endures forever. Psalm 107:1

Sunday, June 21 — Job 38:1–11; Psalm 107:1–3,23–32
2 Corinthians 6:1–13; Mark 4:35–41

Give me neither poverty nor riches; feed me with the food that I need. Proverbs 30:8

Gracious Lord, 528
gracious Lord,
blessed is our lot indeed
in your ransomed congregation;
here we on your merits feed,
and the wellsprings of salvation,
all the needy to revive and cheer,
stream forth here,
stream forth here.

Give us this day our daily bread. Matthew 6:11

Feed us, Jesus, 418*
we in hunger stand.
Feed us, Jesus,
from your timeless hand:
the broken bread of life,
the love that we all need,
O, feed us, Jesus, feed us.

God, it has not been easy to teach us that we cannot live on bread alone; we need to be nourished physically and spiritually. We pray that you provide us with the wisdom to listen and understand your word. Amen.

* © 1975 by David M. Henkelmann

Monday, June 22 — Psalm 78:17–31
Isaiah 1; Galatians 3:6–18

You broaden the path beneath me, so that my ankles do not turn. 2 Samuel 22:37 (NIV)

Lead on, O King eternal: 753
we follow, not with fears,
for gladness breaks like morning
where'er your face appears:
your cross is lifted o'er us;
we journey in its light;
the crown awaits the conquest;
lead on, O God of might!

Jesus saw a man called Matthew sitting at the tax booth; and he said to him, "Follow me." And he got up and followed him. Matthew 9:9

Jesus calls us; o'er the tumult   600
of our life's wild, restless sea,
day by day his voice is sounding,
saying, "Christian, follow me."

Shepherd, you are ever patient with our inaction.
Help us to drown out the noise so that we can hear
your voice. Hold us in your arms so that we can let
go of fears that hold us back. We look forward to
following you. Amen.

— Psalm 78:32–39

ıtians 3:19–29

ıladness in my heart more than in and wine abound. Psalm 4:7

ııame, Jesus' name,   324
ɔource of life and happiness!
In this name true consolation
mourning sinners may possess;
here is found complete salvation.
Blessed Jesus, we your name will praise
all our days, all our days.

Paul wrote: I have learned to be content with whatever I have. Philippians 4:11

Perfect submission, all is at rest,   714
I in my Savior am happy and blessed,
watching and waiting, looking above,
filled with his goodness, lost in his love.
This is my story, this is my song,
praising my Savior all the day long.
This is my story, this is my song,
praising my Savior all the day long.

Lord, you make us feel loved and happy! May we praise you always for the miracle that you are in our lives. Help us to share our joy with everyone. Amen.

Wednesday, June 24 — Psalm 78:40–55
Isaiah 4:2–5:30; Galatians 4:1–16

Return, O faithless children, says the Lord, for I am your master; I will take you, and I will bring you to Zion. Jeremiah 3:14

Dear Lord and Father of mankind,   739
forgive our foolish ways;
reclothe us in our rightful mind;
in purer lives thy service find,
in deeper rev'rence, praise.

In those days John the Baptist appeared in the wilderness of Judea, proclaiming, "Repent, for the kingdom of heaven has come near." Matthew 3:1–2

Seek ye first the kingdom of God   605*
and his righteousness,
and all these things shall be added unto you—
Allelu, alleluia!

Father, at times we think our way is better than yours, and we ignore you. Please be patient, forgive us for being foolish children, and help us to understand your instructions so that we may follow you to your kingdom. Amen.

Thursday, June 25 — Psalm 78:56–64
Isaiah 6,7; Galatians 4:17–27

The Lord waits to be gracious to you. Isaiah 30:18

> He will not always chide;   546
> he will with patience wait;
> his wrath is ever slow to rise
> and ready to abate.

Listen! I am standing at the door, knocking; if you hear my voice and open the door, I will come in to you and eat with you, and you with me. Revelation 3:20

> Long my imprisoned spirit lay   773
> fast bound in sin and nature's night.
> Your sunrise turned that night to day;
> I woke—the dungeon flamed with light!
> My chains fell off, your voice I knew;
> was freed, I rose, and followed you.
> My chains fell off, your voice I knew;
> was freed, I rose, and followed you.

Lord, you may be knocking, but at times we treat you like a stranger and keep the door closed. Help us to be more constant in prayer and in our faith so that we can hear your voice and let you into our hearts. You are our salvation. Amen.

Friday, June 26 — Psalm 78:65–72
Isaiah 8:1–9:7; Galatians 4:28–5:6

Sing for joy, O heavens, and exult, O earth; break forth, O mountains, into singing! For the Lord has comforted his people, and will have compassion on his suffering ones. Isaiah 49:13

> He comes with rescue speedy 263
> to those who suffer wrong,
> to help the poor and needy,
> and bid the weak be strong,
> to give them songs for sighing,
> their darkness turn to light,
> whose souls, condemned and dying,
> were precious in his sight.

The grace of God has appeared, bringing salvation to all. Titus 2:11

> Your lofty themes, all mortals, bring; 551
> in songs of praise divinely sing;
> the great salvation loud proclaim,
> and shout for joy the Savior's name.

Praise God! Your grace and compassion know no boundaries. You are omnipresent in our lives, helping us even when worry and negative thoughts enter our minds. May we always be worthy in your eyes. Amen.

Saturday, June 27 — Psalm 79:1–8
Isaiah 9:8–10:11; Galatians 5:7–18

You have made human beings a little lower than God, and crowned them with glory and honor. Psalm 8:5

Bless your maker, all you creatures,   458
ever under God's control;
all throughout his vast dominion
bless the Lord of all, my soul!

God chose to give us birth through the word of truth, that we might be a kind of firstfruits of all he created. James 1:18 (NIV)

All things bright and beautiful,   467
all creatures great and small,
all things wise and wonderful—
the Lord God made them all.
God gave us eyes to see them,
and lips that we might tell
how great is God Almighty,
who has made all things well.

Lord God, you are the amazing creator of all things. You entrusted us with your creation, but we haven't always been the best or wisest of caretakers. Help us to respect, care, and love that which you created. In your name we pray. Amen.

Fifth Sunday after Pentecost

Watchword for the Week — The steadfast love of the Lord never ceases, his mercies never come to an end. Lamentations 3:22

Sunday, June 28 — Lamentations 3:22–33; Psalm 30
2 Corinthians 8:7–15; Mark 5:21–43

Rise up, O God, plead your cause. Psalm 74:22

When all my prayers no answer seem to bring,   755*
and there is silence in my deepest soul;
when in the wilderness I find no spring,
Lord of the desert places, keep me whole.

For the kingdom of heaven is like a landowner who went out early in the morning to hire laborers for his vineyard. Matthew 20:1

O, to grace how great a debtor   782
daily I'm constrained to be!
Let that grace, Lord, like a fetter,
bind my wand'ring heart to thee.
Prone to wander, Lord, I feel it,
prone to leave the God I love,
here's my heart, O take and seal it;
seal it for thy courts above.

O Ancient of Days, there are times we grow frustrated with your answers. Please forgive us our impatience and ingratitude. Fill us with peace so that our hearts can let go of negativity. Although we may not always agree or understand, help us to know that you answer in love. Amen.

Monday, June 29 — Psalm 79:9–13
Isaiah 10:12–11:9; Galatians 5:19–6:5

The Lord your God turned the curse into a blessing for you, because the Lord your God loved you. Deuteronomy 23:5

No more let sin and sorrow grow,   294
nor thorns infest the ground;
he comes to make his blessings flow
far as the curse is found,
far as the curse is found,
far as, far as the curse is found.

Christ says, "I came not to judge the world, but to save the world." John 12:47

What wondrous love is this,   328
   O my soul, O my soul!
What wondrous love is this, O my soul!
What wondrous love is this
   that caused the Lord of bliss
to bear the dreadful curse for my soul, for my soul,
to bear the dreadful curse for my soul?

Savior, you demonstrated your immense love for us when you sent your only son to save us. Thank you for forgiving us and believing that we could be redeemed. Help us to love and forgive others as you have done for us. Amen.

Tuesday, June 30 — Psalm 80:1–7
Isaiah 11:10–13:22; Galatians 6:6–18

You are my hiding-place and my shield; I hope in your word. Psalm 119:114

Jesus, Lover of my soul,   724
let me to thy bosom fly,
while the raging billows roll,
while the tempest still is high;
hide me, O my Savior, hide
'til the storm of life is past;
safe into the haven guide;
O receive my soul at last!

The Lord is faithful; he will strengthen you and guard you from the evil one. 2 Thessalonians 3:3

O God, our help in ages past,   461
our hope for years to come,
remain our guard while life shall last,
and our eternal home.

Almighty God, you are our refuge and strength. There is nothing to fear when you are near. Forgive us when we forget such faith during troubled times. We pray to remain steadfast in our love and faithfulness to you. Amen.

Wednesday, July 1 — Psalm 80:8–11
Isaiah 14; Ephesians 1:1–10

Is not my word like fire, says the Lord, and like a hammer that breaks a rock in pieces? Jeremiah 23:29

> O Savior, whose almighty word   725
> the winds and waves submissive heard,
> who walked upon the foaming deep
> and calm amid the storm did sleep:
> O hear us when we cry to thee
> for those in peril on the sea.

Jesus said, "I came to bring fire to the earth." Luke 12:49

> Kindle within us and preserve that fire,   377
> which will with holy love our hearts inspire,
> and with an active zeal our souls inflame
> to do your will and glorify your name.

Lord, let us focus on your word as you guide us through life to do what you would have us do. Give us strength and knowledge that your word is our unchanging guide. Amen.

Thursday, July 2 — Psalm 80:12–19
Isaiah 15,16; Ephesians 1:11–23

O God, you are my God, I seek you, my soul thirsts for you. Psalm 63:1

Now my heart sets none above you,   612*
for your grace alone I thirst,
knowing well that if I love you,
you, O Lord, have loved me first.

Christ says, "To the thirsty I will give water as a gift from the spring of the water of life." Revelation 21:6

I heard the voice of Jesus say,   606
"Behold, I freely give
the living water; thirsty one,
stoop down and drink and live."
I came to Jesus, and I drank
of that life-giving stream;
my thirst was quenched, my soul revived,
and now I live in him.

Heavenly Father, you provide the living water we
need to sustain us through each day and each
situation we face. Your life-giving stream restores
us. Amen.

*   © 1982 by Charles P. Price

Friday, July 3 — Psalm 81:1–5
Isaiah 17:1–19:17; Ephesians 2:1–10

This poor soul cried, and was heard by the Lord, and was saved from every trouble. Psalm 34:6

Let me at thy throne of mercy   772
find a sweet relief;
kneeling there in deep contrition,
help my unbelief.
Savior, Savior, hear my humble cry;
while on others thou art calling;
do not pass me by.

A man from the crowd shouted, "Teacher, I beg you to look at my son." Luke 9:38

Jesus comes again in mercy,   p55
when our hearts are bowed with care;
Jesus comes again in answer
to our earnest heartfelt prayer:
alleluia, alleluia!
Comes to save us from despair.

Lord, help us to know you are always present
during times of trouble. Your hope and grace
sustains us through all peril. Amen.

Saturday, July 4 — Psalm 81:6–10
Isaiah 19:18–22:14; Ephesians 2:11–22

O Lord my God, in you I take refuge; save me from all my pursuers, and deliver me. Psalm 7:1

> Now we bring ourselves to you;   741
> cleanse us, Lord, we humbly pray;
> undeserving though we be,
> draw us closer ev'ry day.
> Lord, our refuge, hope, and strength!
> Keep, O keep us safe from harm,
> shield us through our earthly life
> by your everlasting arm.

Blessed are you when people insult you, persecute you and falsely say all kinds of evil against you because of me. Matthew 5:11 (NIV)

> In ev'ry insult, rift, and war,   362*
> where color, scorn, or wealth divide,
> Christ suffers still, yet loves the more,
> and lives, where even hope has died.

Dearest Lord, you are our refuge and strength throughout life's trials. Help us to know this and to help others to know your love. Amen.

Sixth Sunday after Pentecost

Watchword for the Week — Jesus says, "My grace is sufficient for you, for power is made perfect in weakness." 2 Corinthians 12:9

Sunday, July 5 — Ezekiel 2:1–5; Psalm 123
2 Corinthians 12:2–10; Mark 6:1–13

The Lord raises up the poor from the dust.
1 Samuel 2:8

> Thou, O Christ, art all I want;   724
> more than all in thee I find;
> raise the fallen, cheer the faint,
> heal the sick and lead the blind.
> Just and holy is thy name,
> I am all unrighteousness,
> false and full of sin I am,
> thou art full of truth and grace.

Which one of you, having a hundred sheep and losing one of them, does not leave the ninety-nine in the wilderness and go after the one that is lost until he finds it? When he has found it, he lays it on his shoulders and rejoices. Luke 15:4–5

> Tender Shepherd, never leave them,   660
> never let them go astray;
> by your warning love directed,
> may they walk the narrow way!
> Thus direct them, thus defend them,
> lest they fall an easy prey.

Faithful Shepherd, in those times when our faith waivers and we fall away, we know you will find us and lead us back to the flock. Help us always to feel your love and grace. Give us shelter from life's storms and from our own lukewarmness. Amen.

Monday, July 6 — Psalm 81:11–16
Isaiah 22:15–23:18; Ephesians 3:1–13

John Hus Festival† — Isaiah 49:1–7; Psalm 135:1–13
1 Corinthians 1:18–24; Mark 8:34–38

Peace, peace, to the far and the near, says the Lord; and I will heal them. Isaiah 57:19

Forgive the hurts our selfishness inflicted   671*
on those we love and those who love us best.
Christ, heal the scars, and draw us all together
in him whose will is peace and joy and rest.

Christ is our peace. Ephesians 2:14

The peace of Christ makes fresh my heart,   701
a fountain ever springing!
All things are mine since I am his!
How can I keep from singing?
No storm can shake my inmost calm,
while to that Rock I'm clinging.
Since love is Lord of heaven and earth,
how can I keep from singing?

Christ, you are our peace; on this we can depend.
Amen.

---

*   © 1957 by Frank von Christierson. Used by permission of
Pilgrim Press/United Church Press.

†   On July 6, 1415, John Hus was martyred at the Council of Constance

July 7 — Psalm 82:1–4
25; Ephesians 3:14–4:6

your eyes be open toward this temple night
day, this place of which you said, "My name
shall be there." 1 Kings 8:29 (NIV)

I bind unto myself today   p237
the power of God to hold and lead,
his eye to watch, his might to stay,
his ear to hearken to my need,
the wisdom of my God to teach,
his hand to guide, his shield to ward;
the word of God to give me speech,
his heavenly host to be my guard.

**Christ was faithful as a Son over his house—
whose house we are, if we hold fast our
confidence and the boast of our hope firm until
the end. Hebrews 3:6 (NASB)**

O enter then his gates with joy;   539
within his courts his praise proclaim.
Let thankful songs your tongues employ;
O bless and magnify his name.

God, we know you hear our prayers and that you
walk with us through all we face. Help us to trust
in you and to feel your enveloping love as we face
life's challenges. Amen.

Wednesday, July 8 — Psalm 82:5–8
Isaiah 26,27; Ephesians 4:7–16

Your own eyes have seen every great deed that the Lord did. Deuteronomy 11:7

Lord of glory, God most high,   744
man exalted to the sky,
with your love my heart now fill;
prompt me to perform your will!
Then your glory I shall see;
blessed for all eternity.

We declare to you what we have seen and heard so that you also may have fellowship with us. 1 John 1:3

Blessed be the tie that binds   680
our hearts in Christian love;
the fellowship of kindred minds
is like to that above.

Lord, we join together in fellowship as the family
of God to praise and glorify your name. Help us to
include others within our community so they, too,
can come to know you. Amen.

Thursday, July 9 — Psalm 83:1–8
Isaiah 28; Ephesians 4:17–28

Do not be grieved, for the joy of the Lord is your strength. Nehemiah 8:10

The Lord's joy be our strength and stay   734
in our employ from day to day;
our thoughts and our activity
through Jesus' merits hallowed be.

Rejoice in the Lord always; again I will say, Rejoice. Philippians 4:4

He blesses me so sensibly   596
that, though I'm poor and lowly,
yet in him I can rejoice
as my Savior holy.

Father, we rejoice and sing your praise! You are our strength and stay as we seek your blessings and guidance throughout our days. Lord, be with us. Amen.

Friday, July 10 — Psalm 83:9–12
Isaiah 29; Ephesians 4:29–5:7

Look! On the mountains the feet of one who brings good tidings, who proclaims peace! Nahum 1:15

He shall come down like showers   263
upon the fruitful earth,
and love, joy, hope, like flowers,
spring in his path to birth;
before him on the mountains
shall Peace, the herald, go;
and righteousness, in fountains,
from hill to valley flow.

Jesus said to the disciples, "Peace be with you. As the Father has sent me, so I send you." John 20:21

That night the apostles met in fear;   369
among them came their Master dear
and said, "My peace be with you here."
Alleluia!
Alleluia, alleluia,
alleluia, alleluia!

Most gracious Lord and God, your peace surrounds us day and night. Help us to share that peace and love with others as we go about your work in our daily lives. Amen.

July 11 — Psalm 83:13–18
30,31; Ephesians 5:8–20

Naaman said, "Your servant will no longer offer sacrifice to any god except the Lord." 2 Kings 5:17

Salvation to God, who sits on the throne!   565
Let all cry aloud and honor the Son;
the praises of Jesus the angels proclaim,
fall down on their faces and worship the Lamb.

Do not be conformed to this world, but be transformed by the renewing of your minds, so that you may discern what is the will of God—what is good and acceptable and perfect. Romans 12:2

Gracious Spirit, in your wisdom   496*
grant your gifts to us anew;
hallow and transform our living;
breathe through all we say or do.

Lord, help us to discern your will for our lives.
Help us to do what you would have us do as we
encounter temptation and strife. Amen.

*   © 1995 by C. Daniel Crews

Seventh Sunday after Pentecost

Watchword for the Week — Surely God's salvation is at hand for those who fear him, that his glory may dwell in our land. Psalm 85:9

Sunday, July 12 — Amos 7:7–15; Psalm 85:8–13
Ephesians 1:3–14; Mark 6:14–29

In days to come nation shall not lift up sword against nation, neither shall they learn war any more. Isaiah 2:2,4

Lead us, Father, into freedom,   685*
from despair your world release;
that, redeemed from war and hatred,
all may come and go in peace.
Show us how through care and goodness
fear will die and hope increase.

The soldiers asked John, saying, "And what shall we do?" So he said to them, "Do not intimidate anyone or accuse falsely." Luke 3:14 (NKJV)

Love is a gift, a present sweet,   536**
love unfailing and complete.
Bonded in love, we are to stand,
guided by the great command.
Love one another, bear no ill,
share of the bounty, do God's will.
Let us by action love profess,
with our deeds as evidence.

Wise Father, guide us with your wisdom and help us to love one another as you have directed. Help us to redirect our mistrust of others into positive energy and good will toward all. Amen.

*   © 1968 by Hope Publishing Company

** © 1991 by Beth E. Hanson

Monday, July 13 — Psalm 84:1–7
Isaiah 32:1–33:16; Ephesians 5:21–33

Rend your hearts and not your clothing. Return to the Lord, your God. Joel 2:13

And now at length discerning   763*
the evil that I do,
behold me Lord, returning
with hope and trust to you.
In haste you come to meet me
and home rejoicing bring,
in gladness there to greet me
with calf and robe and ring.

The tax collector, standing far off, would not even look up to heaven, but was beating his breast and saying, "God, be merciful to me, a sinner!" Luke 18:13

May we in our guilt and shame   352
still your love and mercy claim,
calling humbly on your name:
hear us, holy Jesus.

Lord, we confess that we sin each day. We ask your forgiveness and your help to live the lives you would have us live, loving one another in all things. Amen.

*   © 1981 by ICEL

Tuesday, July 14 — Psalm 84:8–12
Isaiah 33:17–35:10; Ephesians 6:1–9

Go, and may the Lord be with you! 1 Samuel 17:37

Be present with your servants, Lord;   734
we look to you with one accord;
refresh and strengthen us anew,
and bless what in your name we do.

The peace of God, which surpasses all understanding, will guard your hearts and your minds in Christ Jesus. Philippians 4:7

Jesus, source of lasting pleasure,   588*
truest friend, and dearest treasure,
peace beyond all understanding,
joy into all life expanding:
humbly now, I bow before you,
love incarnate, I adore you;
worthily let me receive you
and, so favored, never leave you.

Jesus, the peace you offer us surrounds us like
a warm blanket on a cold night. We rejoice in
your love and care. Help us to spread your love
throughout our world. Amen.

*   © 1978 by Lutheran Book of Worship. Reprinted by permission of Augsburg Fortress.

Wednesday, July 15 — Psalm 85:1–7
Isaiah 36:1–37:13; Ephesians 6:10–24

Do not put your trust in princes, in mortals, in whom there is no help. Psalm 146:3

In you I trust by faith,   488
my Jesus, God and Savior;
on your atoning death
I shall rely forever.
Your suff'rings shall remain
deep on my heart impressed,
O Son of God and man,
'til I with you shall rest.

Jesus said, "If one blind person guides another, both will fall into a pit." Matthew 15:14

God has called you out of darkness   526*
into this most marvelous light;
bringing truth to live within you,
turning blindness into sight;
let your light so shine around you
that God's name is glorified;
and all find fresh hope and purpose
in Christ Jesus crucified.

God of light, so many times we reject your ways
and seek comfort in earthly treasures. Help us,
gracious One, to see your way and your light.
Amen.

Thursday, July 16 — Psalm 85:8–13
Isaiah 37:14–38; Philippians 1:1–11

For as the heavens are higher than the earth, so are my ways higher than your ways and my thoughts than your thoughts. Isaiah 55:9

> Lord of all life, below, above,   p122
> whose light is truth, whose warmth is love,
> before your ever blazing throne
> we ask no luster of our own.

O the depth of the riches and wisdom and knowledge of God! How unsearchable are his judgments and how inscrutable his ways! Romans 11:33

> O Spirit of the Lord, all life is yours;   516
> now on your church your pow'r and strength outpour,
> that many children may be born to you
> and through your knowledge may be brought anew
> to sing Christ's praise.

Most wise Counselor, help us to see the wisdom of your word and ways and apply them to our daily lives. Help us to spread your word and wisdom so that others might see your treasures. Amen.

Friday, July 17 — Psalm 86:1–10
Isaiah 38:1–40:5; Philippians 1:12–22

Who are they that fear the Lord? He will teach them the way that they should choose. Psalm 25:12

> Be with me, Lord, where'er I go;   733
> teach me what you would have me do;
> suggest whate'er I think or say;
> direct me in the narrow way.

Follow God's example as dearly loved children and walk in the way of love, just as Christ loved us. Ephesians 5:1–2 (NIV)

> Where divine affection lives,   670
> there the Lord his blessing gives;
> there his will on earth is done;
> there his heav'n is half begun.
> Great example from above,
> teach us all like you to love.

Lord, you are our great example. Help us to love one another just as you love us. Amen.

Saturday, July 18 — Psalm 86:11–17
Isaiah 40:6–41:7; Philippians 1:23–2:4

Your eyes beheld my unformed substance. In your book were written all the days that were formed for me. Psalm 139:16

See the Lord, your keeper, stand   729
omnipotently near.
Now he holds you by the hand,
and banishes your fear;
shadows with his wings your head,
guards from all impending harms;
round you and beneath are spread
the everlasting arms.

Nathanael asked Jesus, "Where did you get to know me?" John 1:48

Blessed assurance, Jesus is mine!   714
O what a foretaste of glory divine!
Heir of salvation, purchase of God,
born of his Spirit, washed in his blood.
This is my story, this is my song,
praising my Savior all the day long.
This is my story, this is my song,
praising my Savior all the day long.

Lord, you know our stories from beginning to end, long before we do. We rejoice in knowing that you walk with us and enfold us in your arms throughout our journeys! Help us to know we are never without your care. Amen.

Eighth Sunday after Pentecost

Watchword for the Week — So then you are no longer strangers and aliens, but you are citizens with the saints and members of the household of God. Ephesians 2:19

Sunday, July 19 — Jeremiah 23:1–6; Psalm 23
Ephesians 2:11–22; Mark 6:30–34, 53–56

The Lord will bless his people with peace.
Psalm 29:11 (NKJV)

> Through all the passing years, O Lord,   512
> grant that, when church bells are ringing,
> many may come to hear God's word
> where he this promise is bringing:
> "I know my own, my own know me,
> you, not the world, my face shall see;
> my peace I leave with you." Amen.

Since we are justified by faith, we have peace with God through our Lord Jesus Christ.
Romans 5:1

> Faith in the conscience works for peace,   700
> and bids the mourner's weeping cease,
> by faith the children's place we claim,
> and give all honor to one name.

Most precious Lord and Savior, give us the faith of a child to see your light in our lives so that we might experience and share your peace that surpasses all understanding. Amen.

Monday, July 20 — Psalm 87
Isaiah 41:8–42:9; Philippians 2:5–18

The Lord God will wipe away the tears from all faces. Isaiah 25:8

While life's dark maze I tread,   705
and griefs around me spread,
O, be my guide;
make darkness turn to day,
wipe sorrow's tears away,
nor let me ever stray
from you aside.

Blessed be the God and Father of our Lord Jesus Christ, the Father of mercies and the God of all consolation, who consoles us in all our affliction. 2 Corinthians 1:3–4

Holy Spirit, come, console us   p226*
come as Advocate to plead;
loving Spirit from the Father,
grant in Christ the help we need.
Ponder now the sacred loaf,
bread of God, the food of hope,
broken, blessed, and freely served,
richly giv'n though undeserved.

God of healing and grace, we thank you for your constant vigilance and consolation. Help us to be steadfast in your ways. Help us to feel your grace and share it with others. Amen.

*   © by Faber Music Ltd.

Tuesday, July 21 — Psalm 88:1–5
Isaiah 42:10–43:21; Philippians 2:19–30

The Lord rewards everyone for his righteousness and his faithfulness. 1 Samuel 26:23

As you, Lord, have lived for others,   648
so may we for others live;
freely have your gifts been granted;
freely may your servants give.
Yours the gold and yours the silver,
yours the wealth of land and sea;
we but stewards of your bounty
held in solemn trust will be.

Blessed are those who are persecuted for righteousness' sake, for theirs is the kingdom of heaven. Matthew 5:10

Blessed are the poor in spirit,   595
claiming nothing as their own,
but as giv'n them by their Father
that his goodness may be shown.
Blessed are they who share the sorrow
of their God's unchanging love;
they shall know his presence with them
and his promised comfort prove.

Heavenly Father, make us strong in the face of adversity. Give us courage and strength when we face conflict or persecution. We know you are with us to guide us and we are blessed. Amen.

Wednesday, July 22 — Psalm 88:6–12
Isaiah 43:22–44:23; Philippians 3:1–11

I will add to their numbers, and they will not be decreased; I will bring them honor, and they will not be disdained. Jeremiah 30:19 (NIV)

Come, O Father's saving Son,   265*
who o'er sin the vict'ry won.
Boundless shall your kingdom be;
grant that we its glories see.

Jesus said, "The kingdom of heaven is like a mustard seed that someone took and sowed in his field; it is the smallest of all the seeds, but when it has grown it is the greatest of shrubs and becomes a tree, so that the birds of the air come and make nests in its branches." Matthew 13:31–32

Like a tiny seed of mustard,   702**
stored with life, invisibly,
grows and grows, each day increasing
and becomes a mighty tree.

Blessed Father, we rejoice in your abounding love! Help us to grow in faith each and every day and to share that faith with those who remain in the dark. Amen.

Thursday, July 23 — Psalm 88:13–18
Isaiah 44:24–45:25; Philippians 3:12–4:1

When I sit in darkness, the Lord will be a light to me. Micah 7:8

The radiant sun has vanished,   572
its golden rays are banished
from dark'ning skies of night;
but Christ the Sun of gladness,
dispelling all our sadness,
shines down on us in warmest light.

Christ says, "I have come as light into the world, so that everyone who believes in me should not remain in the darkness." John 12:46

I heard the voice of Jesus say,   606
"I am this dark world's Light;
look unto me, your morn shall rise,
and all your day be bright."
I looked to Jesus, and I found
in him my Star, my Sun;
and in that Light of life I'll walk,
'til trav'ling days are done.

Precious Lord Jesus, your light is a beacon for
all! Let us share the warmth of your light as we
encounter others throughout our daily lives. Help
us to share your love with all people! Amen.

Friday, July 24 — Psalm 89:1–8
Isaiah 46:1–48:6; Philippians 4:2–13

O Lord, I will praise you; though you were angry with me, your anger is turned away, and you comfort me. Isaiah 12:1 (NKJV)

Sing praise to God who reigns above,   537
the God of all creation,
the God of pow'r, the God of love,
the God of our salvation.
My soul with comfort rich he fills,
and ev'ry grief he gently stills:
to God all praise and glory!

Christ says, "Anyone who comes to me I will never drive away." John 6:37

Come, you thirsty, come and welcome,   765
God's free bounty glorify;
true belief and true repentance,
ev'ry grace that brings you nigh.
I will arise and go to Jesus;
he will embrace me in his arms;
in the arms of my dear Savior,
O there are ten thousand charms.

Lord, so many times, we confess that we turn away from your love and care. Help us to repent and to seek your forgiveness for doing so. We know you will welcome us back to the warm, loving embrace of your arms. We are blessed! Amen.

Saturday, July 25 — Psalm 89:9–18
Isaiah 48:7–49:21; Philippians 4:14–23

The Lord kills and brings to life; he brings down to Sheol and raises up. 1 Samuel 2:6

O be our mighty healer still,   736*
O Lord of life and death;
restore and strengthen, soothe and bless,
with your almighty breath:
on hands that work and eyes that see,
your healing wisdom pour,
that whole and sick, and weak and strong,
may praise you evermore.

May the God of peace, who brought back from the dead our Lord Jesus, the great shepherd of the sheep, by the blood of the eternal covenant, make you complete in everything good. Hebrews 13:20–21

Savior, like a shepherd lead us;   731
much we need your tender care;
in your pleasant pastures feed us,
for our use your folds prepare.
Blessed Jesus, blessed Jesus,
you have bought us; yours we are.
Blessed Jesus, blessed Jesus,
you have bought us; yours we are.

Lord, we turn to you in our struggles and in our
good times. Your constant love and care are
things we can be sure of. We rejoice in that blessed
assurance! Amen.

Ninth Sunday after Pentecost

Watchword for the Week — The Lord is faithful in all his words, and gracious in all his deeds. Psalm 145:13

Sunday, July 26 — 2 Kings 4:42–44; Psalm 145:10–18
Ephesians 3:14–21; John 6:1–21

Trust in him at all times, O people; pour out your heart before him; God is a refuge for us. Psalm 62:8

> If you but trust in God to guide you   712
> and place your confidence in him,
> you'll find him always there beside you
> to give you hope and strength within;
> for those who trust God's changeless love
> build on the rock that will not move.

This is the confidence we have in approaching God: that if we ask anything according to his will, he hears us. 1 John 5:14 (NIV)

> Lord, you have been our dwelling place   p147
> in ev'ry generation.
> Your people still have known your grace
> and your blessed consolation.
> Through ev'ry age you heard our cry,
> through ev'ry age we found you nigh,
> our strength and our salvation.

Dearest Lord, we seek your answers to our prayers always. We know that you answer us, sometimes in ways we do not expect. Lord, help us to be patient, to listen, and to understand that your will is above ours. Amen.

Monday, July 27 — Psalm 89:19–29
Isaiah 49:22–51:16; Colossians 1:1–14

Wondrously show your steadfast love, O Savior of those who seek refuge. Psalm 17:7

I am thine, O Lord—I have heard thy voice,   607
and it told thy love to me;
but I long to rise in the arms of faith
and be closer drawn to thee.
Draw me nearer, nearer, blessed Lord,
to the cross where thou hast died;
draw me nearer, nearer, nearer blessed Lord,
to thy precious, bleeding side.

This is how we know what love is: Jesus Christ laid down his life for us. 1 John 3:16 (NIV)

Love divine, all loves excelling,   474
joy of heav'n, to earth come down!
Fix in us your humble dwelling,
all your faithful mercies crown.
Jesus, you are all compassion,
pure, unbounded love impart!

God, you gave your son for us so that our sins might be forgiven! May we honor you and work daily to increase your kingdom so others may experience your love and grace! Amen.

Tuesday, July 28 — Psalm 89:30–37
Isaiah 51:17–53:12; Colossians 1:15–27

**We give thanks to you, O God, we give thanks!
For your wondrous works declare that your
name is near. Psalm 75:1 (NKJV)**

All praise and thanks to God   533
the Father now be given,
the Son and Spirit blessed,
who reign in highest heaven—
the one eternal God,
whom heav'n and earth adore;
for thus it was, is now,
and shall be evermore.

**Joyfully give thanks to the Father, who has
enabled you to share in the inheritance of the
saints in the light. Colossians 1:12**

Riches I heed not nor man's empty praise,   719
thou mine inheritance now and always;
thou and thou only first in my heart,
high King of heaven, my treasure thou art.

Father, we give you thanks for all the joys and
blessings in our lives. The presence of your beautiful
creation surrounds us and we are grateful! Amen.

Wednesday, July 29 — Psalm 89:38–45
Isaiah 54,55; Colossians 1:28–2:10

There is none like you, O Lord; you are great, and your name is great in might. Jeremiah 10:6

Come now, almighty King,   555
help us your name to sing,
help us to praise.
Father all glorious,
ever victorious,
come and reign over us,
Ancient of Days.

Jesus said to the disciples, "But who do you say that I am?" Matthew 16:15

All glory to the Son,   p185
who comes to set us free,
with Father, Spirit, ever one
through all eternity.

Christ our Father, you are the Great I Am! We are blessed by your presence in our lives and the greatness of your love for us. Help us to share that love with others through our actions. Amen.

Thursday, July 30 — Psalm 89:46–52
Isaiah 56,57; Colossians 2:11–23

I am with you, says the Lord, to save you. Jeremiah 30:11

> God is our strength and song,   531
> and his salvation ours;
> then be his love in Christ proclaimed
> with all our ransomed pow'rs.

Paul wrote: I am confident of this, that the one who began a good work among you will bring it to completion by the day of Jesus Christ. Philippians 1:6

> Take my hands, Lord Jesus,   578*
>   let them work for you,
> make them strong and gentle, kind in all I do;
> let me watch you, Jesus, 'til I'm gentle too,
> 'til my hands are kind hands, quick to work for you.

Lord, you are with us always, even when we do not acknowledge you. Sometimes we think we can make our way in this world without you. Even so, you reach out and gather us in your arms, never rejecting us. Your love is awesome! Amen.

Friday, July 31 — Psalm 90
Isaiah 58,59; Colossians 3:1–11

You are the God of my salvation; for you I wait all day long. Psalm 25:5

> God is my strong salvation,   769
> no enemy I fear;
> he hears my supplication,
> dispelling all my care;
> if he, my head and master,
> defend me from above,
> what pain or what disaster
> can part me from his love?

Devote yourselves to prayer, keeping alert in it with thanksgiving. Colossians 4:2

> To him shall endless prayer be made   404
> and praises throng to crowd his head;
> his name like sweet perfume shall rise
> with ev'ry morning sacrifice.

Blessed Jesus, we so often go about our days without speaking with you in prayer and praise. We ask your forgiveness for this. Help us to turn to you constantly in prayer and thanksgiving! Amen.

Saturday, August 1 — Psalm 91:1–8
Isaiah 60,61; Colossians 3:12–25

It is God who executes judgment, putting down one and lifting up another. Psalm 75:7

When a poor one who has nothing   689*
    shares with strangers,
when the thirsty water give unto us all,
when the crippled in their weakness
    strengthen others,
then we know that God still goes that road with us,
then we know that God still goes that road with us.

Yes, O Lord God, the Almighty, your judgments are true and just! Revelation 16:7

When at last all those who suffer   689*
    find their comfort,
when they hope though even hope
    seems hopelessness,
when we love though hate at times
    seems all around us,
then we know that God still goes that road with us,
then we know that God still goes that road with us.

Oh Lord, you are God almighty. You alone are judge of our hearts and souls. May we be set free from our habit of fulfilling our own wills. May we thirst, instead, for your counsel. Amen.

---

* © 1971 by J. A. Olivar, Muguel Manzano y San Pablo Internacional-SSP.
Trans. © 1989 by the United Methodist Publishing House. Used by permission.

Tenth Sunday after Pentecost

Watchword for the Week — Jesus says, "I am the bread of life. Whoever comes to me will never be hungry, and whoever believes in me will never be thirsty." John 6:35

Sunday, August 2 — Exodus 16:2–4,9–15; Psalm 78:23–29
Ephesians 4:1–16; John 6:24–35

They will be my treasured possession. I will spare them, just as a father has compassion and spares his son who serves him. Malachi 3:17 (NIV)

> O may your mighty love prevail   374
> our sinful souls to spare,
> O may we come before your throne
> and find acceptance there,
> and find acceptance there.

Christ loved the church and gave himself up for her, in order to make her holy. Ephesians 5:25–26

> When in the soul this blessed truth resounds,   325r*
> that in Christ's death, for sinners life abounds,
> O how doth this refresh the fainting heart
> and bid all anxious doubts and fears depart.

Divine Sustainer, may we feast this day on your salvation. May Christ's love for the church awaken and embolden our love for you. In Christ's holy name we pray. Amen.

Monday, August 3 — Psalm 91:9–16
Isaiah 62,63; Colossians 4:1–9

The path of the righteous is like the light of dawn, which shines brighter and brighter until full day. Proverbs 4:18

When simplicity we cherish,   717
then the soul is full of light;
but that light will quickly vanish,
when of Jesus we lose sight.

Let your light shine before others, so that they may see your good works and give glory to your Father in heaven. Matthew 5:16

Lord, as thou hast lived for others,   407r
so may we for others live;
freely have thy gifts been granted;
freely may thy servants give.
Thine the gold and thine the silver,
thine the wealth of land and sea,
we but stewards of thy bounty
held in solemn trust for thee.

Lord God, Source of light and life, may we seek your kingdom and righteousness as our own. May Jesus remain our Lord and one essential. May our lives stay true to his eternal light. Amen.

Tuesday, August 4 — Psalm 92:1–8
Isaiah 64,65; Colossians 4:10–1 Thessalonians 1:5a

Have you not known? Have you not heard? The Lord is the everlasting God, the Creator of the ends of the earth. He does not faint or grow weary; his understanding is unsearchable. Isaiah 40:28

> Then let us adore and give him his right,   565
> all glory and pow'r and wisdom and might,
> all honor and blessing, with angels above,
> and thanks never ceasing for infinite love.

To the only wise God be glory forever through Jesus Christ! Romans 16:27 (NIV)

> Born your people to deliver,   262
> born a child and yet a king,
> born to reign in us forever,
> now your gracious kingdom bring.
> By your own eternal Spirit
> rule in all our hearts alone;
> by your all-sufficient merit
> raise us to your glorious throne.

Who are you God? How can we know you? Your ways and your understanding are not like our own, yet you call us to pray, to worship, to serve. Help us to trust in your wisdom. May your grace, known to us in our Lord Jesus Christ, be sufficient. Amen.

Wednesday, August 5 — Psalm 92:9–15
Isaiah 66–Jeremiah 1:7; 1 Thessalonians 1:5b–2:9

Is anything too difficult for the Lord?
Genesis 18:14 (NASB)

God of the earthquake   462*
God of the storm
God of the trumpet blast
how does the creature cry woe
how does the creature cry save

Do not fear, only believe. Mark 5:36

I know not where his islands lift   539r
their fronded palms in air;
I only know I cannot drift
beyond his love and care.

O eternal God, Hallelujah! Your Spirit conquers
death itself. Direct the gaze of our hearts away from
ourselves. Lift the eyes of our souls to you. Set us
free from fears that distract us from an ever growing
trust in you. In Jesus' name we pray. Amen.

*   © 1983 by Jaroslav J. Vajda

Thursday, August 6 — Psalm 93
Jeremiah 1:8–2:19; 1 Thessalonians 2:10–20

After the suffering of his soul, he will see the light of life and be satisfied. Isaiah 53:11 (NIV)

> Through many dangers, toils, and snares,　　　783
> I have already come;
> 'tis grace has brought me safe thus far,
> and grace will lead me home.

Christ humbled himself and became obedient to the point of death—even death on a cross. Therefore God also highly exalted him. Philippians 2:8–9

> He who slumbered in the grave　　　360
> is exalted now to save;
> now through Christendom it rings
> that the Lamb is King of kings.
> Alleluia!

Dear Lord, your humility is our salvation. Your surrender is our strength. We are resurrected by your burial. Your cross is our salvation. May we exalt you by faithfulness to your eternal servant spirit. Amen.

Friday, August 7 — Psalm 94:1–11
Jeremiah 2:20–3:13; 1 Thessalonians 3

Samuel said to Saul, "Stop here yourself for a while, that I may make known to you the word of God." 1 Samuel 9:27

> Still will I wait, O Lord, on you,   721
> 'til in your light I see anew;
> 'til you in my behalf appear,
> to banish ev'ry doubt and fear.

Let everyone be quick to listen, slow to speak, slow to anger. James 1:19

> O give me Samuel's ear!   609
> The open ear, O Lord,
> alive and quick to hear
> each whisper of thy word;
> like him to answer at thy call,
> and to obey thee first of all.

Slow us down, Lord. Slow our racing minds and anxious hearts. Help us to be still and know that you are God and we are not. Strengthen and comfort us we pray. In Jesus' name. Amen.

Saturday, August 8 — Psalm 94:12–23
Jeremiah 3:14–4:22; 1 Thessalonians 4:1–12

They have turned their backs to me, and not their faces. But in the time of their trouble they say, "Come and save us!" Jeremiah 2:27

> Come, you weary, heavy laden,   765
> lost and ruined by the fall;
> if you tarry 'til you're better,
> you will never come at all.
> I will arise and go to Jesus;
> he will embrace me in his arms;
> in the arms of my dear Savior,
> O there are ten thousand charms.

Christ says, "Abide in my love." John 15:9

> Therefore I pray, while here I stay   596
> and look to him with yearning:
> fixed in him may I abide,
> kept from ever turning.

Forgive us, Lord, for we have sinned. We speak of faith and live by willfulness. We hunger for your love. We ache for your forgiveness. We pray for your transforming spirit. May we abide in Christ's love. Amen.

Eleventh Sunday after Pentecost

Watchword for the Week — Jesus says, "Very truly, I tell you, whoever believes has eternal life." John 6:47

Sunday, August 9 — 1 Kings 19:4–8; Psalm 34:1–8
Ephesians 4:25–5:2; John 6:35, 41–51

The Lord searches every mind, and understands every plan and thought. 1 Chronicles 28:9

Be still, my soul: your God will undertake   757
to guide the future, as in ages past.
Your hope, your confidence let nothing shake;
all now mysterious shall be bright at last.
Be still, my soul: the waves and winds still know
the Christ who ruled them while he dwelt below.

When you pray, go into your room, close the door and pray to your Father, who is unseen. Then your Father, who sees what is done in secret, will reward you. Matthew 6:6 (NIV)

Sometimes, when I pray,   41s*
I bow my head, cup my hands,
and hold them out in front of me as though I were:
Raising Living Water to my lips
Waiting to receive the Bread of Life
Offering up my heart, my soul, my strength
Sheltering a small spark of the Light of the World
Setting free a cloud-white dove to find us
     a token of Peace
Sometimes when I pray.

Lord, we are embarrassed by the clutter in our prayer closet, but you are not. We get stuck in shame even as you offer eternal grace. Your reward is freedom from fear. Your salvation heals our duplicity. May we trust you wholly. Amen.

*   © by Brian Dixon

Monday, August 10 — Psalm 95
Jeremiah 4:23–5:25; 1 Thessalonians 4:13–5:3

Nothing can hinder the Lord from saving by many or by few. 1 Samuel 14:6

Eternal Father, strong to save, 725
whose arm has bound the restless wave,
who bade the mighty ocean deep
its own appointed limits keep:
O hear us when we cry to thee
for those in peril on the sea.

Strive first for the kingdom of God and his righteousness, and all these things will be given to you as well. Matthew 6:33

Ask and it shall be given unto you, 605*
seek and you shall find,
knock and the door shall be opened unto you—
Allelu, alleluia!

You alone are worthy, Lord. Your ways bring life to the oppressed, humility to the proud, and justice to the nations. We see through a glass darkly; you see through an eternal lens. Open our eyes to your sovereign presence. Amen.

Tuesday, August 11 — Psalm 96:1–9
Jeremiah 5:26–6:30; 1 Thessalonians 5:4–15

The Lord said to Moses, "Assemble the people for me, and I will let them hear my words, so that they may learn to fear me as long as they live on the earth, and may teach their children to do so." Deuteronomy 4:10

Like Moses and his wand'ring band,   46s*
I journey with my Lord.
Who trusted God out in the sand,
I journey with my Lord.
And what I need God will supply;
abundant grace I can't deny.
The great I AM is my ally,
I journey with the Lord.

When Barnabas came and saw the grace of God, he rejoiced, and he exhorted them all to remain faithful to the Lord with steadfast devotion. Acts 11:23

Rejoice, all those in Christ's command!   24s**
Again, we say, rejoice!
With hearts and minds and adoration,
proudly lift your voice.
Declare good news to all the world;
from mountains, shout and sing!
With ev'ry breath, give all you are
to Christ, our Lord and King!

Gracious God, we thank you for the saints that have proclaimed your salvation throughout history. Open our ears to the voice of your servant leaders today. Calm our fears. Awaken our hopes and dreams. You are God of all. Amen.

Wednesday, August 12 — Psalm 96:10–13
Jeremiah 7; 1 Thessalonians 5:16–28

Therefore revere the Lord, and serve him in sincerity and in faithfulness; put away the gods that your ancestors served, and serve the Lord. Joshua 24:14

> We are called to be God's servants,   635*
> working in his world today;
> taking his own task upon us,
> all his sacred words obey.
> Let us rise, then, to his summons,
> dedicate to him our all,
> that we may be faithful servants,
> quick to answer now his call.

I want you to be wise about what is good, and innocent about what is evil. Romans 16:19 (NIV)

> Build up each other in the faith,   60s**
> push evil thoughts aside;
> encourage others, as you do,
> thus we in Christ abide.

Forgive us, Lord, for in our zeal we put our trust in yesterday's faith. We cling to tradition and stability rather than your living, transforming presence. Save us from the false god of predictability. Instill in us the courage to seek you anew this day. Amen.

Thursday, August 13 — Psalm 97:1–6
Jeremiah 8:1–9:9; 2 Thessalonians 1

August Thirteenth Festival † —Joshua 24:16–24; Psalm 133
1 John 4:1–13; John 17:1–2, 6–19

Great is our Lord, and abundant in power; his understanding is beyond measure. Psalm 147:5

God of grace and God of glory,   751
on your people pour your power;
crown your ancient Church's story;
bring its bud to glorious flower.
Grant us wisdom, grant us courage
for the facing of this hour,
for the facing of this hour.

We know that in all things God works for the good of those who love him. Romans 8:28 (NIV)

God wants us to see how the world will be   *
when no one lacks bread, nor homes for a bed.
God's kingdom will come as divine will is done.
A world without hate is what God does create.

Holy Spirit, fall fresh on your church. Empower us
to overcome timid hearts and divisive tongues. In
all things may your love reign. Amen.

* © 2007 by Konnoak Hills Moravian Youth. To the tune of Hymn 565.
  Used by permission.

† At the conclusion of a Holy Communion service in the church at Berthelsdorf,
  Germany, on August 13, 1727, the residents of Herrnhut were united into the
  Renewed Brethren's Church through the Spirit of God.

Friday, August 14 — Psalm 97:7–12
Jeremiah 9:10–10:16; 2 Thessalonians 2:1–12

You have made the Lord your refuge. Psalm 91:9

Lord, your body ne'er forsake,   p86
ne'er your congregation leave;
we in you our refuge take,
of your fullness we receive:
ev'ry other help be gone,
you are our support alone;
for on your supreme commands
all the universe depends.

Jesus prays, "I am not asking you to take them out of the world, but I ask you to protect them from the evil one." John 17:15

Pass me not, O gentle Savior,   772
hear my humble cry;
while on others thou art smiling,
do not pass me by.
Savior, Savior, hear my humble cry;
while on others thou art calling;
do not pass me by.

Gracious God, under your wings we find comfort and protection. Though storms may come we know that we are in your loving care. Evil is real, but is no match for your resurrection power. We pray to put our trust in you always. Amen.

Saturday, August 15 — Psalm 98
Jeremiah 10:17–11:23; 2 Thessalonians 2:13–3:5

O Lord, do your eyes not look for truth?
Jeremiah 5:3

As twig is bent, so grows the tree.   78s*
As child is nurtured, she will be.
Within each soul a servant sleeps;
awake the love that childhood keeps.

Remember your leaders, those who spoke the word of God to you; consider the outcome of their way of life, and imitate their faith. Hebrews 13:7

In simple trust like theirs who heard,   739
beside the Syrian sea,
the gracious calling of the Lord,
Let us, like them, without a word
rise up and follow thee.

God of history and eternity, we praise you for the inspired lives of those upon whose shoulders we stand. Empower us to also live lives of courage and practical faith. May you be glorified. In Christ's name. Amen.

Twelfth Sunday after Pentecost

Watchword for the Week — Lay aside immaturity, and live, and walk in the way of insight. Proverbs 9:6

Sunday, August 16 — Proverbs 9:1–6; Psalm 34: 9–14
Ephesians 5:15–20; John 6:51–58

Joseph's brothers begged him, "Please forgive the crime of the servants of the God of your father." Genesis 50:17

> Much forgiven, may I learn   779
> love for hatred to return;
> then my heart assured shall be
> you, my God, have pardoned me.

Peter came to Jesus and asked, "Lord, how many times shall I forgive my brother or sister who sins against me? Up to seven times?" Jesus answered, "I tell you, not seven times, but seventy-seven times." Matthew 18:21–22 (NIV)

> "Forgive our sins as we forgive,"   777
> you taught us, Lord, to pray;
> but you alone can grant us grace
> to live the words we say,
> to live the words we say.

Dear God, we are often too slow or too quick to forgive. We pray that your Spirit would guide our response to hurt and resentment that we hold close. Help us to love with both the honesty and wisdom of Christ this day. Amen.

Monday, August 17 — Psalm 99
Jeremiah 12:1–13:19; 2 Thessalonians 3:6–18

When words are many, transgression is not lacking, but the prudent are restrained in speech. Proverbs 10:19

Keep me from saying words   615
that later need recalling;
guard me, lest idle speech
may from my lips be falling;
but when, within my place,
I must and ought to speak,
then to my words give grace,
lest I offend the weak.

By your words you will be justified, and by your words you will be condemned. Matthew 12:37

When our joy fills up our cup to overflowing,   689*
when our lips can speak no words other than true,
when we know that love for simple things is better,
then we know that God still goes that road with us,
then we know that God still goes that road with us.

God, help us. Amen.

Tuesday, August 18 — Psalm 100
Jeremiah 13:20–14:22; 1 Timothy 1:1–11

I will give them one heart, and put a new spirit within them. Ezekiel 11:19

Lord Jesus, for our call of grace,   437
to praise your name in fellowship
we humbly meet before your face
and in your presence love-feast keep.
Shed in our hearts your love abroad,
your Spirit's blessing now impart;
grant we may all, O Lamb of God,
in you be truly one in heart.

You received the Spirit of adoption by whom we cry out, "Abba, Father." Romans 8:15 (NKJV)

Father, now your sinful child   779
through your love is reconciled.
By your pard'ning grace I live;
daily still I cry, forgive.

Abba, Father, instill in us a new and right spirit. Eradicate fear and awaken faith. Give us the audacity to claim the promise and presence of Christ our Savior and Brother. You are near. May we live close to you. Amen.

Wednesday, August 19 — Psalm 101
Jeremiah 15:1–16:13; 1 Timothy 1:12–2:7

The Lord is good, a stronghold in the day of trouble; and he knows those who trust in him. Nahum 1:7 (NKJV)

> Be still, my soul: the Lord is on your side.   757
> Bear patiently the cross of grief or pain;
> leave to your God to order and provide;
> in ev'ry change God faithful will remain.
> Be still, my soul: your best, your heav'nly friend
> through thorny ways leads to a joyful end.

Paul wrote: Epaphroditus was indeed so ill that he nearly died. But God had mercy on him, and not only on him but on me also, so that I would not have one sorrow after another. Philippians 2:27

> Be still, my soul: the hour is hast'ning on   757
> when we shall be forever with the Lord,
> when disappointment, grief, and fear are gone,
> sorrow forgot, love's purest joys restored.
> Be still, my soul: when change and tears are past,
> all safe and blessed we shall meet at last.

Dear God, we grow tired of hardship. Do you? We sometimes feel that sorrow may drown us. Awaken us to your own broken heart. May we trust the truth of your power revealed through the cross. In the name of our Christ we pray. Amen.

Thursday, August 20 — Psalm 102:1–11
Jeremiah 16:14–17:27; 1 Timothy 2:8–3:7

Truly, you are a God who hides himself, O God of Israel, the Savior. Isaiah 45:15

O, send your Spirit, Lord,   502
now unto me,
that he may touch my eyes
and make me see.
Show me the truth concealed
within your word;
and in your book revealed
I see my Lord.

Jesus said, "The Son of Man will be handed over to the Gentiles; and he will be mocked and insulted and spat upon. After they have flogged him, they will kill him, and on the third day he will rise again." But the Twelve understood nothing about all these things; in fact, what he said was hidden from them. Luke 18:32–34

Resting from his work today,   220b
in the tomb the Savior lay;
still he slept, from head to feet,
shrouded in the winding-sheet,
lying in the rock alone,
hidden by the sealed stone.

Have mercy Lord, for we do not see the world as you do. Your wisdom is infinite. In Christ alone do we know the fullness of your eternal being as one of us. Christ, and him crucified, is our confession. Amen.

Friday, August 21† — Psalm 102:12–22
Jeremiah 18:1–19:9; 1 Timothy 3:8–16

God knows what is in the darkness, and light dwells with him. Daniel 2:22

> Morning Star, your cheering light   323
> can dispel the gloom of night.
> Morning Star, your cheering light
> can dispel the gloom of night;
> Jesulein, come and shine;
> come and shine, Jesulein,
> in this darksome heart of mine.

Do not pronounce judgment before the time, before the Lord comes, who will bring to light the things now hidden in darkness and will disclose the purposes of the heart. 1 Corinthians 4:5

> Show God's mercy, show God's mercy   52s*
> unto one and all;
> without judging, without judging
> as we heed our call;
> this is how our church shall be:
> filled with love and liberty,
> in the Spirit, in the Spirit
> of our Savior's law.

Dear God, we praise you that your light shines in darkness of any kind. As Christ loved all, may we love all. May our witness be to his extraordinary love for the stranger and the neighbor, the friend and the foe alike. Amen.

†   On this day in 1732, the first missionaries departed from Herrnhut bound for St. Thomas.

*   © 2013 by Interprovincial Board of Communication and Moravian Music Foundation

Saturday, August 22 — Psalm 102:23–28
Jeremiah 19:10–21:10; 1 Timothy 4:1–10

The Lord is good to those who wait for him, to the soul that seeks him. Lamentations 3:25

Because the Lord our God is good,   539
his mercy is forever sure.
His truth at all times firmly stood,
and shall from age to age endure.

Indeed you have tasted that the Lord is good. 1 Peter 2:3

We come to you, our Father,   433
with thoughts of thanks and praise,
for your abundant mercy,
and all your love and grace;
we praise you for your goodness
and for your loving care,
for daily show'rs of blessing,
for answers to our prayers.

God of grace, God of glory, your delight is our joy.
Our delight is to be loved by you. Open wide our
hearts to receive your goodness in our lives. Amen.

Thirteenth Sunday after Pentecost

Watchword for the Week — Jesus says, "The words that I have spoken to you are spirit and life." John 6:63

Sunday, August 23 — Joshua 24:1–2a,14–18; Psalm 34:15–22
Ephesians 6:10–20; John 6:56–69

He gives power to the faint, and strengthens the powerless. Isaiah 40:29

> Spirit, fill me with your strength;   48s*
> my own resolve will fail me at length.
> Set my spirit free to wait upon you patiently.
> Spirit fill me with your strength.

Therefore I am content with weaknesses, insults, hardships, persecutions, and calamities for the sake of Christ; for whenever I am weak, then I am strong. 2 Corinthians 12:10

> Restrain me lest I harbor pride,   733
> lest I in my own strength confide;
> though I am weak, show me anew
> I have my pow'r, my strength from you.

God of strength and tenderness, we seek you by our surrender. We praise you in our weakness. May Christ lead on through perils dark. May grace alone be our light. Amen.

Monday, August 24 — Psalm 103:1–5
Jeremiah 21:11–22:30; 1 Timothy 4:11–5:8

The Lord has bared his holy arm before the eyes of all the nations; and all the ends of the earth shall see the salvation of our God. Isaiah 52:10

O God of ev'ry nation,   p142*
of ev'ry race and land,
redeem your whole creation
with your almighty hand;
where hate and fear divide us
and bitter threats are hurled,
in love and mercy guide us,
and heal our strife-torn world.

The true light, which enlightens everyone, was coming into the world. John 1:9

As with gladness men of old   p190
did the guiding star behold;
as with joy they hailed its light,
leading onward, beaming bright;
so, most gracious Lord, may we
evermore your splendor see.

Open our eyes, Lord, to see you throughout the world. Teach us the language of your Holy Spirit that inspires, unites, and empowers all. Heal our divided hearts and divided world. In Christ's name we pray. Amen.

* © by the Hymn Society

Tuesday, August 25 — Psalm 103:6–18
Jeremiah 23:1–32; 1 Timothy 5:9–16

In response to his people the Lord said: I am sending you grain, wine, and oil, and you will be satisfied. Joel 2:19

> We come to you, O Lord, 65s*
> with songs of gratitude,
> for all that you have given us,
> our life, our food.
> Our prayers ascend for this our native land
> that it will choose your will.

Taking the five loaves and the two fish and looking up to heaven, Jesus gave thanks and broke the loaves. Then he gave them to the disciples, and the disciples gave them to the people. They all ate and were satisfied. Matthew 14:19–20 (NIV)

> Let your heart be broken 582**
> for a world in need—
> feed the mouths that hunger,
> soothe the wounds that bleed;
> give the cup of water
> and the loaf of bread—
> be the hands of Jesus,
> serving in his stead.

Lord, may gratitude and generosity be our daily joy. We pray that your spirit will overcome the fears that diminish our faith. May the bounty of your provision be all we seek. Amen.

* © 2013 by Interprovincial Board of Communication and Moravian Music Foundation

** © 1975 by The Evangelical Covenant Church

Wednesday, August 26 — Psalm 103:19–22
Jeremiah 23:33–25:14; 1 Timothy 5:17–6:2

Inquire first for the word of the Lord.
2 Chronicles 18:4

> Give us your Holy Spirit, Lord;   17s*
> we would disciples be,
> and know, as we obey your word,
> the truth that makes us free.

These are the ones sown on the good soil: they hear the word and accept it and bear fruit.
Mark 4:20

> All the world is God's own field,   450
> fruit unto his praise to yield,
> wheat and weeds together sown,
> unto joy or sorrow grown;
> first the blade, and then the ear,
> then the full corn shall appear;
> Lord of harvest, grant that we
> wholesome grain and pure may be.

Giver of all joy, we celebrate the diversity of your gifts. May we lift up those who differ from us. May your word be secure in our hearts and your glory be revealed in our words and deeds. Amen.

*   © 2013 by Interprovincial Board of Communication and Moravian Music Foundation

Thursday, August 27 — Psalm 104:1–9
Jeremiah 25:15–26:9; 1 Timothy 6:3–16

Those who oppress the poor insult their maker.
Proverbs 14:31

Give me your courage, Lord, to speak   p150*
whenever strong oppress the weak.
Should I myself as victim live,
rememb'ring you, may I forgive.

Paul wrote: Even though my illness was a trial to you, you did not treat me with contempt or scorn. Instead, you welcomed me as if I were an angel of God, as if I were Christ Jesus himself. Galatians 4:14 (NIV)

Mighty God, we humbly pray,   586
let your pow'r now lead the way
that in all things we may show
that we in your likeness grow.

God of the poor and rich alike, we pray for your compassion to unite us. May our work bear fruit in your kingdom so that greed and injustice fall away. In the name of the servant Christ we pray. Amen.

*   © by Concordia Publishing House

Friday, August 28 — Psalm 104:10–18
Jeremiah 26:10–27:22; 1 Timothy 6:17–2 Timothy 1:7

I am going to gather them from the farthest parts of the earth, among them the blind and the lame, those with child and those in labor, together; a great company, they shall return here. Jeremiah 31:8

> All people of each time and place   p134*
> receive the promise of God's grace.
> O praise God! Alleluia!
> And all who have not heard God's voice,
> we now invite you, "Come! Rejoice!"
> O praise God! Alleluia!
> O praise God! Alleluia! Alleluia!

The master said to the slave, "Go out into the roads and lanes, and compel people to come in, so that my house may be filled." Luke 14:23

> We bid you welcome in the name   432
> of Jesus, our exalted Head.
> Come as a servant; so he came,
> and we receive you in his stead.

God, we are embarrassed by our prejudices. We hide under the veil of innocence even though you know our inner hostility. Help us to see those who are vulnerable as your chosen ones. Help us to glorify you through outrageous hospitality. Amen.

* © by Glen Stoudt

Saturday, August 29 — Psalm 104:19–23
Jeremiah 28:1–29:14; 2 Timothy 1:8–18

Your people say, "The way of the Lord is not just," when it is their own way that is not just. Ezekiel 33:17

Bring justice to our land,   681
that all may dwell secure,
and finely build for days to come
foundations that endure.

And lead us not into temptation. Matthew 6:13 (NIV)

Go to dark Gethsemane,   349
all who feel the tempter's pow'r;
your Redeemer's conflict see,
watch with him one bitter hour.
Turn not from his griefs away;
learn of Jesus Christ to pray.

Help us, Lord. We are such easy prey to the tempters' wiles. We so quickly blame you for our own willful ways. May we repent with broken hearts and be renewed by your forgiveness. In Christ our Savior we pray. Amen.

Fourteenth Sunday after Pentecost

Watchword for the Week — Let everyone be quick to listen, slow to speak, slow to anger. James 1:19

Sunday, August 30 — Deuteronomy 4:1–2, 6–9; Psalm 15
James 1:17–27; Mark 7:1–8,14–15,21–23

I am merciful, says the Lord; I will not be angry forever. Only acknowledge your guilt, that you have rebelled against the Lord your God. Jeremiah 3:12–13

> When I survey the wondrous cross   350
> on which the Prince of glory died,
> my richest gain I count but loss,
> and pour contempt on all my pride

The Lord is patient with you, not wanting any to perish, but all to come to repentance. 2 Peter 3:9

> What a friend we have in Jesus,   743
> all our sins and griefs to bear!
> What a privilege to carry
> ev'rything to God in prayer!
> O what peace we often forfeit,
> O what needless pain we bear,
> all because we do not carry
> ev'rything to God in prayer.

Eternal God, we cannot fathom the depth and width of your grace. We strive to earn that which is freely given. We sin when judging our neighbors' souls. Your patience with us is our salvation. Amen.

Monday, August 31 — Psalm 104:24–30
Jeremiah 29:15–30:11; 2 Timothy 2:1–13

The Lord said to Moses, "All the people among whom you live shall see the work of the Lord." Exodus 34:10

> God of our weary years, God of our silent tears,   707
> thou who hast brought us thus far on the way,
> thou who hast by thy might led us into the light,
> keep us forever in the path, we pray.
> Lest our feet stray from the places,
> our God, where we met thee,
> lest our hearts, drunk with the wine of the world,
> we forget thee, shadowed beneath thy hand,
> may we forever stand, true to our God,
> true to our native land.

Many who heard him were astounded. They said, "Where did this man get all this? What is this wisdom that has been given to him? What deeds of power are being done by his hands! Is not this the carpenter, the son of Mary?" Mark 6:2–3

> By Galilee I met the Savior;   50s*
> by Galilee I heard him call;
> by Galilee I felt his presence,
> and I'll never be the same again.
> By Galilee I saw the splendor
> of all the love he has to give.
> It filled my cup to overflowing,
> and I'll never be the same again.

How amazing are your ways, O God. We marvel at your designs. In Christ you have shown us the awesome, divine presence that is ours. May our heavenly humanity be a witness to your earthly divinity. Amen.

* Lahoma Gray (1985)

Tuesday, September 1 — Psalm 104:31–35
Jeremiah 30:12–31:22; 2 Timothy 2:14–26

With my mouth I will give great thanks to the Lord; I will praise him in the midst of the throng. Psalm 109:30

All apostles join the strain   386
as your sacred name they hallow;
prophets swell the glad refrain,
and the blessed martyrs follow,
and from morn to set of sun,
through the church the song goes on.

Anna came, and began to praise God and to speak about the child to all who were looking for the redemption of Jerusalem. Luke 2:38

Hail to the Lord's anointed!   263
Great David's greater Son!
Hail in the time appointed,
his reign on earth begun!
He comes to break oppression,
to set the captive free,
to take away transgression,
and rule in equity.

Redeemer of the world, we come before you with praise and thanksgiving for your everlasting love. May we carry the news of your salvation to all those we meet. Amen.

Wednesday, September 2 — Psalm 105:1–7
Jeremiah 31:23–32:15; 2 Timothy 3:1–9

And all the people responded with a great shout when they praised the Lord, because the foundation of the house of the Lord was laid. Ezra 3:11

> Christ is our cornerstone, 517
> on him alone we build;
> with his true saints alone
> the courts of heav'n are filled;
> on his great love our hopes we place
> of present grace and joys above.

Day by day, as they spent much time together in the temple, they broke bread at home and ate their food with glad and generous hearts, praising God and having the goodwill of all the people. Acts 2:46–47

> One bread, one cup, one body we, p228
> rejoicing in our unity,
> proclaim your love until you come
> to bring your scattered loved ones home.

Christ, you are our true foundation. Build our community of believers and call us to join together as one: in our homes, in our churches, in the world. In your name. Amen.

Thursday, September 3 — Psalm 105:8–15
Jeremiah 32:16–33:5; 2 Timothy 3:10–4:8

Behold, your King is coming to you; He is just and having salvation, lowly and riding on a donkey. Zechariah 9:9 (NKJV)

Ride on! Ride on in majesty!   343
Hear all the tribes hosanna cry;
O Savior meek, your road pursue,
   with palms and scattered garments strewed.

He, though he was in the form of God, did not regard equality with God as something to be exploited, but emptied himself, taking the form of a slave. Philippians 2:6–7

The everlasting Son   p185
incarnate stoops to be,
takes on himself the servant's form
to set his people free.

Servant God, help us remember that you sent your Son to lead through humility, not might. Give us the desire to serve, not to be served. Amen.

Friday, September 4 — Psalm 105:16–22
Jeremiah 33:6–34:7; 2 Timothy 4:9–22

May God continue to bless us; let all the ends of the earth revere him. Psalm 67:7

From all that dwell below the skies   551
let the Creator's praise arise;
let the Redeemer's name be sung
through every land, by every tongue.

You are worthy, our Lord and God, to receive glory and honor and power, for you created all things, and by your will they existed and were created. Revelation 4:11

All your works with joy surround you,   544
earth and heav'n reflect your rays,
stars and angels sing around you,
center of unbroken praise;
field and forest, vale and mountain,
flowr'y meadow, flashing sea,
chanting bird and flowing fountain,
praising you eternally!

Creator and Sustainer of all, we are awed and
blessed by all you have made. May the whole
of creation, to the ends of the earth, praise you
forever! Amen.

Saturday, September 5 — Psalm 105:23–36
Jeremiah 34:8–35:19; Titus 1:1–9

Remember, O Lord, your great mercy and love for they are from of old. Psalm 25:6 (NIV)

> The God Abraham praise,   468
> who reigns enthroned above,
> the Ancient of eternal days,
> the God of love!
> The Lord, the great I Am,
> by earth and heav'n confessed—
> we bow before his holy name
> forever blessed.

In this is love, not that we loved God but that he loved us and sent his Son to be the atoning sacrifice for our sins. 1 John 4:10

> To God be the glory—great things he has done!   550
> So loved he the world that he gave us his Son,
> who yielded his life an atonement for sin,
> and opened the life-gate that all may go in.
> Praise the Lord, praise the Lord,
> let the earth hear his voice!
> Praise the Lord, praise the Lord,
> let the people rejoice!
> O come to the Father through Jesus the Son,
> and give him the glory—great things he has done!

Eternal God, we thank you for your steadfast love. We often fall short of the life we are called to live, yet your mercy and grace are never lost to us. Let the love you show us be in the love we show others. Amen.

Fifteenth Sunday after Pentecost

Watchword for the Week — I will praise the Lord as long as I live;
I will sing praises to my God all my life long. Psalm 146:2

Sunday, September 6 — Isaiah 35:4–7a; Psalm 146
James 2:1–10,(11–13),14–17; Mark 7:24–37

We will tell to the coming generation the glorious deeds of the Lord, and his might, and the wonders that he has done. Psalm 78:4

Good news is ours to tell!   p160*
Let no one fail to hear!
God gives us life;
God conquers death!
What's left for us to fear?

Freely you have received; freely give. Matthew 10:8 (NIV)

As you, Lord, have lived for others,   648
so may we for others live;
freely have your gifts been granted;
freely may your servants give.
Yours the gold and yours the silver,
yours the wealth of land and sea;
we but stewards of your bounty
held in solemn trust will be.

Giver of all gifts, help us remember that you are
the source of all. We have freely received your
abundance; in turn, help us share that abundance
with those who come after us. Amen.

* © by Jane Parker Huber

Monday, September 7 — Psalm 105:37–45
Jeremiah 36; Titus 1:10–2:5

Lord, plead my cause and redeem me; revive me according to your word. Psalm 119:154 (NKJV)

O God of ev'ry nation   683*
of ev'ry race and land,
redeem your whole creation
with your almighty hand;
where hate and fear divide us,
and bitter threats are hurled,
in love and mercy guide us,
and heal our strife-torn world.

Paul wrote: Hold to the standard of sound teaching that you have heard from me, in the faith and love that are in Christ Jesus. 2 Timothy 1:13

Holy Lord, holy Lord,   506
thanks and praise be yours, O Lord,
that your word to us is given,
teaching us with love outpoured
that as Lord of earth and heaven,
everlasting life for us to gain,
you were slain, you were slain.

Divine Teacher and Redeemer, fill our hearts with your love. Show us how to live our lives so that we may reflect your truth in all we say and do. Guide our lives forever. Amen.

Tuesday, September 8 — Psalm 106:1–5
Jeremiah 37:1–38:13; Titus 2:6–3:2

Deliverance belongs to the Lord; may your blessing be on your people! Psalm 3:8

Come, Almighty to deliver;   p218
let us all your life receive;
suddenly return, and never,
nevermore your temples leave.
Lord, we would be always blessing,
serve you as your hosts above,
pray, and praise you without ceasing,
glory in your precious love.

May mercy, peace, and love be yours in abundance. Jude 2

The peace which God alone reveals   p33
and by his word of grace imparts,
which only the believer feels,
direct, and keep, and cheer our hearts!
And may the holy Three-in-One,
the Father, Word, and Comforter,
pour an abundant blessing down
on ev'ry soul assembled here!

Holy Deliverer, we ask that you make us aware of your abundant blessings in our lives. Open our eyes and hearts to see and understand all that you have done, and continue to do, for us. Reveal your mercy, peace, and love. Amen.

Wednesday, September 9 — Psalm 106:6–12
Jeremiah 38:14–39:18; Titus 3:3–15

Let us lift up our hearts as well as our hands to God in heaven. Lamentations 3:41

> Join hearts and voices as we lift   p154*
> our gratitude for ev'ry gift,
> and multiply each gift with praise
> to God who gives us all our days.

Let us therefore approach the throne of grace with boldness, so that we may receive mercy and find grace to help in time of need. Hebrews 4:16

> Jesus, great High Priest of our profession   400
> we in confidence draw near;
> grant us, then, in mercy, the confession
> of our grateful hearts to hear;
> you we gladly own in ev'ry nation,
> Head and Master of your congregation,
> conscious that in ev'ry place
> you are giving life and grace.

Joyfully and boldly we come before you, Lord, to offer our praise. You are our All-in-all, our steadfast Source of life, and mercifully your grace knows no bounds. Thank you! Amen.

*   © by Jane Parker Huber

Thursday, September 10 — Psalm 106:13–23
Jeremiah 40,41; Philemon 1:1–11

I the Lord do not change. Malachi 3:6

O word of God incarnate,   505
O wisdom from on high,
O truth unchanged, unchanging,
O light of our dark sky:
we praise you for the radiance
that from the scripture's page,
a lantern to our footsteps,
shines on from age to age.

"I am the Alpha and the Omega," says the Lord God, who is and who was and who is to come, the Almighty. Revelation 1:8

Hail, Alpha and Omega, hail,   703
O Author of our faith,
the Finisher of all our hopes,
the Truth, the Life, the Path.

O great I Am, ground us in the constancy of your truth and grace. Help us to remember in times of distress or instability that you are an ever-present comfort and guide. Amen.

Friday, September 11 — Psalm 106:24–31
Jeremiah 42,43; Philemon 1:12–25

Many nations shall join themselves to the Lord on that day, and shall be my people. Zechariah 2:11

Rejoice, rejoice, the kingdom comes;　　　　260*
be glad, for it is near.
It comes with joy surprising us;
it triumphs o'er our fears.
Give thanks, for as the kingdom comes
it brings God's own shalom,
a state of peace and justice
where all with God are one.

The same Lord is Lord of all and is generous to all who call on him. Romans 10:12

Good news! Our Christ has come!　　　　630**
His arms reach out and plead
to share God's blessings
with a lonely world in need.
God's Spirit comes to all who ask,
to ev'ry heart that seeks release.

Christ, you came to claim all peoples as your own. Your kingdom may be found on earth if we open our eyes to see past divisions that too often define and separate us. Remind us that the blessing of your salvation is available to all. Amen.

* © 1987 by M. Lynnette Delbridge

** © 1988 by Sharon M. Benson. Used by permission.

Saturday, September 12 — Psalm 106:32–39
Jeremiah 44; Hebrews 1:1–9

Give me an undivided heart to revere your name.
Psalm 86:11

Take my life, O Lord, renew,   610
consecrate my heart to you.
Take my self, and I will be
yours for all eternity,
yours for all eternity.

Remember Jesus Christ, raised from the dead.
2 Timothy 2:8

Eternal thanks we sing,   488
great author of salvation,
who sinful hearts did bring
to heed your invitation.
We are your property.
O may we yours remain;
this is our only plea,
since you for us were slain.

Loving Savior, we pledge our hearts to you. Mend
our broken, fractured hearts, and make us whole in
you. Let our lives revere and reflect your love and
mercy. Amen.

Sixteenth Sunday after Pentecost

Watchword for the Week — Jesus asks, "But who do you say that I am?" Mark 8:29

Sunday, September 13 — Isaiah 50:4–9a; Psalm 116:1–9
James 3:1–12; Mark 8:27–38

Incline your ear, and come to me; listen, so that you may live. Isaiah 55:3

O let me hear you speaking   603
in accents clear and still,
above the storms of passion,
the murmurs of self-will.
O speak to reassure me,
to hasten or control;
and speak to make me listen,
O guardian of my soul.

If you continue in my word, you are truly my disciples; and you will know the truth, and the truth will make you free. John 8:31–32

Thanks we give and adoration   559
for your gospel's joyful sound.
May the fruits of your salvation
in our hearts and lives abound.
Ever faithful, ever faithful
to your truth may we be found.

Author of our faith, let us hear you when you impart your truth to us through your word. Let us live faithfully as your disciples, listening to your will for our lives, and freely following where you lead. Amen.

Monday, September 14 — Psalm 106:40–48
Jeremiah 45,46; Hebrews 1:10–2:8a

You will not abandon me to the realm of the dead. Psalm 16:10 (NIV)

> I fear no foe with you at hand to bless,   807
> though ills have weight, and tears their bitterness.
> Where is death's sting? Where, grave, your victory?
> I triumph still, if you abide with me.

Paul wrote: Wretched man that I am! Who will rescue me from this body of death? Thanks be to God through Jesus Christ our Lord! Romans 7:24–25

> Amazing grace!   783
> How sweet the sound
> that saved a wretch like me!
> I once was lost,
> but now am found,
> was blind, but now I see.

Abiding God, you give us victory over death! You raise us above the trials of earthly life through the promise of eternal life with you. Let us not despair, as you will never abandon us, no matter how wretched we believe we are. In your grace. Amen.

Tuesday, September 15 — Psalm 107:1–9
Jeremiah 47:1–48:25; Hebrews 2:8b–18

So Abram went, as the Lord had told him. Genesis 12:4

> Blessed be the day when I must roam   794
> far from my country, friends, and home,
> an exile, poor and mean;
> my fathers' God will be my Guide,
> will angel guards for me provide,
> my soul, my soul in danger screen.

By faith Abraham obeyed when he was called to set out for a place that he was to receive as an inheritance; and set out, not knowing where he was going. Hebrews 11:8

> My God will lead me to a spot   794
> where, all my cares and griefs forgot,
> I shall enjoy sweet rest.
> As pants for cooling streams the hart,
> I languish for my heavenly part,
> for God, for God, my Refuge blessed.

God of Abraham, you call each of us to follow you,
though we often do not know the way. Give us faith
to go, and give us trust in your guidance. Amen.

Ministers' Covenant Day†

Wednesday, September 16 — Psalm 107:10–16
Jeremiah 48:26–49:16; Hebrews 3:1–15

O Lord, you are God, you alone, of all the kingdoms of the earth; you have made heaven and earth. 2 Kings 19:15

What rush of hallelujahs   394
fills all the earth and sky!
What ringing of a thousand harps
bespeaks the triumph nigh!
O day, for which creation
and all its tribes were made!
O joy, for all its former woes
a thousand-fold repaid!

The kingdom of the world has become the kingdom of our Lord and of his Messiah, and he will reign forever and ever. Revelation 11:15

Praise the Lord, God our salvation,   298
praise him who retrieved our loss;
sing, with awe and love's sensation,
hallelujah, God with us.

Emmanuel, you came to be the light of the world, to fulfill the promise for all creation, to reign as our Chief Elder forever. Hallelujah! We celebrate your presence with us as we remember this day of covenant. Amen.

† During a synodal conference in London, Jesus Christ was recognized as chief elder of the Brethren's Church. The day is observed as a covenanting day for servants of the church.

Thursday, September 17 — Psalm 107:17–22
Jeremiah 49:17–38; Hebrews 3:16–4:5

You hem me in, behind and before, and lay your hand upon me. Psalm 139:5

He leadeth me: O blessed thought!   787
O words with heav'nly comfort fraught!
Whate'er I do, where're I be,
still 'tis God's hand that leadeth me.
He leadeth me, he leadeth me;
by his own hand he leadeth me,
his faithful foll'wer I would be,
for by his hand he leadeth me.

Now may the Lord of peace himself give you peace at all times in all ways. The Lord be with all of you. 2 Thessalonians 3:16

Jesus, Prince of Peace, be near us;   556
fix in all our hearts your home;
with your gracious presence cheer us;
let your sacred kingdom come;
raise to heav'n our expectation,
give our favored souls to prove
glorious and complete salvation
in the realms of bliss above.

Eternal Guide, lead us down the paths you
would have us go. Let us feel your hand upon us,
reminding us that we are never alone. Give us
peace and assurance to trust and follow you at all
times. Amen.

Friday, September 18 — Psalm 107:23–32
Jeremiah 50:1–40; Hebrews 4:6–16

Do not spurn us, for your name's sake; do not dishonor your glorious throne. Jeremiah 14:21

Sure as your truth shall last,   513
to Zion shall be given
the brightest glories earth can yield
and brighter bliss of heaven.

The God of all grace, who called you to his eternal glory in Christ, after you have suffered a little while, will himself restore you and make you strong, firm and steadfast. 1 Peter 5:10 (NIV)

Take up your cross, let not its weight   758
fill your weak spirit with alarm;
his strength shall bear your spirit up,
and brace your heart, and nerve your arm.

Forgiving Lord, thank you for your grace. Thank
you for not turning away from us when we stumble
in our walks with you. Let us look to you for truth
and steadfastness. Amen.

Saturday, September 19 — Psalm 107:33–43
Jeremiah 50:41–51:23; Hebrews 5

Those who cling to worthless idols turn away from God's love for them. Jonah 2:8 (NIV)

> Jesus calls us from the worship   600
> of the vain world's golden store,
> from each idol that would keep us,
> saying, "Christian, love me more."

I do not set aside the grace of God. Galatians 2:21 (NIV)

> O my soul, bless God, the Father;   458
> all within me bless his name;
> bless the Father, and forget not
> all his mercies to proclaim.

Redeemer, you call us to a higher purpose than that which the world offers. Lead us away from the daily temptations that all too often become easy idols, and grant us the grace to claim your eternal treasure. Amen.

Seventeenth Sunday after Pentecost

Watchword for the Week — Jesus says, "Whoever wants to be first must be last of all and servant of all." Mark 9:35

Sunday, September 20 — Jeremiah 11:18–20; Psalm 54
James 3:13–4:3,7–8a; Mark 9:30–37

Keep my steps steady according to your promise, and never let iniquity have dominion over me. Psalm 119:133

> Faithful soul, pray, always pray,   729
> and still in God confide;
> he your stumbling steps shall stay,
> and shall not let you slide;
> safe from known or secret foes,
> free from sin and Satan's hold,
> when the flesh, earth, hell oppose,
> he'll keep you in his fold.

Do not be children in your thinking; yet in evil be infants, but in your thinking be mature. 1 Corinthians 14:20 (NASB)

> O come, O Wisdom from on high,   274
> and order all things far and nigh;
> to us the path of knowledge show,
> and teach us in her ways to go.
> Rejoice! Rejoice! Immanuel
> shall come to you, O Israel!

Divine Wisdom, lead us down paths of understanding. Keep our steps steady and sure as we seek spiritual maturity, and open our hearts to the teachings of your word. Amen.

Monday, September 21 — Psalm 108:1–5
Jeremiah 51:24–64; Hebrews 6:1–12

Let us come into his presence with thanksgiving; let us make a joyful noise to him with songs of praise! For the Lord is a great God. Psalm 95:2–3

Sing hallelujah, praise the Lord!   543
Sing with a cheerful voice;
exalt our God with one accord,
and in his name rejoice.
Ne'er cease to sing, O ransomed host,
praise Father, Son, and Holy Ghost,
until in realms of endless light
your praises shall unite.

The King of kings and Lord of lords, who alone is immortal and who lives in unapproachable light, whom no one has seen or can see—to him be honor and might forever. 1 Timothy 6:15–16 (NIV)

Hark! those bursts of acclamation!   406
Hark! those loud triumphant chords!
Jesus takes the highest station;
O, what joy the sight affords!
Crown him! Crown him!
Crown him! Crown him!
King of kings and Lord of lords.

Hallelujah! Praise the Lord! He has sent his Son to be our Savior, calling us into his eternal presence, a gift for which we have abundant joy. Thank you, thank you! Amen.

Tuesday, September 22 — Psalm 108:6–13
Jeremiah 52; Hebrews 6:13–7:3

Bring the homeless poor into your house. Isaiah 58:7

"Come now, you blessed; eat at my table,"   p149*
Christ Jesus said to the righteous above.
"When I was hungry, thirsty, and homeless,
sick and in prison you showed me your love."

I was a stranger and you welcomed me, I was naked and you gave me clothing, I was sick and you took care of me. Matthew 25:35–36

Christ, when we see you out on life's highways,   p149*
looking to us in the faces of need,
then may we know you, welcome and show you
love that is faithful in word and in deed.

Source of all hope, open our hearts to extend your
welcoming grace to all we meet, especially those
whom the world routinely shuns. Let us not be
hesitant or afraid to extend hospitality and care
to those who need food, shelter, medicine, and the
comfort of human connection. Amen.

Wednesday, September 23 — Psalm 109:1–7
Lamentations 1:1–15; Hebrews 7:4–17

Lord, save us! Lord, grant us success! Psalm 118:25 (NIV)

> Come now, Incarnate Word,   555
> our just and mighty Lord,
> our prayer attend.
> Come and your people bless
> and give your word success;
> strengthen your righteousness,
> Savior and Friend!

May the God of peace work in us what is pleasing to him, through Jesus Christ, to whom be glory forever and ever. Hebrews 13:20,21

> Thanks we give and adoration   p36
> for the gospel's joyful sound;
> may the fruits of your salvation
> in our hearts and lives abound;
> may your presence, may your presence,
> with us evermore be found.

Lord, through the saving grace of Jesus Christ, you have given us the secret to success. Nurture us, work within us, and inspire us to bear the fruits of love and salvation so we may be living witnesses to others and bring glory to you. Amen.

Thursday, September 24 — Psalm 109:8–20
Lamentations 1:16–2:10; Hebrews 7:18–28

Who is like you, O Lord, among the gods? Who is like you, majestic in holiness, awesome in splendor, doing wonders? Exodus 15:11

Come now, almighty King,   555
help us your name to sing,
help us to praise.
Father all glorious,
ever victorious,
come and reign over us,
Ancient of Days.

There are varieties of activities, but it is the same God who activates all of them in everyone. 1 Corinthians 12:6

I bind unto myself the name,   p237
the strong name of the Trinity,
by invocation of the same,
the three in one, and one in three.
Of whom all nature has creation,
eternal Father, Spirit, Word,
Praise to the Lord of my salvation;
salvation is of Christ the Lord.

Omnipotent Lord, you made all things, rule over all things, and provide all things. Every gift you give us is from you and is meant to work in concert to your glory. Help us celebrate the diversity of gifts we see in our communities. Amen.

Friday, September 25 — Psalm 109:21–31
Lamentations 2:11–3:15; Hebrews 8

He guards the lives of his faithful; he rescues them from the hand of the wicked. Psalm 97:10

> O God, our help in ages past,   461
> our hope for years to come,
> remain our guard while life shall last,
> and our eternal home.

Christ says, "Because you have kept my word of patient endurance, I will keep you from the hour of trial that is coming on the whole world." Revelation 3:10

> Lord, nothing from your arms of love   p147
> shall your own people sever.
> Our helper never will remove;
> our God will fail us never.
> Your people, Lord, have dwelt secure;
> our dwelling place you will endure
> forever and forever.

Everlasting God, you promise us safety and surety in the face of all that is to come. In our moments of doubt, give us courage and reassurance that our faithful, patient service to you will be rewarded for all eternity. Amen.

Saturday, September 26 — Psalm 110
Lamentations 3:16–66; Hebrews 9:1–10

Lord, you silence the song of the ruthless.
Isaiah 25:5 (NIV)

> I need thee ev'ry hour;   740
> stay thou nearby;
> temptations lose their pow'r
> when thou art nigh.
> I need thee, O I need thee,
> ev'ry hour I need thee!
> O bless me now, my Savior—
> I come to thee!

Mary said, "He has shown strength with his arm; he has scattered the proud in the thoughts of their hearts. He has brought down the powerful from their thrones, and lifted up the lowly."
Luke 1:51–52

> Come, O long-expected Jesus,   262
> born to set your people free;
> from our fears and sins release us;
> O, in you our rest shall be.
> Israel's strength and consolation,
> hope to all the earth impart,
> dear desire of ev'ry nation,
> joy of ev'ry longing heart.

Blessed Savior, you came to free us from life's temptations. Let us not fall prey to the siren songs of the world, but rather hear your word deep in our heart, calling us to joy. Amen.

Eighteenth Sunday after Pentecost

Watchword for the Week — The precepts of the Lord are right, rejoicing the heart; the commandment of the Lord is clear, enlightening the eyes. Psalm 19:8

Sunday, September 27 — Numbers 11:4–6,10–16,24–29; Psalm 19:7–14 James 5:13–20; Mark 9:38–50

The Lord confirms the word of his servant, and performs the counsel of his messengers. Isaiah 44:26 (NKJV)

O holy God,   p155*
whose gracious pow'r redeems us,
make us, by faith,
true stewards of your grace;
help us to hear
and heed Christ's great commission,
sharing good news
in this our time and place.

These Jews (from Beroea) welcomed the message very eagerly and examined the scriptures every day to see whether these things were so. Acts 17:11

Proclaim to ev'ry people, tongue, and nation   618
that God, in whom they live and move, is love;
tell how he stooped to save his lost creation,
and died on earth that we might live in love.
Publish glad tidings, tidings of peace,
tidings of Jesus, redemption, and release.

Confirm your word in us, O Lord, as we set forth into the world to proclaim the good news of your salvation. Counsel us as we seek to follow your lead, guiding our steps to those who need to hear of your grace and love. Amen.

* © by Jane Parker Huber

Monday, September 28 — Psalm 111
Lamentations 4,5; Hebrews 9:11–22

Before I was humbled I went astray, but now I keep your word. Psalm 119:67

Now we bring ourselves to you;   741
cleanse us, Lord, we humbly pray;
undeserving though we be,
draw us closer ev'ry day.
Lord, our refuge, hope, and strength!
Keep, O keep us safe from harm,
shield us through our earthly life
by your everlasting arm.

As Paul was going along and approaching Damascus, suddenly a light from heaven flashed around him. He fell to the ground and heard a voice saying to him, "Saul, Saul, why do you persecute me?" Acts 9:3–4

Just as I am, poor, wretched, blind;   762
sight, riches, healing of the mind,
yea, all I need, in thee to find,
O Lamb of God, I come, I come!

Merciful Savior, humble us now, we pray. Challenge our ways of living when we do not live for you and when we do not act with love. Father, forgive us and grant us grace, and keep us in your word. Amen.

Tuesday, September 29 — Psalm 112
Ezekiel 1,2; Hebrews 9:23–10:4

The Lord is your keeper; the Lord is your shade at your right hand. The sun shall not strike you by day, nor the moon by night. Psalm 121:5–6

> What God's almighty pow'r has made,   537
> in mercy he is keeping;
> by morning glow or evening shade
> his eye is never sleeping.
> And where he rules in kingly might,
> there all is just and all is right:
> to God all praise and glory!

An angel of the Lord appeared to Joseph in a dream and said, "Get up, take the child and his mother, and flee to Egypt, and remain there until I tell you; for Herod is about to search for the child, to destroy him." Matthew 2:13

> In mercy, Lord, this grace bestow,   643
> that in your service we may do
> with gladness and a willing mind
> whatever is for us assigned.

Keeper of us all, you protect us by day and by night. Strengthen us to respond when you call, regardless of the uncertainty we face. Let us trust in you. Amen.

Wednesday, September 30 — Psalm 113
Ezekiel 3–4:5; Hebrews 10:5–18

You, O Lord, are our father; our Redeemer from of old is your name. Isaiah 63:16

O for a thousand tongues to sing   548
my great Redeemer's praise,
the glories of my God and King,
the triumphs of his grace!

Blessed be the God and Father of our Lord Jesus Christ! By his great mercy he has given us a new birth into a living hope through the resurrection of Jesus Christ from the dead. 1 Peter 1:3

The Lord is ris'n again,   356
who on the cross did bleed;
he lives to die no more, amen,
the Lord is ris'n indeed!
He truly tasted death
to give us hope again,
in bitter pangs resigned his breath,
but now has ris'n. Amen!

Alpha and Omega, you are everything that has
been, is, and will be. We are humbly blessed to
be given the promise of eternal hope through the
sacrifice and redemption of your Son. Thank you!
Amen.

Thursday, October 1 — Psalm 114
Ezekiel 4:6–6:7; Hebrews 10:19–31

The Lord will send his angel before you. Genesis 24:7

> Angels help us to adore him,   529
> who behold him face to face.
> Sun and moon bow down before him;
> all who dwell in time and space.
> Alleluia! Alleluia!
> Praise with us the God of grace.

An angel of the Lord said to Philip, "Get up and go toward the south to the road that goes down from Jerusalem to Gaza." (This is a wilderness road.) So he got up and went. Acts 8:26–28

> This child of God, though young or old,   410*
> we welcome now into Christ's fold,
> to know with us God's loving care,
> here all our joys and sorrows share.

O God, as the angels before us, we welcome your call. In our hearts and minds write your will. Give us your voice that we may proclaim our Lord's Holy Sacrifice. Amen.

---

* © 1980 by Jane Parker Huber from A Singing Faith. Used by permission from Westminster John Knox Press.

Friday, October 2 — Psalm 115:1–8
Ezekiel 6:8–7:27; Hebrews 10:32–11:3

I will tell of your name to my brothers and sisters. Psalm 22:22

O for the living flame,   531
from his own altar brought,
to touch our lips, our minds inspire,
and wing to heav'n our thought!

How are they to believe in one of whom they have never heard? And how are they to hear without someone to proclaim him? Romans 10:14

Trusting only in thy merit,   772
would I seek thy face;
heal my wounded, broken spirit,
save me by thy grace.
Savior, Savior, hear my humble cry;
while on others thou art calling;
do not pass me by.

Father of all earth's children, to you the glory! May
we never be silent in our love for your holy word.
Let us remain, against all fire, sword, and wind, in
your blessings. Amen.

Saturday, October 3 — Psalm 115:9–18
Ezekiel 8,9; Hebrews 11:4–16

Behold, here I am, let the Lord do to me what seems good to Him. 2 Samuel 15:26

Hushed was the evening hymn,   609
the temple courts were dark,
the lamp was burning dim
before the sacred ark,
when suddenly a voice divine
rang through the silence of the shrine.

If we live, we live to the Lord, and if we die, we die to the Lord. Romans 14:8

All our days, O Jesus,   770
hallow unto you;
may our lives be given
in your service true;
let us all experience,
to the end of days,
your abiding presence
and your loving grace.

Dear God, may we for all eternity be yours, made from you to return to you. May our lives, through our thoughts, words, and actions reflect the light you brought to the world in Christ, our Savior. Amen.

Nineteenth Sunday after Pentecost

Watchword for the Week — I will proclaim your name to my brothers and sisters, in the midst of the congregation I will praise you. Hebrews 2:12

Sunday, October 4 — Genesis 2:18–24; Psalm 8
Hebrews 1:1–4;2:5–12; Mark 10:2–16

Let your eyes be open to the plea of your servant, and to the plea of your people Israel, listening to them whenever they call to you. 1 Kings 8:52

> While the prayers of saints ascend, 553
> God of love, to mine attend.
> Hear me, for your Spirit pleads;
> hear, for Jesus intercedes.

Ask, and it will be given to you; search, and you will find; knock, and the door will be opened for you. Matthew 7:7

> Seek ye first the kingdom of God 605*
> and his righteousness,
> and all these things shall be added unto you—
> Allelu, alleluia!

O Lord, hear our prayer; not in our own strength do we move. Let us become living witnesses, reaching to you. Savior, may we hear your call as instruments of your compassion and truth, and as ambassadors of reconciliation. Amen.

Monday, October 5 — Psalm 116:1–7
Ezekiel 10:1–11:15; Hebrews 11:17–28

Our God turned the curse into a blessing. Nehemiah 13:2

Hungry and thirsty, faint and weak,	411
as you when here below,	
our souls the joys celestial seek,	
that from your sorrows flow	

In Christ, God was reconciling the world to himself, not counting their trespasses against them, and entrusting the message of reconciliation to us. 2 Corinthians 5:19

My Lord, what you did suffer	345
was all for sinners' gain;	
mine, mine was the transgression,	
but yours the deadly pain.	
So here I kneel, my Savior,	
for I deserve your place;	
look on me with your favor	
and save me by your grace.	

Welcome O my Savior now! Clothed in elements of salvation, we await earth's deliverance. Though we cannot earn it, you bless us with divine forgiveness. In your mercy we have found favor with you. Jesus, come alive within us! Amen.

Tuesday, October 6 — Psalm 116:8–14
Ezekiel 11:16–12:28; Hebrews 11:29–40

Thus says the Lord, "Seek me and live." Amos 5:4

You are the Way to God,   p78*
your blood our ransom paid;
in you we face our judge
and maker unafraid.
Before the throne absolved we stand,

A man was there by the name of Zacchaeus; he was a chief tax collector and was wealthy. He wanted to see who Jesus was. Luke 19:2–3 (NIV)

'Twas grace that taught my heart to fear   783
and grace my fears relieved;
how precious did that grace appear
the hour I first believed.

Lord Jesus, mold us for God's witness! Empower
us to recognize, maintain, and restore the power
that comes from living in you. Fashion us into true
believers. Let us see you, Prince of Peace, and purify
us in our commitment! Amen.

Wednesday, October 7 — Psalm 116:15–19
Ezekiel 13:1–14:11; Hebrews 12:1–13

Like birds hovering overhead, so the Lord of hosts will protect Jerusalem; he will protect and deliver it, he will spare and rescue it. Isaiah 31:5

> Enrich me always with your love;   733
> my kind protector ever prove;
> Lord, put your seal upon my heart,
> that I from you may not depart.

If God is for us, who can be against us? Romans 8:31 (NIV)

> Perfect submission, all is at rest,   714
> I in my Savior am happy and blessed,
> watching and waiting, looking above,
> filled with his goodness, lost in his love.
> This is my story, this is my song,
> praising my Savior all the day long.
> This is my story, this is my song,
> praising my Savior all the day long.

Gracious God, our Father, we owe all that we have to you. Reveal the work you have set before us and preserve us in true faith. Freely may we give, in the joys of discipleship, to the glory of your kingdom. Amen.

Thursday, October 8 — Psalm 117
Ezekiel 14:12–15:8; Hebrews 12:14–24

The Lord says, "I desire steadfast love and not sacrifice, the knowledge of God rather than burnt-offerings." Hosea 6:6

What language shall I borrow 345
to thank you, dearest friend,
for this, your dying sorrow,
your mercy without end?
Lord, make me yours forever,
a loyal servant true,
and let me never, never
outlive my love for you.

Love must be sincere. Hate what is evil; cling to what is good. Be devoted to one another in love. Honor one another above yourselves. Romans 12:9–10 (NIV)

We covenant with hand and heart p183
to follow Christ, our Lord;
with world, and sin, and self to part,
and to obey his word;
to love each other heartily,
in truth and with sincerity,
and under cross, reproach, and shame,
to glorify his name.

Blessed Christ Jesus, you have our eternal thanks. You understand our deepest needs and present them, with love, to God. May we choose to be living witnesses, to present our hearts in prayer, and to gratefully celebrate the lives we've been blessed to have. Amen.

Friday, October 9 — Psalm 118:1–9
Ezekiel 16:1–42; Hebrews 12:25–13:6

The Lord is gracious and merciful, slow to anger, and abounding in steadfast love, and relents from punishing. Joel 2:13

O God of mercy, hear us,   806*
in steadfast love draw near us,
from age to age the same;
that we, by grace defended,
when early days are ended,
may live to praise a Savior's name.

You have heard of the endurance of Job, and you have seen the purpose of the Lord, how the Lord is compassionate and merciful. James 5:11

We've a story to tell to the nations,   621
that shall turn their hearts to the right,
a story of truth and mercy,
a story of peace and light,
a story of peace and light.
For the darkness shall turn to dawning,
and the dawning to noonday bright;
and Christ's great kingdom shall come on earth,
the kingdom of love and light.

Master Jesus, you reveal God's boundless love. Bring near your great salvation! Break our hearts that we may see the tribulations of others and show them compassion, love, and grace, in order to serve and love you best of all. Amen.

Saturday, October 10 — Psalm 118:10–14
Ezekiel 16:43–17:10; Hebrews 13:7–19

He will regard the prayer of the destitute, and will not despise their prayer. Psalm 102:17

O Lord, hear my prayer,745
O Lord, hear my prayer:
when I call answer me.
O Lord, hear my prayer,
O Lord, hear my prayer.
Come and listen to me.

And will not God grant justice to his chosen ones who cry to him day and night? Luke 18:7

May the God of hope go with us ev'ry day,708
filling all our lives with love and joy and peace.
May the God of justice speed us on our way,
bringing light and hope to ev'ry land and race.
Praying, let us work for peace,
singing, share our joy with all.
Working for a world that's new,
faithful when we hear Christ's call.

Lord, Father, Maker, and Redeemer, we labor to proclaim salvation to the ends of the earth, our faith forever sharing. In grace, invite us to join with Christians everywhere to touch, teach, comfort, and feed, sharing your love with the world. Amen.

Twentieth Sunday after Pentecost

Watchword for the Week — Since we have a great high priest who has passed through the heavens, Jesus, the Son of God, let us hold fast to our confession. Hebrews 4:14

Sunday, October 11 — Amos 5:6–7,10–15; Psalm 90:12–17 Hebrews 4:12–16; Mark 10:17–31

God, you have shaken the land and torn it open; mend its fractures, for it is quaking. Psalm 60:2 (NIV)

Spirit, working in creation,   p223*
bringing order out of strife:
come among God's gathered people,
giving harmony and life.
Spirit, wind, and flame, empowering,
fearless witness to the lost:
come unite, renew your wonders;
give us a new Pentecost.

God did not send the Son into the world to condemn the world, but in order that the world might be saved through him. John 3:17

Love divine, all loves excelling,   474
joy of heav'n, to earth come down!
Fix in us your humble dwelling,
all your faithful mercies crown.
Jesus, you are all compassion,
pure, unbounded love impart!
Visit us with your salvation,
enter ev'ry trembling heart.

All praise to you, Eternal Lord; your Advent has our freedom won! How shall we meet you? Once you came in blessing, still you remain within us. Make us rise to fall no more! Amen.

* © by John Richards

Monday, October 12 — Psalm 118:15–21
Ezekiel 17:11–18:18; Hebrews 13:20–James 1:8

When Pharaoh saw that the rain and the hail and the thunder had ceased, he sinned once more and hardened his heart. Exodus 9:34

> Glorious Lord, yourself impart!   558
> Light of light, from God proceeding,
> open now our ears and heart,
> help us by your Spirit's pleading;
> hear the cry that we are raising;
> hear and bless our prayers and praising.

See to it that no one fails to obtain the grace of God. Hebrews 12:15

> Here may we gain from heav'n   517
> the grace which we implore;
> and may that grace, once giv'n,
> be with us evermore,
> until that day when all the blessed
> to endless rest are called away.

Soften our hearts, O Lord. Lead us to have compassion for all others and show us the good in everyone and everything. Your grace is our salvation and we will bask in its warmth and share it with all. Amen.

Tuesday, October 13 — Psalm 118:22–29
Ezekiel 18:19–19:14; James 1:9–18

Happy are those who keep his decrees, who seek him with their whole heart. Psalm 119:2

Early let us seek your favor;   731
early let us do your will;
blessed Lord and only Savior,
with your love our spirits fill.
Blessed Jesus, blessed Jesus,
you have loved us, love us still.
Blessed Jesus, blessed Jesus,
you have loved us, love us still.

Blessed are those who hunger and thirst for righteousness, for they shall be satisfied. Matthew 5:6 (NASB)

Blessed Jesus, at your word   558
we are gathered all to hear you;
let our hearts and souls be stirred
now to seek and love and fear you;
by your teachings true and holy,
drawn from earth to love you solely.

Lord, joyous are we in your arms! With Christ, life is worth living and we seek his pure truth. He feeds us with his grace and we are sated. May we always look to share his holy vision with those around us. Amen.

Wednesday, October 14 — Psalm 119:1–8
Ezekiel 20:1–29; James 1:19–27

The Lord gave, and the Lord has taken away; blessed be the name of the Lord. Job 1:21

> Great is thy faithfulness, O God my Father, 460*
> there is no shadow of turning with thee;
> thou changest not, thy compassions they fail not;
> as thou has been thou forever wilt be.
> Great is thy faithfulness! Great is thy faithfulness!
> Morning by morning new mercies I see;
> all I have needed thy hand hath provided;
> great is thy faithfulness, Lord, unto me!

We know that suffering produces perseverance; perseverance, character; and character, hope. Romans 5:3–4 (NIV)

> My hope is built on nothing less 771
> than Jesus' blood and righteousness;
> no merit of my own I claim
> but wholly lean on Jesus' name.
> On Christ the solid rock, I stand;
> all other ground is sinking sand,
> all other ground is sinking sand.

Lord, we are with you; we want for nothing. O God, you have known us better than we will ever know ourselves. How do we press on through difficult times without your leading? We will follow you and clear the way for others. Amen.

Thursday, October 15 — Psalm 119:9–16
Ezekiel 20:30–21:17; James 2:1–13

Who can say, "I have made my heart clean; I am pure from my sin"? Proverbs 20:9

Clearer still and clearer,   778
dawns the light from heav'n,
in our sadness bringing
news of sin forgiv'n.
Life has lost its shadows,
pure the light within;
you have shed your radiance
on a world of sin.
Savior, blessed Savior,
listen while we sing,
hearts and voices raising
praises to our King.

All have sinned and fall short of the glory of God, and all are justified freely by his grace through the redemption that came by Christ Jesus. Romans 3:23–24 (NIV)

Jesus, may our hearts be burning   331
with more fervent love for you;
may our eyes be ever turning
to behold your cross anew;
'til in glory, parted never
from the blessed Savior's side,
graven in our hearts forever,
dwell the cross, the Crucified.

Heavenly Father, we are sinners, familiar with life's
desires. Yet, you still show us your compassion.
In this world we are never to follow our will,
but instead we are to follow you and your pure
example. We can fearlessly cast off our weight and
love freely. Amen.

Friday, October 16 — Psalm 119:17–24
Ezekiel 21:18–22:22; James 2:14–26

Upon your walls, O Jerusalem, I have posted sentinels; all day and all night they shall never be silent. Isaiah 62:6

Zion hears the watchmen singing,   258
and in her heart new joy is springing.
She wakes, she rises from her gloom.
For her Lord comes down all glorious,
the strong in grace, in truth victorious
Her star's arising light has come!
"Now come, O blessed one,
Lord Jesus, God's own Son.
Hail, hosanna!
We answer all in joy your call,
we follow to the wedding hall."

Pray without ceasing. 1 Thessalonians 5:17

When morning gilds the skies,   552
my heart awaking cries:
may Jesus Christ be praised!
in all my work and prayer
I ask his loving care:
may Jesus Christ be praised!

Dearest Father, we rejoice in the warmth and glow radiated by your great love! You fill our days and they become worth living. We shall be ever prayerful and always anticipate being with you. Hear us as we pray! Amen.

Saturday, October 17 — Psalm 119:25–32
Ezekiel 22:23–23:27; James 3:1–12

No one shall be found among you who practices divination, or is a soothsayer, or an augur, or a sorcerer. Whoever does these things is abhorrent to the Lord. Deuteronomy 18:10,12

> Visit, then, this soul of mine, 475
> pierce the gloom of sin and grief;
> fill me, radiancy divine;
> scatter all my unbelief;
> more and more yourself display,
> shining to the perfect day!

Claiming to be wise, they became fools; and they exchanged the glory of the immortal God for images. Romans 1:22–23

> My Father, I have wandered 763*
> and hidden from your face;
> in foolishness have squandered
> your legacy of grace.
> But now, in exile dwelling,
> I rise with fear and shame,
> as distant but compelling,
> I hear you call my name.

Jesus, we have placed value on the things of this world instead of on our spiritual gifts. Only by your grace and contact shall we be free of the shackles this life puts on us. Hold us close to your heart, Lord. We are yours. Amen.

* © 1981 by ICEL

Twenty-First Sunday after Pentecost

Watchword for the Week — For the Son of Man came not to be served but to serve, and to give his life a ransom for many. Mark 10:45

Sunday, October 18 — Isaiah 53:4–12; Psalm 91:9–16 Hebrews 5:1–10; Mark 10:35–45

Those who look to him are radiant; their faces are never covered with shame. Psalm 34:5 (NIV)

Jesus, Master, I am yours;   614
keep me faithful, keep me near;
as your radiance through me pours
all my homeward way to cheer.
Jesus, at your feet I fall.
O be now my all in all!

May the God of hope fill you with all joy and peace in believing, so that you may abound in hope by the power of the Holy Spirit. Romans 15:13

Spirit of the living God   p96*
fall afresh on me;
Spirit of the living God,
fall afresh on me.
Melt me, mold me, fill me, use me.
Spirit of the living God,
fall afresh on me.

Holy Triumvirate, we live in you! All our joys and tribulations are part of our preparation for the place you prepared for us in heaven. Through your power alone may we be saved from this world and held for eternity in your grace. Amen.

Monday, October 19 — Psalm 119:33–40
Ezekiel 23:28–24:8; James 3:13–4:6

The Lord watches over the strangers; he upholds the orphan and the widow. Psalm 146:9

"Fear not, I am with you; O be not dismayed,   709
for I am your God and will still give you aid;
I'll strengthen you, help you, and cause you to stand
upheld by my righteous, omnipotent hand."

Religion that God our Father accepts as pure and faultless is this: to look after orphans and widows in their distress and to keep oneself from being polluted by the world. James 1:27 (NIV)

To comfort and to bless,   657
to find a balm for woe,
to tend those lost in loneliness
is angels' work below.

Lord Christ, soften our hearts to do your loving will. Let us see through the eyes of others, that we may know what they have lived, find common purpose, and spread your grace and love. Amen.

Tuesday, October 20 — Psalm 119:41–48
Ezekiel 24:9–25:14; James 4:7–17

There is no Holy One like the Lord, no one besides you. 1 Samuel 2:2

> Through all the tumult and the strife,   701
> I hear that music ringing.
> It sounds and echoes in my soul;
> how can I keep from singing?
> No storm can shake my inmost calm,
> while to that Rock I'm clinging.
> Since love is Lord of heaven and earth,
> how can I keep from singing?

To the King of the ages, immortal, invisible, the only God, be honor and glory forever and ever. Amen. 1 Timothy 1:17

> Immortal, invisible, God only wise,   457
> in light inaccessible hid from our eyes,
> most blessed, most glorious, O Ancient of Days,
> almighty, victorious, your great name we praise.

Can we live our lives without you, Lord? Never are we without you, though we may wish to dismiss you. Thank you, Lord, for never giving up on us, even when we give up on ourselves. Our lives belong to you, Jesus! Use us as you will. Amen.

Wednesday, October 21 — Psalm 119:49–56
Ezekiel 25:15–27:11; James 5:1–12

Joseph remained there in prison. But the Lord was with him. Genesis 39:20–21

If dangers gather round,   615
still keep me calm and fearless;
help me to bear the cross
when life is bleak and cheerless,
to overcome my foes
with words and actions kind;
O God, your will disclose,
your counsel let me find.

Remember those who are in prison, as though you were in prison with them. Hebrews 13:3

Blessings abound where'er he reigns,   404
the pris'ners leap to lose their chains,
the weary find eternal rest,
and all who suffer want are blessed.

Father, as this world holds us prisoner from you, so
may we be divorced from society. The separation
can only be breached through your love, O
God. Bring your concern, through us, to those
incarcerated by place and by reason. Amen.

Thursday, October 22 — Psalm 119:57–64
Ezekiel 27:12–28:10; James 5:13–20

The nations are like a drop from a bucket, and are accounted as dust on the scales. Isaiah 40:15

> Bless your maker, all your creatures,   458
> ever under God's control;
> all throughout his vast dominion
> bless the Lord of all, my soul!

I saw another angel flying in mid-heaven, with an eternal gospel to proclaim to those who live on the earth—to every nation and tribe and language and people. Revelation 14:6

> Now shall the church, this time of celebration,   830*
> give thanks to God for each new revelation,
> for gospel truth and promise of salvation:
> to God be endless praise!

We are but flashes in the span of your universe, Great Maker. Yet, we each have a cosmic reason for being, to be revealed in its own time. Let our flashes be noticeable and admirable, stimulating other flashes of blinding faith. Amen.

Friday, October 23 — Psalm 119:65–72
Ezekiel 28:11–29:12; 1 Peter 1:1–12

The counsel of the Lord stands forever.
Psalm 33:11

Lord, you bless with words assuring: 617*
"I am with you to the end."
Faith and hope and love restoring,
may we serve as you intend,
and, amid the cares that claim us,
hold in mind eternity;
with the Spirit's gifts empower us
for the work of ministry.

Christ says, "Heaven and earth will pass away,
but my words will not pass away." Matthew 24:35

When ends life's transient dream,   705
when death's cold, sullen stream
rolls over me,
blessed Savior, then, in love,
fear and distrust remove;
O bear me safe above,
redeemed and free!

Father, you are the Great I Am! Though we may
not ever understand why you love us so much, we
can feel that you do. Alpha and Omega, with no
beginning or end, we long for your timeless love
beyond compare. Amen.

Saturday, October 24 — Psalm 119:73–80
Ezekiel 29:13–30:26; 1 Peter 1:13–25

The Lord your God you shall follow, him alone you shall fear, his commandments you shall keep, his voice you shall obey, him you shall serve, and to him you shall hold fast. Deuteronomy 13:4

> Grant by guidance from above   586
> that obedience, faith, and love
> show our hearts to you are giv'n,
> that our treasure is in heav'n.

Jesus said, "You are my friends if you do what I command you." John 15:14

> God, grant me strength to do   615
> with ready heart and willing,
> whatever you command,
> my calling here fulfilling;
> and do it when I ought,
> with zeal and joyfulness;
> and bless the work I've wrought,
> for you must give success.

Jesus, we long for your way, proven blameless and pure. What could be, in this world, were we all of like mind and heart? We seek to obey your will. May we learn to love as you have, Savior Christ! Amen.

Twenty-Second Sunday after Pentecost

Watchword for the Week — The Lord has done great things for us. Psalm 126:3

Sunday, October 25 — Jeremiah 31:7–9; Psalm 126
Hebrews 7:23–28; Mark 10:46–52

Let him who walks in the dark, who has no light, trust in the name of the Lord. Isaiah 50:10 (NIV)

The people who in darkness walked   320
have seen a glorious light;
on them broke forth the heav'nly dawn
who dwelt in death and night

Jesus spoke to the disciples, "Take heart, it is I; do not be afraid." Matthew 14:27

See the Lord, your keeper, stand   729
omnipotently near.
Now he holds you by the hand,
and banishes your fear;
shadows with his wings your head,
guards from all impending harms;
round you and beneath are spread
the everlasting arms.

Savior, fear and doubt rise at every turn to cloud our minds to your loving ways. We seek the fearlessness your love provides, Lord Jesus! All without you is uncertainty, mistrust, bewilderment. In you we know happiness and worth. Amen.

Monday, October 26 — Psalm 119:81–88
Ezekiel 31:1–32:16; 1 Peter 2:1–12

God saw my affliction and the labor of my hands. Genesis 31:42

> Church, unite for the right;   631
> let your foes behold your stand;
> rebuke them for their error;
> inspire with hope and fervor;
> declare the Savior's merit
> and how the Holy Spirit
> by his power,
> by his power, ev'ry hour,
> will direct us and protect us
> in a world of sin and strife.

Mary said, "My soul magnifies the Lord, and my spirit rejoices in God my Savior, for he has looked with favor on the lowliness of his servant." Luke 1:46–48

> O my God, be ever near me;   568
> for your rest, for your feast,
> more and more prepare me.
> Still assure me of my calling;
> keep me near, in your care,
> saved from final falling.

Creator, Sustainer, Reconciler, our spirits cry out in your language, as you have taught it to us. We love to speak the "God-talk" and to feel its effects on our hearts and souls. May we always strengthen our skills in your loving ways. Amen.

Tuesday, October 27 — Psalm 119:89–96
Ezekiel 32:17–33:20; 1 Peter 2:13–25

Lord, forgive the iniquity of this people according to the greatness of your steadfast love. Numbers 14:19

> Am I of my salvation   795
> assured through thy great love?
> May I on each occasion
> to thee more faithful prove.
> Hast thou my sins forgiven?
> Then, leaving things behind,
> may I press on to heaven
> and bear the prize in mind.

Jesus Christ is the atoning sacrifice for our sins, and not for ours only but also for the sins of the whole world. 1 John 2:2

> O perfect Love, all human thought transcending,   427
> lowly we kneel in prayer before your throne,
> that theirs may be the love which knows no ending,
> whom you forevermore unite in one.

Sinners, doubters, lost souls we are. God, we seek your divine guidance. Held down by the ways of the world, we conform, making us spiritually ill. Transform us to do your will and we shall live, instead, for you! Amen.

Wednesday, October 28 — Psalm 119:97–104
Ezekiel 33:21–34:19; 1 Peter 3:1–7

The days are surely coming, says the Lord, when I will make a new covenant with the house of Israel and the house of Judah. Jeremiah 31:31

The covenant, so long revealed 339*
to those of faith in former time,
Christ by his own example sealed,
the Lord of love, in love sublime.

God prepared beforehand for glory, even us, whom he also called, not from among Jews only, but also from among Gentiles. Romans 9:23–24 (NASB)

Hail, the heav'n-born Prince of Peace! 295
Hail, the Sun of Righteousness!
Light and life to all he brings,
ris'n with healing in his wings.
Mild he lays his glory by,
born that we no more may die,
born to raise us from the earth,
born to give us second birth.
Hark! The herald angels sing:
"Glory to the newborn King!"

Lord, we long for the peace of understanding and a way back to you. In our noisy lives, it is sometimes hard to discern your voice. Allow us to perfect our listening to hear your call so that we may glorify you. Amen.

* © by Geoffrey Chapman, an imprint of Cassell PLC

Thursday, October 29 — Psalm 119:105–112
Ezekiel 34:20–36:7; 1 Peter 3:8–22

Thus says the Lord: Do not let the wise boast in their wisdom, do not let the mighty boast in their might, do not let the wealthy boast in their wealth; but let those who boast boast in this, that they understand and know me. Jeremiah 9:23–24

> Forbid it, Lord, that I should boast,   350
> save in the death of Christ, my God;
> all the vain things that charm me most,
> I sacrifice them to his blood.

Paul wrote: I am not ashamed of the gospel; it is the power of God for salvation to everyone who has faith. Romans 1:16

> Come in praise and adoration,   p37*
> all who on Christ's name believe;
> worship him with consecration,
> grace and love you will receive.
> For his grace give him the glory,
> for the Spirit and the word,
> and repeat the gospel story
> 'til all souls his name have heard.

How wonderful, knowing wisdom is learned and not imparted! God, in the Spirit you have provided the way, the resolve, and the reward. We have heard your message. Let us take up our cross for Christ and make the world ready for his coming. Amen.

Friday, October 30 — Psalm 119:113–120
Ezekiel 36:8–36; 1 Peter 4

The Lord our God may not leave us or abandon us. 1 Kings 8:57

Sing, pray, and keep his ways unswerving,   712
offer your service faithfully,
and trust his word; though undeserving,
you'll find his promise true to be.
God never will forsake in need
the soul that trusts in him indeed.

Indeed God is not far from each one of us. Acts 17:27

God is here! As we your people   564*
meet to offer praise and prayer,
may we find in fuller measure
what it is in Christ we share.
Here, as in the world around us,
all our varied skills and arts
wait the coming of the Spirit
into open minds and hearts.

God, be with us every minute we are on earth.
Christ be our staff and stay, your teachings and
examples to emulate. Spirit, fill us, that we cannot
contain the joy of salvation. Give us hope. Give us
love. Give us joy. Give us life! Amen.

Reformation Day

Saturday, October 31 — Psalm 119:121–128
Ezekiel 37:1–38:6; 1 Peter 5

Return, O my soul, to your rest, for the Lord has dealt bountifully with you. Psalm 116:7

> Endow us richly with your gifts and grace　　377
> to fit us for the duties of our place;
> so open now our lips, our hearts so raise,
> that both our hearts and lips may give you praise.

Your Father knows what you need before you ask him. Matthew 6:8

> Only be still and wait his pleasure　　712
> in cheerful hope with heart content.
> He fills your needs to fullest measure
> with what discerning love has sent;
> doubt not our inmost wants are known
> to him who chose us as his own.

Father, we look forward to the Great Rest. We know that you will be there to take us home when we are done here. We shout with joy, knowing you have made the perfect place for us. May we earn it. Amen.

All Saints Day

Twenty-Third Sunday after Pentecost

Watchword for All Saints Day — Salvation belongs to our God who is seated on the throne, and to the Lamb! Revelation 7:10

Watchword for the Week — Hear, O Israel: The Lord is our God, the Lord alone. You shall love the Lord your God with all your heart, and with all your soul, and with all your might. Deuteronomy 6:4–5

Sunday, November 1 — Deuteronomy 6:1–9; Psalm 119:1–8
Hebrews 9:11–14; Mark 12:28–34

All Saints Day — Isaiah 25:6–9; Psalm 24
Revelation 21:1–6a; John 11:32–44

You are wearied with your many consultations. Isaiah 47:13

> Here, O my Lord, I see you face to face! 421
> Here would I touch and handle things unseen,
> here grasp with firmer hand eternal grace,
> and all my weariness upon you lean.

Jesus asked the disciples, "What were you arguing about on the way?" But they were silent, for on the way they had argued with one another about who was the greatest. Mark 9:33–34

> Is this our high calling, harmonious to dwell, 675
> and thus in sweet concert Christ's praises to tell,
> in peace and blessed union our moments to spend
> and live in communion with Jesus our Friend?

Guiding Light of the world, may we be inspired by the courage, spirit, and commitment of the saints who have gone before us. Let us celebrate our common call to serve and love you above all. Amen.

Monday, November 2 — Psalm 119:129–136
Ezekiel 38:7–39:13; 2 Peter 1:1–11

If you seek me with all your heart, I will let you find me, says the Lord. Jeremiah 29:13–14

Ready, Lord, I'm ready, Lord,   601*
to follow where you lead.
Show me, Lord, just show me, Lord,
the service you will need.
Ready, Lord, I'm ready, Lord,
I'm ready, come what may,
so call me, Lord, just call me, Lord,
and I'll be on your way.

If two of you agree on earth about anything you ask, it will be done for you by my Father in heaven. Matthew 18:19

Christian hearts, in love united,   673
seek alone in Jesus rest;
has he not your love excited?
Then let love inspire each breast.
Members—on our Head depending,
lights—reflecting him, our Sun,
brethren—his commands attending,
we in him, our Lord, are one.

Gracious One, do not stop calling us to open
ourselves to your unimaginable love. Help us to
come together that our witness of faith may be
unified for all the world to know of your great
compassion. Amen.

Tuesday, November 3 — Psalm 119:137–144
Ezekiel 39:14–40:16; 2 Peter 1:12–21

The Lord will guide you continually, and satisfy your needs in parched places. Isaiah 58:11

Holy God of all creation,   84s*
give us vision, love, and nerve
to respond to our first calling
on this earth to care and serve.
Show the world by our example
how to live each waking hour,
as we strive to humbly follow,
sharing your creative power.

My God will fully satisfy every need of yours according to his riches in glory in Christ Jesus. Philippians 4:19

You are the bread of life,   502
O Lord, to me.
Your holy word the truth
that rescues me.
Give me to eat and live
with you above;
teach me to love your truth,
for you are love.

Holy One, help us to see our need for you and for one another. May we be filled with your vision and act through your love towards your whole creation that all may be satisfied. Amen.

* © 2013 by Interprovincial Board of Communication and Moravian Music Foundation

Wednesday, November 4 — Psalm 119:145–152
Ezekiel 40:17–49; 2 Peter 2:1–10

Keep these words that I am commanding you today in your heart. Recite them to your children and talk about them. Deuteronomy 6:6–7

> I love to tell the story,   625
> for those who know it best
> seem hungering and thirsting
> to hear it, like the rest.
> And when, in scenes of glory,
> I sing the new, new song,
> I'll sing the old, old story
> that I have loved so long.
> I love to tell the story;
> I'll sing this theme in glory
> and tell the old, old story
> of Jesus and his love.

Be doers of the word, and not merely hearers who deceive themselves. James 1:22

> And we believe your word,   657
> though dim our faith may be.
> Whate'er we do for you, O Lord,
> we do it gratefully.

God, may your presence empower us to live boldly and to do the work you call us to do with energy and hope for your future! Amen.

Thursday, November 5 — Psalm 119:153–160
Ezekiel 41:1–42:9; 2 Peter 2:11–22

Into your hand I commit my spirit; you have redeemed me, O Lord God of truth. Psalm 31:5 (NKJV)

Abide with me; fast falls the eventide;   807
the darkness deepens; Lord, with me abide.
When other helpers fail and comforts flee,
help of the helpless, O abide with me.

We will be with the Lord forever. Therefore encourage one another with these words. 1 Thessalonians 4:17–18

Lord, our God, Lord, our God,   506
may your precious saving word,
'til our days on earth are ended,
light unto our path afford;
then, among your saints ascended,
we for your redeeming love shall raise
ceaseless praise, ceaseless praise.

Lord, let our lives be testaments to our trust in you. Let our hearts be shaped by your love and our lives known by it. Amen.

Friday, November 6 — Psalm 119:161–168
Ezekiel 42:10–43:21; 2 Peter 3:1–13

You are the God who sees me. Genesis 16:13 (NIV)

I am Jesus' little lamb;   723
ever glad at heart I am;
for my Shepherd gently guides me,
knows my need and well provides me,
loves me ev'ry day the same,
even calls me by my name.

As Jesus was walking along, he saw Levi son of Alphaeus sitting at the tax booth, and he said to him, "Follow me." Mark 2:14

Come, come, come,   412*
Christ Jesus bids us come.
O come to his table, all who love him,
think of his grace, and pray to receive him;
come, come, come,
Christ Jesus bids us come.

Saving God, as we are known along this, Jesus' way, we learn of your care for us and for the world. Give us strength to follow you wherever the path may lead. Amen.

* © 1993 by Albert H. Frank. Used by permission.

Saturday, November 7 — Psalm 119:169–176
Ezekiel 43:22–44:27; 2 Peter 3:14–1 John 1:4

You shall love the alien as yourself. Leviticus 19:34

Make us more giving,   535*
make us more open,
fill us for living
each day with love;
pour out your Spirit,
strengthen our witness,
'til earth inherit
heaven above.

Peter said, "God has shown me that I should not call anyone profane or unclean." Acts 10:28

Strike from our feet the fetters that bind.   489
Lift from our lives the weight of our wrong.
Teach us to love with heart, soul, and mind.
Spirit of God, your love makes us strong.

God of the Stranger, invite us to share your love
of the "other" and challenge us to live your all-
embracing way of life each day. Give us eyes to see
your face in everyone we meet. Amen.

*   © 1993 by C. Daniel Crews

Twenty-Fourth Sunday after Pentecost

Watchword for the Week — The Lord lifts up those who are bowed down; the Lord loves the righteous. Psalm 146:8

Sunday, November 8 — 1 Kings 17:8–16; Psalm 146
Hebrews 9:24–28; Mark 12:38–44

The alien who resides with you shall be to you as the citizen among you. Leviticus 19:34

Chosen and sent by the Father   639*
    before earth's creation,
Christ came from heaven in mercy
    to bring us salvation'
now he sends you
God's mighty plan to pursue:
go in the strength of his Spirit!

Whatever you did for one of the least of these brothers and sisters of mine, you did for me. Matthew 25:40 (NIV)

Friends, welcome one another   59s**
as Christ has welcomed you.
Say "yes" to sister, brother,
and that way live anew.
Our life together is a sign
of life to come in God's design.
The strong and weak will live as one,
thanks to the risen Son.

Welcome all creation, O God, into your ways of love and compassion. Remind us that we have all been strangers made friends through Jesus Christ. Help us embrace one another as you embrace us all. Amen.

Monday, November 9 — Psalm 120
Ezekiel 44:28–45:25; 1 John 1:5–2:11

The Lord will keep you from all evil; he will keep your life. Psalm 121:7

Holy Spirit, Lord of love,   426
who descended from above,
gifts of blessing to bestow
on your waiting church below,
once again in love draw near
to your servants gathered here;
from their bright baptismal day
you have led them on their way.

Even the hairs of your head are all counted. So do not be afraid. Matthew 10:30–31

Christians, dismiss your fear;   356
let hope and joy succeed;
the joyful news with gladness hear:
"The Lord is ris'n indeed!"
The promise is fulfilled
in Christ our only Head;
now justice, mercy, reconciled,
he lives who once was dead.

Redeeming God, you are always bringing light into our darkness and hope into our hearts. May we live with gratitude and faithfulness in your way and truth. Amen.

Tuesday, November 10 — Psalm 121
Ezekiel 46:1–47:12; 1 John 2:12–17

You brought up my life from the pit, O Lord my God. Jonah 2:6

Amen, yea, my lasting praises,   808
Jesus, unto you are giv'n,
that a place by you prepared
is for me secured in heav'n;
blessed my case, O truly blessed,
when to heav'nly glory raised,
I from pain and sorrow free
in your presence safe shall be.

The Son of God was revealed for this purpose, to destroy the works of the devil. 1 John 3:8

Jesus, your arms are open   54s*
to children filled with fear,
who want for love and nurture.
To your side draw them near.
From tow'ring threats deliver,
preserve them from all harm,
stretch out our hands with your love;
their quiet fears disarm.

Gracious Savior, when we forget your gift of grace
we can struggle to see your presence in our world.
Help us to remember the times you have shown us
new life and new ways. Amen.

* © 2000 by Mary White Rights

Wednesday, November 11 — Psalm 122
Ezekiel 47:13–48:22; 1 John 2:18–29

Make haste to help me, O Lord, my salvation. Psalm 38:22

God is our refuge, strength, and home,   20s*
our help and peace today.
Though pow'rs may fail and sorrows come,
God's light will show the way.

Paul wrote: But the Lord stood by me and gave me strength. 2 Timothy 4:17

Lord, grant that we impelled by love   643
in smallest things may faithful prove;
'til we depart, our lives be true,
devoted wholly unto you.

Loving Parent, your presence in our world and in our churches calls us to serve your children. May we have the strength to love your family and welcome them into your salvation now and in the life to come. Amen.

* © 2013 by Interprovincial Board of Communication and Moravian Music Foundation

Thursday, November 12 — Psalm 123
Ezekiel 48:23–Daniel 1:21; 1 John 3:1–10

Woe to you shepherds who only take care of yourselves! Should not shepherds take care of the flock? Ezekiel 34:2 (NIV)

Come as a shepherd; guard and keep   432
your fold from all that fosters sin,
and nourish lambs, and feed the sheep,
the wounded heal, the lost bring in.

If your gift is serving, then serve. Romans 12:7 (NIV)

New life for some means food and warmth,   481*
for some the right to speak,
for some the comfort of a friend
or loving God to meet.
So help us, Christ, as now we join
with Christians ev'rywhere
to touch and teach, to comfort, feed,
your love the world to share.

Holy God, when we miss the mark and fail to love our neighbors, show us your way. Give us the courage to love with Jesus' hands and feet in the places where we meet your beloved children. Amen.

* © 1987 by M. Lynnette Delbridge.

Chief Elder Festival

Friday, November 13 — Psalm 124
Daniel 2:1–33; 1 John 3:11–24

Chief Elder Festival† — Ezekiel 34:11–16,23–24; Psalm 8
Hebrews 4:14–16; John 10:1–10

I am coming to gather all nations and tongues; and they shall come and shall see my glory. Isaiah 66:18

Let the whole creation cry,   p127
"Glory to the Lord on high!"
Heav'n and earth awake and sing,
"Praise to our almighty King!"
Praise God, angel hosts above,
ever bright and fair in love;
sun and moon, lift up your voice;
night and stars, in God rejoice.

When the Son of Man comes in his glory, and all the angels with him, then he will sit on the throne of his glory. All the nations will be gathered before him. Matthew 25:31–32

Let us follow our Lamb who is still leading on,   79s*
Jesus Christ, the Messiah, our God's own dear Son.
He's the One who has conquered
    the struggle life gives,
and who never gave up but in faithfulness lives.

Chief Elder, give us vision for your future and let us know our part to play. May we witness to your love with everything we do. In grace we ask for your guidance of our words and actions. Amen.

† On November 13, 1741, announcement was made to the congregations of the Brethren's Church of the Chief Eldership of Jesus Christ.

* © 2010 by Sharon Michel Benson

Saturday, November 14 — Psalm 125
Daniel 2:34–3:18; 1 John 4:1–16a

Worship the Lord with gladness; come into his presence with singing. Psalm 100:2

Sing for joy! Sing passionately strong.   40s*
Sing as though your greatest gift
of love could be your song.
Sing for peace. Sing quietly, but clear.
Sing a gentle phrase as though
you're whisp'ring in God's ear.
Music is a prayer.
Sing it ev'rywhere.
God is ev'rywhere,
listening to a prayer.
Come to God through a melody.

Whatever you do, do everything for the glory of God. 1 Corinthians 10:31

Gather together, sing as one,   536**
raising up a joyful song
high and loud, into the air,
broadcast praises ev'rywhere.
Deep in our heart we tend the flame,
and as your servant we remain.
By this, we will our voice unite,
bring glory day and night.

Amazing God, you fill our days with joy and hope!
May we sing of your glory even in days of sorrow.
Let our voices carry to those in need of your hope
and give them reprieve. Amen.

*   © 2011 by Christine Sobania Johnson

** © 1991 by Beth E. Hanson

Twenty-fifth Sunday after Pentecost

Watchword for the Week — Let us hold fast to the confession of our hope without wavering, for God who has promised is faithful. Hebrews 10:23

Sunday, November 15 — Daniel 12:1–3; Psalm 16 Hebrews 10:11–14,(15–18),19–25; Mark 13:1–8

Happy are those who live in your house, ever singing your praise. Psalm 84:4

Thus may our lips your praises sound,   519
our hearts in steadfast hope abound;
'til you to heaven our steps shall bring
where saints and angels hail you King.

Through Jesus, then, let us continually offer a sacrifice of praise to God, that is, the fruit of lips that confess his name. Hebrews 13:15

But not for us alone this news   543
was brought by Christ our Lord.
'Twas meant for all the world to hear
and thus with one accord
with all God's children everywhere
his name and sign with pride we bear.
To us, to us, this task is giv'n:
to spread God's word. Amen.

Faithful God, your word of challenge to live in praise of all you have done comes to us this day. Give us strength and courage to live fully in Jesus' way. Amen.

Monday, November 16 — Psalm 126
Daniel 3:19–4:18; 1 John 4:16b–5:5

Your eyes are open to all the ways of mortals.
Jeremiah 32:19

                                                        77s*

We're called to take the risky step,
align with those in need,
to vision the new thing God's doing
within community.
The challenge is to not rely
on raw reality
that shrouds our hope, obscuring all
that God would have us see.

In him we live and move and have our being.
Acts 17:28

                                                        59s**

Our model is the Savior
whose grace is labeled "free."
We offer to the neighbor
Christ's hospitality.
In this way God is glorified,
not by the vict'ry of "our side."
We welcome just as Christ,
and then we praise the Lord! Amen.

Creator, you made us with a capacity to live in
relationship with you and with one another. Help
us to follow Jesus' example as we live in your world,
loving one another freely and completely. Amen.

*   © 2007 by Judith M. Ganz

** © 2013 by Interprovincial Board of Communication and Moravian Music Foundation

Tuesday, November 17 — Psalm 127
Daniel 4:19–5:16; 1 John 5:6–21

Moses said, "See, I am setting before you today a blessing and a curse: the blessing, if you obey the commandments of the Lord your God that I am commanding you today; and the curse, if you do not obey the commandments of the Lord your God." Deuteronomy 11:26–28

Jesus calls us; by your mercies,   600
Savior, may we hear your call,
give our hearts to your obedience,
serve and love you best of all.

Jesus says, "I am the way, and the truth, and the life. No one comes to the Father except through me. John 14:6

O Joy, all joys excelling,   484
the Bread of Life, the Way,
you came to make your dwelling
in sinful hearts to stay.
My spirit's hungry craving
you can forever still;
from deepest anguish saving,
with bliss my cup can fill.

Jesus, you have shown us what it means to live as God intends. May our lives show your love, mercy, and compassion to all those we meet as we seek to be your disciples. Amen.

Wednesday, November 18 — Psalm 128
Daniel 5:17–6:18; 2 John

I will make a covenant of peace with them; it shall be an everlasting covenant with them.
Ezekiel 37:26

> We covenant with hand and heart　　　　　　　p209
> to follow Christ our Lord;
> with world, and sin, and self to part,
> and to obey his word;
> to love each other heartily,
> in truth and with sincerity,
> and under cross, reproach, and shame,
> to glorify his name.

In Jesus Christ every one of God's promises is a "Yes." For this reason it is through him that we say the "Amen," to the glory of God.
2 Corinthians 1:20

> God of grace and God of glory,　　　　　　　751
> on your people pour your power;
> crown your ancient Church's story;
> bring its bud to glorious flower.
> Grant us wisdom, grant us courage
> for the facing of this hour,
> for the facing of this hour.

Holy God, you keep your promises and we entrust our lives to you. Help us to share your love and grace as you have shared it with us. To you all glory on earth and heaven be given! Amen.

Thursday, November 19 — Psalm 129
Daniel 6:19–7:22; 3 John

**Do not let your heart envy sinners, but always
continue in the fear of the Lord. Proverbs 23:17**

> Your love and peace will rule our hearts;   93s*
> unite us into one.
> Your word dwells richly in our souls,
> our thankfulness to you o'erflows.
> In the name of Jesus, where
> his wisdom we can share.

**Your Father in heaven makes his sun rise on
the evil and on the good, and sends rain on the
righteous and on the unrighteous. Matthew 5:45**

> Make it known to folks among us.   73s**
> Do it now, this very hour.
> Let us listen, love, and serve them,
> acting in the Spirit's pow'r.
> Make it known to those outside us,
> where the seed of faith is sown.
> We will pray and work together
> as we make the Lord's love known.

Gracious One, let us not forget that your love
shelters all. Help us to reach out to your children
with love and grace for each one. Transform our
lives to show your love in everything we do. Amen.

*   © 1995 by Barbara Strauss

** © 1993 by Darryl Bell

Friday, November 20 — Psalm 130
Daniel 7:23–8:27; Jude 1:1–10

O mountains of Israel, see now, I am for you; I will turn to you, and you shall be tilled and sown. Ezekiel 36:8–9

> Love of God is a fragrant garden,   83s*
> full of color, life, and fruit.
> Throughout its annual cycle,
> we find seed and bulb and shoot.
> Hiding under the snows of winter,
> soaking up the rain of spring,
> bathing in the gold of summer,
> they an autumn harvest bring.

He has helped his servant Israel, in remembrance of his mercy, according to the promise he made to our ancestors, to Abraham and to his descendants forever. Luke 1:54–55

> Water has touched us,   408
> fresh on our foreheads,
> showing an inward,
> spiritual grace.
> Into God's fam'ly,
> we have been welcomed.
> As sons and daughters,
> we take our place.

Faithful One, you sustain and nurture us in life that we may have the energy and nerve to share the good news of your love. Enable us to do your will and live your promise of life for all. Amen.

*   © 2011 by C. Riddick Weber

Saturday, November 21 — Psalm 131
Daniel 9:1–10:7; Jude 1:11–25

Sing to the Lord, bless his name; tell of his salvation from day to day. Psalm 96:2

Sing we now with joyfulness,   55s*
our voices joined as one.
Christ is our true happiness;
all praise to God's dear Son.
We lift our voices singing
in grateful thanks and praise
to Christ whose love surrounds us
throughout our lifelong days.

Sing psalms and hymns and spiritual songs among yourselves, singing and making melody to the Lord in your hearts. Ephesians 5:19

Sing hallelujah, praise the Lord!   543
Sing with a cheerful voice;
exalt our God with one accord,
and in his name rejoice.
Ne'er cease to sing, O ransomed host,
praise Father, Son, and Holy Ghost,
until in realms of endless light
your praises shall unite.

Giver of joy, we are filled with songs of praise and thanksgiving! Give us grace to honor you in all we do and say. May your love be known by others as our hands and feet serve you. Amen.

* © 2004 by Thom Stapleton

Reign of Christ (Christ the King Sunday)

Watchword for the Week — "I am the Alpha and the Omega," says the Lord God, who is and who was and who is to come, the Almighty. Revelation 1:8

Sunday, November 22 — Daniel 7:9–10,13–14; Psalm 93
Revelation 1:4b–8; John 18:33–37

You in your mercy have led forth the people whom you have redeemed. Exodus 15:13 (NKJV)

76s*

Come, be with our friend Jesus,
our God in human form,
who came to earth to save us,
and to make love the norm.
He guides us by the Spirit,
and leads us on our way,
to be a place of safety,
and welcome ev'ry day.

Our citizenship is in heaven, and it is from there that we are expecting a Savior, the Lord Jesus Christ. Philippians 3:20

76s*

Let us with all creation
now dance and celebrate.
God wants you at the party,
so please don't hesitate.
For this is where all people
will join and sing one song.
All welcome in one fam'ly,
to know that all belong.

Lord of all, hear our praises and our songs! Thank you for all the gifts of abundant life here today and with you tomorrow. Shape us in your likeness to share this good news with all the world. Amen.

* © 2013 by Interprovincial Board of Communication and Moravian Music Foundation

Monday, November 23 — Psalm 132
Daniel 10:8–11:19; Revelation 1:1–8

One who is slow to anger is better than the mighty, and one whose temper is controlled than one who captures a city. Proverbs 16:32 (NIV)

> When peace, like a river, attendeth my way,   754
> when sorrows like sea billows roll;
> whatever my lot, you have taught me to say,
> it is well, it is well with my soul.
> It is well with my soul,
> it is well, it is well with my soul.

Blessed are the peacemakers, for they will be called children of God. Matthew 5:9

> Faith in the conscience works for peace,   700
> and bids the mourner's weeping cease,
> by faith the children's place we claim,
> and give all honor to one name.

Patient Teacher, we are sometimes distracted from your hope for the world by anger, mistrust, and doubt. Send us your peace that the burdens we carry may be released so we can follow you well. Amen.

Tuesday, November 24 — Psalm 133
Daniel 11:20–12:7; Revelation 1:9–20

They have all gone astray, they are all alike perverse; there is no one who does good, no, not one. Psalm 14:3

> God meets us where we are;   23s*
> God comes to bring us grace.
> God comes to make one family
> of the whole human race.

Deliver us from evil. Matthew 6:13 (NASB)

> Jesus, Lord of Life and Light,   26s**
> ev'ry soul's salvation,
> glowing hope in sin's dark night,
> love's bright affirmation:
> on the earth of Christmas night
> you were born in meekness,
> leaving all your heav'nly might
> to embrace our weakness.

Lord of grace, we cannot comprehend the gift of your salvation for the world. May our lives express the gratitude for this tremendous gift of love and may we share that love with others. Amen.

* © 2008 by R. L. Rominger, III

** © 2013 by Interprovincial Board of Communication and Moravian Music Foundation

Wednesday, November 25 — Psalm 134
Daniel 12:8–Hosea 2:15; Revelation 2:1–11

Honor the Lord with your wealth.
Proverbs 3:9 (NIV)

> We give you but your own   657
> in any gifts we bring;
> all that we have is yours alone,
> a trust from you, our King.

In the parable, the rich man says, "Soul, you have ample goods laid up for many years; relax, eat, drink, be merry." But God said to him, "You fool!" Luke 12:19–20

> Riches I heed not nor man's empty praise,   719
> thou mine inheritance now and always;
> thou and thou only first in my heart,
> high King of heaven, my treasure thou art.

Generous God, your gifts are abundant! Open our hearts to show your generosity by sharing with and caring for those who know the reality of "not enough." In Jesus' name. Amen.

Thursday, November 26 — Psalm 135:1–12
Hosea 2:16–4:19; Revelation 2:12–23

The Lord will vindicate his people, and have compassion on his servants. Psalm 135:14

> God is love; and love enfolds us,   463
> all the world in one embrace;
> with unfailing grasp God holds us,
> ev'ry child of ev'ry race.
> And when human hearts are breaking
> under sorrow's iron rod,
> then we find that selfsame aching
> deep within the heart of God.

Christ Jesus became for us wisdom from God, and righteousness and sanctification and redemption. 1 Corinthians 1:30

> On him we'll venture all we have,   479
> our lives, our all, to him we owe.
> None else is able us to save,
> naught but the Savior will we know;
> this we subscribe with heart and hand,
> resolved through grace thereby to stand.

Guiding Savior, you show us how to live and share your love. Help us remember this call to justice in your name through graceful action and service with your children at home and in the world. Amen.

Friday, November 27 — Psalm 135:13–21
Hosea 5,6,7; Revelation 2:24–3:6

I will bless the Lord at all times; his praise shall continually be in my mouth. Psalm 34:1

Then let us adore and give him his right,   565
all glory and pow'r and wisdom and might,
all honor and blessing, with angels above,
and thanks never ceasing for infinite love.

Are any among you suffering? They should pray. Are any cheerful? They should sing songs of praise. James 5:13

Christ for the world we sing!   640
The world to Christ we bring
with loving zeal;
the poor and them that mourn,
the faint and overborne,
sin-sick and sorrow-worn,
whom Christ does heal.

Amazing God, we find ourselves faced with many challenges and opportunities to share your good news. Be with us in the sharing as we offer all we have to you. Amen.

Saturday, November 28 — Psalm 136
Hosea 8,9; Revelation 3:7–18

All these things my hand has made, and so all these things are mine, says the Lord. But this is the one to whom I will look, to the humble and contrite in spirit, who trembles at my word. Isaiah 66:2

What splendid rays of truth and grace,   596
all other light excelling!
This I know when he in love
makes my heart his dwelling!

Paul said; "Now I commit you to God and to the word of his grace, which can build you up." Acts 20:32 (NIV)

O Jesus, you have promised   603
to all who follow you
that where you are in glory
your servants shall be too.
And Jesus, I have promised
to serve you to the end;
O give me grace to follow,
my master and my friend.

Gracious Lord, help us to follow your direction and live our lives in peace. Fill the hearts of all humankind with love, faith, and hope that the world may know the fullness of your grace. Amen.

First Sunday of Advent

Watchword for the Week — Jesus says, "Heaven and earth will pass away, but my words will not pass away." Luke 21:33

Sunday, November 29 — Jeremiah 33:14–16; Psalm 25:1–10
1 Thessalonians 3:9–13; Luke 21:25–36

How precious is your steadfast love, O God! All people may take refuge in the shadow of your wings. Psalm 36:7

> All praise to you, my God, this night   569
> for all the blessings of the light.
> Keep me, O keep me, King of kings,
> beneath the shelter of your wings.

See what love the Father has given us, that we should be called children of God; and that is what we are. 1 John 3:1

> Join hands, disciples of the faith,   523
> whate'er your race may be.
> All children of the living God
> are surely kin to me.

Coming Christ, we begin this journey of light and hope with your Spirit. Open our hearts, eyes, and minds to the call of new birth and new life given to all. Thank you for coming to us. Amen.

Monday, November 30 — Psalm 137
Hosea 10,11,12; Revelation 3:19–4:8

In overflowing wrath for a moment I hid my face from you, but with everlasting love I will have compassion on you, says the Lord, your Redeemer. Isaiah 54:8

> Light of the world, you are the way;   38s*
> to you ourselves we give,
> to share your death on this dark day,
> and by your light to live.

By grace you have been saved through faith, and this is not your own doing; it is the gift of God. Ephesians 2:8

> Triumphant hosts on high   468
> give thanks to God and sing,
> and "Holy, holy, holy," cry,
> "Almighty King!"
> Hail, Abraham's God and ours!
> One mighty hymn we raise.
> All pow'r and majesty be yours
> and endless praise!

Holy One, thank you for your grace and love that we could never earn. May we find ways to love one another with the fullness of your embrace. In Jesus' name. Amen.

Tuesday, December 1 — Psalm 138:1–5
Hosea 13,14; Revelation 4:9–5:10

Truly my soul finds rest in God; my salvation comes from him. Psalm 62:1 (NIV)

I fully am persuaded   769
and joyfully declare
I'm never left unaided,
my Father hears my prayer;
his comforts never fail me,
he stands at my right hand;
when tempests fierce assail me,
they're calm at his command.

The Spirit helps us in our weakness; for we do not know how to pray as we ought, but that very Spirit intercedes with sighs too deep for words. Romans 8:26

The ground of my profession   769
is Jesus and his blood;
he gives me the possession
of everlasting good.
To me his Holy Spirit
speaks many a precious word
of rest to one who's seeking
a refuge in the Lord.

The spinning turbulence of life pulls us from you, O Center of Being. We are out of control, powerless to save ourselves. Words fail us. O Spirit of Calm, draw us into your saving sphere and voice the words we long to speak. Amen.

Wednesday, December 2 — Psalm 138:6–8
Joel 1:1–2:14; Revelation 5:11–6:8

Help us, O Lord our God, for we rely on you. 2 Chronicles 14:11

> Jesus, Lover of my soul,   724
> let me to thy bosom fly,
> while the raging billows roll,
> while the tempest still is high;
> hide me, O my Savior, hide
> 'til the storm of life is past;
> safe into the haven guide;
> O receive my soul at last!

The Lord will rescue me from every evil attack and will bring me safely to his heavenly kingdom. 2 Timothy 4:18 (NIV)

> Tenderly he shields and spares us,   529
> well our feeble frame he knows,
> in his hands he gently bears us,
> rescues us from all our foes.
> Alleluia! Alleluia!
> Widely as his mercy flows.

Evil attacks us, O Shield of our souls. All those less-than-Christlike thoughts, desires, and actions can contribute to a life of anger and despair. Savior, only you can deliver us from sin. Lead us to your kingdom we pray. Amen.

Thursday, December 3 — Psalm 139:1–6
Joel 2:15–3:21; Revelation 6:9–7:8

Our God whom we serve is able to deliver us from the furnace of blazing fire; and he will deliver us. But even if he does not, let it be known to you, O king, that we are not going to serve your gods or worship the golden image. Daniel 3:17–18 (NASB)

> O, to grace how great a debtor   782
> daily I'm constrained to be!
> Let that grace, Lord, like a fetter,
> bind my wand'ring heart to thee.
> Prone to wander, Lord, I feel it,
> prone to leave the God I love,
> here's my heart, O take and seal it;
> seal it for thy courts above.

Christ says, "I know your works. Look, I have set before you an open door, which no one is able to shut. I know that you have but little power, and yet you have kept my word and have not denied my name." Revelation 3:8

> Faith finds in Christ our ev'ry need   700
> to save or strengthen us indeed;
> we now receive the grace sent down,
> which makes us share his cross and crown.

All-seeing God, as feeble as our attempts are to follow Jesus, you know we are trying to walk in the light of his truth. As we move forward this Advent season, may we keep our eyes fixed on the path he illuminates. Amen.

Friday, December 4 — Psalm 139:7–12
Amos 1,2; Revelation 7:9–17

The haughty eyes of people shall be brought low, and the pride of everyone shall be humbled; and the Lord alone will be exalted in that day. Isaiah 2:11

> While we, deeply humbled,   746
> own we're oft to blame,
> this remains our comfort,
> you are still the same.
> In you all the needy
> have a friend most dear,
> whose love and forbearance
> unexampled are.

God shows no partiality. Romans 2:11

> Lord of all nations, grant me grace   686
> to love all people, ev'ry race,
> to see each mortal as I ought,
> my kindred, whom your love has bought.

Impartial God, too often we use the Advent season to pat ourselves on the back for helping "the needy." We take pride in being generous. Help us to see that in your eyes we all need your saving grace. Humble us, loving Lord. Amen.

Saturday, December 5 — Psalm 139:13–16
Amos 3,4; Revelation 8

You shall worship before the Lord your God; and you shall rejoice in all the good which the Lord your God has given you and your household. Deuteronomy 26:10,11 (NKJV)

> All people that on earth do dwell,   539
> sing to the Lord with cheerful voice;
> serve him with joy, his praises tell,
> come now before him and rejoice.

Give thanks in all circumstances; for this is the will of God in Christ Jesus for you. 1 Thessalonians 5:18

> We'll bring him hearts that love him,   658
> we'll bring him thankful praise,
> and souls forever striving
> to follow in his ways:
> and these shall be the treasures
> we offer to the King,
> and these are gifts that even
> our grateful hearts may bring.

What do you want from us, O Giver of Life, except to glorify you with lives of gratitude for your everlasting grace as shown to us through our Savior Jesus Christ? We give thanks and rejoice with grateful hearts. Amen.

Second Sunday of Advent

Watchword for the Week — Blessed be the Lord God of Israel, for he has looked favorably on his people and redeemed them. Luke 1:68

Sunday, December 6 — Malachi 3:1–4; Luke 1:68–79
Philippians 1:3–11; Luke 3:1–6

Arise, shine; for your light has come, and the glory of the Lord has risen upon you. Isaiah 60:1

> Praise the Lord, whose saving splendor   298
> shines into the darkest night;
> O what praises shall we render
> for this never-ceasing light.

You are all children of light and children of the day. 1 Thessalonians 5:5

> Great Father of glory, pure Father of light,   457
> your angels adore you, all veiling their sight;
> all praise we would render, O lead us to see
> the light of your splendor, your love's majesty.

Morning Star, when the days grow short and dim and our lives feel empty and dark, remind us that we are offered the true and everlasting light of your love which enables us to shine so that the world may see your glory. Amen.

Monday, December 7 — Psalm 139:17–24
Amos 5; Revelation 9:1–11

The earth will be full of the knowledge of the Lord as the waters cover the sea. Isaiah 11:9

> Isaiah the prophet has written of old   682*
> how God's earthly kingdom shall come.
> Instead of the thorn tree the fir tree shall grow;
> the wolf shall lie down with the lamb.
> The mountains and hills shall break forth into song,
> the peoples be led forth in peace;
> for the earth shall be filled with the knowledge of God
> as the waters cover the seas.

God our Savior desires everyone to be saved and to come to the knowledge of the truth. 1 Timothy 2:3–4

> O come, O wisdom from on high,   274
> and order all things far and nigh;
> to us the path of knowledge show,
> and teach us in her ways to go.
> Rejoice! Rejoice! Immanuel
> shall come to you, O Israel!

Jesus, triumphant witness to the power of the Holy One's saving love for all creation, grant us wisdom to understand that what we know now is merely a glimpse of the glory of the Almighty which will be ours to share by your grace. Amen.

Tuesday, December 8 — Psalm 140:1–5
Amos 6,7; Revelation 9:12–21

Long ago you laid the foundation of the earth, and the heavens are the work of your hands. Psalm 102:25

Praise we all our God eternal   637*
who created land and sea
bringing forth the human story,
life and love that's true and free.
Alleluia! Through this journey
let our lives inspired be.

Worship him who made heaven and earth, the sea and the springs of water. Revelation 14:7

O Lord my God, when I in awesome wonder   465**
consider all the works thy hands have made,
I see the stars, I hear the mighty thunder,
thy pow'r throughout the universe displayed.
Then sings my soul, my Savior God, to thee;
how great thou art, how great thou art!
Then sings my soul, my Savior God, to thee:
how great thou art, how great thou art.

From microorganisms to the majestic mountains,
from molten minerals to frozen tundra, nothing
exists except by your will, O Creator God.
We worship you with humble awe and with
thanksgiving for all that you provide today and
always. Amen.

Wednesday, December 9 — Psalm 140:6–13
Amos 8,9; Revelation 10

My eyes are fixed on you, O Sovereign Lord; in you I take refuge—do not give me over to death. Psalm 141:8 (NIV)

God is my strong salvation,   769
no enemy I fear;
he hears my supplication,
dispelling all my care;
if he, my head and master,
defend me from above,
what pain or what disaster
can part me from his love?

Jesus was in the stern, asleep on the cushion; and the disciples woke him up and said to him, "Teacher, do you not care that we are perishing?" Mark 4:38

Lord, your body ne'er forsake,   p86
ne'er your congregation leave;
we in you our refuge take,
of your fullness we receive:
ev'ry other help be gone,
you are our support alone;
for on your supreme commands
all the universe depends.

There is no refuge for us, O Ruler of the Elements, when we seek protection from fear and death by our own devices. Only when we rely on you can we weather the trials of life. In this Advent season we focus on Jesus, whose power calms all our storms. Amen.

Thursday, December 10 — Psalm 141:1–4
Obadiah 1; Jonah 1,2; Revelation 11:1–14

The lot is cast into the lap, but the decision is the Lord's alone. Proverbs 16:33

Be still, my soul: the Lord is on your side.   757
Bear patiently the cross of grief or pain;
leave to your God to order and provide;
in ev'ry change God faithful will remain.
Be still, my soul: your best, your heav'nly friend
through thorny ways leads to a joyful end.

Are not two sparrows sold for a penny? Yet not one of them will fall to the ground unperceived by your Father. Matthew 10:29

What God's almighty pow'r has made,   537
in mercy he is keeping;
by morning glow or evening shade
his eye is never sleeping.
And where he rules in kingly might,
there all is just and all is right:
to God all praise and glory!

Nothing we decide to say or do escapes you, ever-vigilant Spirit. All our choices are detected as you move among us, seeking to guide us from self-indulgence and self-centeredness toward sacrificial love. We welcome your presence as we prepare our hearts for the coming Christ. Amen.

Friday, December 11 — Psalm 141:5–10
Jonah 3,4; Revelation 11:15–12:6

My words that I have put in your mouth shall not depart out of your mouth, or out of the mouths of your children, or out of the mouths of your children's children. Isaiah 59:21

God's word alive and active,   503*
proclaimed throughout the years,
still comforts us when hurting
and calms our hidden fears.
God's word of truth and justice
sets weary captives free,
and joins God's holy people
in new community.

Pay close attention to yourself and to your teaching; continue in these things, for in doing this you will save both yourself and your hearers. 1 Timothy 4:16

How shall the young direct their way?   510
What light shall be their perfect guide?
Your word, O Lord, will safely lead
if in its wisdom they confide.

We fondly recall annual Sunday school Christmas programs designed to honor you, O Child Divine. No matter how many, the years have not diminished the importance of telling of your birth. With joy we repeat the message of your love for the world, celebrate your coming, and share the good news. Amen.

* © by American Bible Society

Saturday, December 12 — Psalm 142
Micah 1–3:7; Revelation 12:7–18

The angel of the Lord encamps around those who fear him, and delivers them. Psalm 34:7

O ye, beneath life's crushing load,   286
whose forms are bending low,
who toil along the climbing way
with painful steps and slow;
look now! for glad and golden hours
come swiftly on the wing.
O rest beside the weary road,
and hear the angels sing.

During the night an angel of the Lord opened the doors of the jail and brought them out. Acts 5:19 (NIV)

Hail to the Lord's anointed!   263
Great David's greater Son!
Hail, in the time appointed,
his reign on earth begun!
He comes to break oppression,
to set the captive free,
to take away transgression,
and rule in equity.

Mysterious God, in this scientific age we often
struggle with the idea of angels moving among
us to accomplish your will. Help us grow in faith
to trust and accept what we cannot understand or
explain. Cast out our unbelief. Amen.

Third Sunday of Advent

Watchword for the Week — Bear fruits worthy of repentance.
Luke 3:8

Sunday, December 13 — Zephaniah 3:14–20; Isaiah 12:2–6
Philippians 4:4–7; Luke 3:7–18

The fear of the Lord is instruction in wisdom.
Proverbs 15:33

> You are the truth; your word alone   661
> true wisdom can impart;
> you only can inform the mind
> and purify the heart.

Who is wise and understanding among you?
Show by your good life that your works are done
with gentleness born of wisdom. James 3:13

> Help us our priesthood understand,   440*
> that we can make the simple grand,
> and with a gentle, caring deed,
> prepare the soil and plant the seed.
> Fill us with urgency to search
> beyond the windows of the church
> to love and touch and lay the hand,
> and walk as Christians in this land.

Fount of all Wisdom, today, as we worship, we
remember the gentleness of your nature—how you
hold us in your hand, offer us shelter, and whisper
words of comfort and encouragement. May we
model this gentleness as we live our faith. Amen.

* © 1994 by Ralph E. Freeman

Monday, December 14 — Psalm 143:1–6
Micah 3:8–5:15; Revelation 12:18–13:10

Mortals look on the outward appearance, but the Lord looks on the heart. 1 Samuel 16:7

Create in me a clean heart, O God,   p79
and renew a right Spirit within me.
Cast me not away from your presence,
and take not your Holy Spirit from me.
Restore unto me the joy of salvation;
anoint me with your Spirit free.
Create in me a clean heart, O God,
and renew a right Spirit within me.

The angel said to her, "Do not be afraid, Mary, for you have found favor with God." Luke 1:30

Bless, O Lord, we pray, your congregation;   445
bless each home and family;
bless the youth, the rising generation;
blessed may your dear children be;
bless your servants, grant them help and favor;
you to glorify be their endeavor.
Lord, on you we humbly call;
let your blessing rest on all.

God, you see through the artifice of our attempts to impress the world. As we contemplate Mary, mother of Jesus, we realize that you honor those whose hearts are filled with humble faith and perfect obedience. May we strive for hearts like that. Amen.

Tuesday, December 15 — Psalm 143:7–12
Micah 6,7; Revelation 13:11–14:5

O give thanks to the Lord, for he is good; for his steadfast love endures forever. Psalm 106:1

> For the harvest of the Spirit, 449*
> thanks be to God.
> For the good we all inherit,
> thanks be to God.
> For the wonders that astound us,
> for the truths that still confound us,
> most of all, that love has found us,
> thanks be to God.

And whatever you do, in word or deed, do everything in the name of the Lord Jesus, giving thanks to God the Father through him. Colossians 3:17

> Then let us praise the Father 391
> and worship God the Son
> and sing to God the Spirit,
> eternal Three in One,
> 'til all the ransomed number
> who stand before the throne
> ascribe all pow'r and glory
> and praise to God alone.

Christ, fill our minds and hearts so that all we think, say, or do is a reflection of you. We thank you for the everlasting life we have received through your sacrificial grace. Amen.

Wednesday, December 16 — Psalm 144:1–4
Nahum 1,2; Revelation 14:6–16

I will put my Spirit in you and you will live, and I will settle you in your own land. Then you will know that I the Lord have spoken, and I have done it, declares the Lord. Ezekiel 37:14 (NIV)

Breath of God, O life-giving Spirit,   499*
yours the truth that we seek this day.
Yours the wisdom, yours the understanding,
yours the guidance on life's dark way.
Source of courage when hearts are weary,
source of strength for the day's long journey,
Spirit God, our hope and our faith,
breathe now within us your holy breath.

Jesus welcomed them, and spoke to them about the kingdom of God, and healed those who needed to be cured. Luke 9:11

Let the earth now praise the Lord,   261
who has truly kept his word
and at last to us did send
Christ, the sinner's help and friend.

Benevolent God, by the power of your Spirit your attention to all our needs knows no bounds. Moreover, through your Son, you have provided for our greatest need—our salvation. Thank you. Amen.

* © 1989 by Kieran Sawyer

Thursday, December 17 — Psalm 144:5–8
Nahum 3; Habakkuk 1; Revelation 14:17–15:8

The revelation awaits an appointed time; though it lingers, wait for it. Habakkuk 2:3 (NIV)

O give me Samuel's heart!   609
A lowly heart that waits
where in thy house thou art,
or watches at thy gates
by day and night, a heart that still
moves at the breathing of thy will.

You also must be patient. Strengthen your hearts, for the coming of the Lord is near. James 5:8

Still will I wait, O Lord, on you,   721
'til in your light I see anew;
'til you in my behalf appear,
to banish ev'ry doubt and fear.

Patience is not our strong suit, O Lord. We want instant gratification and easy answers. May these weeks of Advent waiting teach us once again to have patient trust in the perfect timing of your plans for us. Amen.

Friday, December 18 — Psalm 144:9–15
Habakkuk 2,3; Revelation 16:1–11

If you will only obey the Lord your God: blessed shall you be when you come in, and blessed shall you be when you go out. Deuteronomy 28:1,6

> You have kindly led us   p205
> through our joys and tears;
> now accept our praises
> and remove our fears.
> Grant us all with gladness
> to obey your voice;
> let your will and pleasure
> be our only choice.

Abraham was fully convinced that God was able to do what he had promised. Romans 4:21

> Let us greet our God with gladness   392*
> filled with joy for faith today.
> Though not seeing, yet believing
> in the Truth, the Life, the Way.
> As we now by faith move forward,
> Christ our Lord we will obey.

Our right relationship with you, O Promise Keeper, is the foundation of our faith and the incentive for our trusting obedience. We give our utmost thanks for your Son whose coming to earth convinces us of your eternal love and grace. Amen.

Saturday, December 19 — Psalm 145:1–7
Zephaniah 1,2; Revelation 16:12–21

Turn back to the Lord whom you have deeply betrayed. Isaiah 31:6

For the herald's voice is crying   264
in the desert far and near,
calling us to true repentance,
since the Kingdom now is here.
O, that warning cry obey!
Now prepare for God a way!
Let the valleys rise to meet him,
and the hills bow down to greet him!

Where sin increased, grace abounded all the more. Romans 5:20

Plenteous grace with thee is found,   724
grace to cover all my sin;
let the healing streams abound;
make and keep me pure within.
Thou of life the fountain art,
freely let me take of thee;
spring thou up within my heart,
rise to all eternity.

Jesus Christ, Son of God, we acknowledge our
sinfulness and come to you with repentant hearts.
By your abundant grace, have mercy on us. Amen.

Fourth Sunday of Advent

Watchword for the Week — God has brought down the powerful from their thrones, and lifted up the lowly. Luke 1:52

Sunday, December 20 — Micah 5:2–5a; Luke 1:46b–55
Hebrews 10:5–10; Luke 1:39–45,(46–55)

Praise him for his acts of power; praise him for his surpassing greatness. Psalm 150:2 (NIV)

Praise to the Lord!   530
    O, let all that is in me adore him!
All that has life and breath,
    come now with praises before him!
Let the amen sound from his people again.
Gladly forever adore him!

Glory to God in the highest heaven, and on earth peace among those whom he favors! Luke 2:14

All glory be to God on high,   296
and to the earth be peace;
good will henceforth from heav'n to all
begin and never cease,
begin and never cease.

Infinite One, Creator and Ruler of all, may we glorify you not only in our worship today, but every day, with our whole selves, for that is the purpose of our lives. Amen.

Monday, December 21 — Psalm 145:8–16
Zephaniah 3; Haggai 1; Revelation 17:1–8

If you offer your food to the hungry and satisfy the needs of the afflicted, then your light shall rise in the darkness. Isaiah 58:10

> Today we all are called to be   696*
> disciples of the Lord,
> to help to set the captive free,
> make plowshare out of sword,
> to feed the hungry, quench their thirst,
> make love and peace our fast,
> to serve the poor and homeless first,
> our ease and comfort last.

Let your gentleness be known to everyone. The Lord is near. Philippians 4:5

> Blessed are the strong but gentle,   595
> trained to serve a higher will,
> wise to know th'eternal purpose
> which their Father shall fulfill.
> Blessed are they who with true passion
> strive to make the right prevail,
> for the earth is God's possession
> and his purpose will not fail.

Jesus, grant us the gentle strength we need to be
steadfast in our compassionate conduct toward the
suffering people of this world. May our persistent
actions shed light on the plight of the hungry and
thirsty, so others may see and act on their behalf.
Amen.

Tuesday, December 22 — Psalm 145:17–21
Haggai 2; Revelation 17:9–18

When an alien resides with you in your land, you shall not oppress the alien. Leviticus 19:33

You offered hope to those oppressed;   28s*
to captives, brought release.
You lived your life in righteousness,
for justice, love, and peace.

Welcome one another, therefore, just as Christ has welcomed you, for the glory of God. Romans 15:7

Grant, Lord, that with thy direction,   673
"Love each other," we comply,
aiming with unfeigned affection
thy love to exemplify;
let our mutual love be glowing;
thus the world will plainly see
that we, as on one stem growing,
living branches are in thee.

As we prepare our homes and hearts to welcome you again, Divine Savior, may we do as much to offer welcoming aid to the stranger in need, native or immigrant. Remind us of our call to serve you to the glory of God. Amen.

Wednesday, December 23 — Psalm 146
Zechariah 1,2; Revelation 18:1–10

I held out my hands all day long to a rebellious people, who walk in a way that is not good, following their own devices. Isaiah 65:2

> O Lord of all the living,   763*
> both banished and restored,
> compassionate, forgiving
> and ever caring Lord,
> grant now that my transgressing,
> my faithlessness may cease.
> Stretch out your hand in blessing,
> in pardon and in peace.

While the son was still far off, his father saw him and was filled with compassion; he ran and put his arms around him and kissed him. Luke 15:20

> My Father, I have wandered   763*
> and hidden from your face;
> in foolishness have squandered
> your legacy of grace.
> But now, in exile dwelling,
> I rise with fear and shame,
> as distant but compelling,
> I hear you call my name.

Benevolent Father, how reassuring it is to know that you always welcome us home with open, expectant arms. Your infinite, immeasurable love overwhelms us with joyous thanksgiving. As we celebrate Jesus' birth, may we remember we are celebrating your love for us. Amen.

*   © 1981 by ICEL

Christmas Eve

Thursday, December 24 — Psalm 147:1–6
Zechariah 3–5; Revelation 18:11–24

Your sins have hidden the Lord's face from you so that he does not hear. Isaiah 59:2

> Now Christ, the Lord, our God, is born!   306*
> As solace to a world forlorn,
> he comes as Savior, peace to win,
> and he will cleanse you from all sin.

The angel of the Lord said to Joseph, "Mary will bear a son, and you are to name him Jesus, for he will save his people from their sins." Matthew 1:21

> O holy Child of Bethlehem,   282
> descend to us, we pray;
> cast out our sin, and enter in,
> be born in us today.
> We hear the Christmas angels
> the great glad tidings tell;
> O come to us, abide with us,
> our Lord Immanuel.

It is easy to concentrate on the beauty of this holy night as we recite the story of your birth, Jesus. But as we light candles and sing carols of joy, let us not forget the reason you came to earth: to save us from sin. Thank you, Shepherd of our souls. Amen.

Nativity of the Lord (Christmas Day)

Watchword for Christmas Day — And the Word became flesh and lived among us, and we have seen his glory, the glory as of a father's only son, full of grace and truth. John 1:14

Nativity of the Lord — Isaiah 52:7-10; Psalm 98
Hebrews 1:1-4, (5-12); John 1:1-14

Friday, December 25 — Psalm 147:7–14
Zechariah 6,7; Revelation 19:1–8

David and all Israel were dancing before God with all their might, with song and lyres and harps and tambourines and cymbals and trumpets. 1 Chronicles 13:8

Rejoice in glorious hope;   372
for Christ, the Judge, shall come
to gather all his saints
to their eternal home.
We soon shall hear the archangel's voice;
the trump of God shall sound, rejoice!

The shepherds returned, glorifying and praising God for all they had heard and seen. Luke 2:20

Rejoice, O heav'ns and earth reply;   278
with praise, you sinners, fill the sky,
for this, his incarnation.
Incarnate God, put forth your pow'r;
ride on, ride on, great Conqueror,
'til all know your salvation.
Amen, amen! Hallelujah!
Hallelujah! Praise be given
evermore by earth and heaven.

Loving Giver of life, receive our words and deeds of celebration as offerings of praise and thanksgiving for the magnificent gift of your Son, our Savior, Jesus Christ. Please accept our undying gratitude for his life, death, and resurrection. Amen.

Saturday, December 26 — Psalm 147:15–20
Zechariah 8,9; Revelation 19:9–21

**Even the stork in the heavens knows its times;
and the turtle-dove, swallow, and crane observe
the time of their coming; but my people do not
know the ordinance of the Lord. Jeremiah 8:7**

> O, happy towns and blessed lands   272*
> that live by their true King's commands.
> And blessed be the hearts he rules,
> the humble places where he dwells.
> He is the rightful Son of bliss
> who fills our lives and makes us his,
> Creator of the world,
> our only strength for good.

**Therefore we must pay greater attention to what
we have heard, so that we do not drift away from
it. Hebrews 2:1**

> Come, Lord, our Savior, Jesus Christ;   272*
> our hearts are open wide in trust.
> O, show us now your lovely grace,
> upon our sorrows shine your face,
> and let your Holy Spirit guide
> our journey in your grace so wide.
> We praise your holy name,
> from age to age the same!

Lord, remind us that Christmas isn't over! We
know the story of Christ's coming must not be
packed away with the nativity figures. Help us stay
focused on the message of salvation we are called to
celebrate and share every day, all year long. Amen.

First Sunday after Christmas

Watchword for the week — Let them praise the name of the Lord, for his name alone is exalted; his glory is above earth and heaven. Psalm 148:13

Sunday, December 27—1 Samuel 2:18–20, 26; Psalm 148
Colossians 3:12–17; Luke 2:41–52

The Lord said to Moses, "Who gives speech to mortals? Is it not I, the Lord?" Exodus 4:11

> Your bountiful care what tongue can recite?   566
> It breathes in the air; it shines in the light;
> it streams from the hills; it descends to the plain,
> and sweetly distills in the dew and the rain.

You did not choose me but I chose you. And I appointed you to go and bear fruit. John 15:16

> O Holy Spirit, stir us now,   299
> inspire our hearts to make this vow:
> we will go forth into the night
> and share with all your gift of light.

Who, us, Lord? You chose us? But we are too small, too old, too young, too poor, too busy to heed your call. Forgive our excuses and fill us, instead, with your Spirit of unselfish commitment and action so that we bear fruit for your kingdom. Amen.

Monday, December 28 — Psalm 148:1–6
Zechariah 10,11; Revelation 20:1–10

The Lord our God we will serve, and him we will obey. Joshua 24:24

> Let all mortal flesh keep silence,   271
> and with fear and trembling stand,
> ponder nothing earthly minded,
> for with blessing in his hand
> Christ our God to earth descended
> our full homage to demand.

Be steadfast, immovable, always excelling in the work of the Lord, because you know that in the Lord your labor is not in vain. 1 Corinthians 15:58

> Forth in your name, O Lord, I go   638
> my daily labor to pursue—
> you only, Lord, resolved to know
> in all I think or speak or do.

Tireless Creator, often we succumb to post-celebration doldrums. We lose our enthusiasm for service and witness. Help us remember that even in the dullness of daily routine we can share your grace. Rekindle the coals of our hearts with the fire of your love. Amen.

Tuesday, December 29 — Psalm 148:7–14
Zechariah 12–13:6; Revelation 20:11–21:8

God gives wisdom to the wise and knowledge to those who have understanding. Daniel 2:21

Breath of God, O life-giving Spirit,   499*
yours the truth that we seek this day.
Yours the wisdom, yours the understanding,
yours the guidance on life's dark way.
Source of courage when hearts are weary,
source of strength for the day's long journey,
Spirit God, our hope and our faith,
breathe now within us your holy breath.

Do not be foolish, but understand what the will of the Lord is. Ephesians 5:17

The task your wisdom has assigned   638
here let me cheerfully fulfill,
in all my work your presence find
and prove your good and perfect will.

It is difficult to discern your will, God of Wisdom.
The Scriptures inform us, but interpretations can
be controversial, even adversarial. Forgive our
allowance of such disagreements to obstruct the
work of your Spirit in us. Show us how to live the
way, the truth, and the life of sacrificial love. Amen.

* © 1989 by Kieran Sawyer

Wednesday, December 30 — Psalm 149
Zechariah 13:7–14:21; Malachi 1; Revelation 21:9–22:7

He heals the broken-hearted, and binds up their wounds. Psalm 147:3

Have we trials and temptations?   743
Is there trouble anywhere?
We should never be discouraged;
take it to the Lord in prayer!
Can we find a friend so faithful
who will all our sorrows share?
Jesus knows our ev'ry weakness;
take it to the Lord in prayer!

When evening came, many who were demon-possessed were brought to him, and he drove out the spirits with a word and healed all the sick. Matthew 8:16 (NIV)

O be our mighty healer still,   736*
O Lord of life and death;
restore and strengthen, soothe and bless,
with your almighty breath:
on hands that work and eyes that see,
your healing wisdom pour,
that whole and sick and weak and strong,
may praise you evermore.

Mighty Healer, we live in a world of great pain. Injustice, war, disaster, disease, selfishness, and hard-heartedness inflict injuries only you can heal. May your love soothe all wounded bodies and souls and may your example of compassion inspire us to offer that same love to those in distress. Amen.

Thursday, December 31 — Psalm 150
Malachi 2–4; Revelation 22:8–21

For you who revere my name the sun of righteousness shall rise, with healing in its wings. Malachi 4:2

Welcome among your flock of grace   p200
with joyful acclamation,
our Shepherd whom we now confess!
Come, feed your congregation.
We own the doctrine of your cross
to be our sole foundation;
accept from ev'ry one of us
the deepest adoration.

Your kingdom come. Your will be done, on earth as it is in heaven. Matthew 6:10

Hear our prayer, O Lord,   825
hear our prayer, O Lord,
incline your ear to us,
and grant us your peace. Amen.

Trusting you completely is a daily, sometimes hourly, struggle, Jesus. The mystery of your incarnation and your resurrection competes with our desire for proof. When tough times and unanswered prayers weaken our faith, grant us the strength to pray the prayer that never fails: "Thy will be done." Amen.

DIRECTORY AND STATISTICS

Moravian Church in North America
Northern and Southern Provinces

2015

THE MORAVIAN CHURCH IN NORTH AMERICA

1021 Center Street, Bethlehem, PA 18018
459 South Church Street, Winston-Salem, NC 27101

Published by the Interprovincial Board of Communication

Moravian Church in North America

www.moravian.org

CONTENTS

ADDRESSES OF CHURCHES

Churches are listed alphabetically by state and then alphabetically by city of physical location.

NP = Northern Province
SP = Southern Province

CD = Canadian District
ED = Eastern District
WD = Western District

ALBERTA, CANADA (NP, CD):
BRUDERHEIM -
Bruderheim Church
Highway 45
Mail: Box 208
Bruderheim, AB T0B 0S0
Canada
O: 780.796.3775
F: 780.796.9736
email:
admin.bruderheimmoravian@shaw.ca
www.bruderheimmoravian.org

CALGARY -
Christ Church
600 Acadia Drive SE
Calgary, AB T2J 0B8
Canada
O: 403.271.2700
F: 403.271.2810
email: moravian@nucleus.com
www.christmoravian.com

Good Shepherd Community Church
6311 Norfolk Drive NW
Calgary, AB T2K 5J8
Canada
O: 403.274.4888
F: 403.451.1556
email:
admin@goodshepherdmoravian.org
www.goodshepherdmoravian.org

EDMONTON -
Edmonton Church
9540 83 Avenue
Edmonton, AB T6C 1B9
Canada
O: 780.439.1063
F: 780.756.7898
email: edmontonmoravian@shaw.ca
www.edmontonmoravian.com

Millwoods Church
2304 38th Street
Edmonton, AB T6L 4K9
Canada
O: 780.463.7427
F: 780.461.3058
email: office@mcchurch.ca
www.mcchurch.ca

Rio Terrace Church
15108 76 Avenue
Edmonton, AB T5R 2Z9
Canada
O/F: 780.487.0211
email: rioterracechurch@shaw.ca
www.rioterracechurch.org

LEDUC COUNTY -
Heimtal Church
51117 Range Road 250
Leduc County, AB T9G 0B3
Canada
O: 780.955.7305
F: 780.955.7988
email: heimtal@telus.net
www.heimtal.com

SHERWOOD PARK -
Good News Church
2 Primrose Boulevard
Sherwood Park, AB T8H 1G2
Canada
O: 780.467.0337
email: goodnewschurch@yahoo.com
www.goodnewschurch.ca

CALIFORNIA (NP, WD):
BANNING -
Morongo Church
47765 Foothill Road
Banning, CA 92220
Mail: PO Box 352
Banning, CA 92220-0352
O: 951.849.3067
email: morongomoravian@verizon.net

DOWNEY-
Downey Church
10337 Old River School Road
Downey, CA 90241-2057
O: 562.927.0718
F: 562.927.0858
email: revchristiemelbygibbons@gmail.com
www.downeymoravian.org

DISTRICT OF COLUMBIA
(NP, ED):
WASHINGTON -
Faith Church
405 Riggs Road NE
Washington, DC 20011-2515
O: 202.635.9012
F: 202.635.9014
email:
writetous@faithmoravianchurch.org
www.faithmoravianchurch.org

FLORIDA (SP):
LONGWOOD-
Rolling Hills Church
1525 State Road 434 W
Longwood, FL 32750-3877
O: 407.332.8380
email: rhmcoffice@centurylink.net
www.rhmoravian.org

MIAMI-
King of Kings Church
1880 NW 183rd Street
Miami, FL 33056
email: kokmoravian@att.net

New Hope Church
6001 SW 127th Avenue
Miami, FL 33183-1427
O/F: 305.273.4047
email: nhmiami@yahoo.com

Prince of Peace Church
1880 NW 183rd Street
Miami, FL 33056
O: 305.628.2061
F: 305.625.5365
email: popmc@bellsouth.net
www.princeofpeacemoravianchurch.org

WEST PALM BEACH -
Palm Beach Church
297 27th Street
West Palm Beach, FL 33407
O: 561.832.1363
F: 561.832.1363 (call first)
email: pbmoravian@yahoo.com

GEORGIA (SP):
STONE MOUNTAIN -
First Church of Georgia
4950 Hugh Howell Road
Stone Mountain, GA 30087
O: 770.491.7250
F: 770.414.5678
email: firstmoravianga@gmail.com
www.gamoravian.org

ILLINOIS (NP, WD):
WEST SALEM -
West Salem Church
PO Box 27
West Salem, IL 62476-0027
O: 618.456.8532
email: wsmor12@gmail.com

INDIANA (NP, WD):
HOPE -
Hope Church
202 Main Street
Hope, IN 47246
O: 812.546.4641
email: pastor@hopemoravianchurch.org
www.hopemoravianchurch.org

MARYLAND (NP, ED):
NEW CARROLLTON -
Trinity Church
7011 Good Luck Road
New Carrollton, MD 20784
O: 301.441.1814
email: trinitymoravian@aol.com
www.trinitymoravianchurch.org

THURMONT -
Graceham Church
8231-A Rocky Ridge Road
Thurmont, MD 21788
O: 301.271.2379
F: 301.271.4241
www.gracehammoravian.org

UPPER MARLBORO -
St. Paul's Church
8505 Heathermore Boulevard
Upper Marlboro, MD 20772
O: 301.627.4200
F: 301.627.4204
email: spmoravian@gmail.com
www.spmoravian.org

MICHIGAN (NP, WD):
DAGGETT -
Daggett Church
102 Old US Highway 41
Daggett, MI 49821
Mail: c/o G. Straughan
2201 Libal Street
Green Bay, WI 54301
O: 906.753.6995
email: daggett@new.rr.com

UNIONVILLE -
Unionville Church
2711 Cass Street
Unionville, MI 48767
O: 989.674.8686
F: 989.674.0115
email: office@unionvillemoravian.org
www.unionvillemoravian.org

WESTLAND -
Grace Church
31133 Hively Avenue
Westland, MI 48185
O/F: 734.721.9290
email: gracemoravian@gmail.com

MINNESOTA (NP, WD):
ALTURA -
Our Savior's Church
PO Box 161
Altura, MN 55910-0161
O: 507.796.5612
email: osmoravian@centurylink.net
www.oursaviorsmoravian.org

CHASKA -
Chaska Church
115 E 4th Street
Chaska, MN 55318
O: 952.448.4000
F: 952.448.6016
email: chaskamoravian@embarqmail.com
www.chaskamoravian.org

MAPLE GROVE -
Christ's Community Church
13250 93rd Avenue
Maple Grove, MN 55369
O: 763.420.7187
email:
christscommunitymoravian@gmail.com
www.ccc-mg.org

NORTHFIELD -
Northfield (Main Street) Church
713 Division Street
Northfield, MN 55057
O: 507.645.7566
email:
mainstreetmoravianchurch@yahoo.com

SAINT CHARLES -
Berea Church
1270 Berea Drive
St. Charles, MN 55972
Mail: PO Box 402
Saint Charles, MN 55972-0402
O: 507.932.3584

VICTORIA -
Lake Auburn Church
7460 Victoria Drive
PO Box 160
Victoria, MN 55386
O/F: 952.443.2051
email:
lakeauburnchurch@centurylink.net
www.lakeauburnchurch.embarqspace.com

WACONIA -
Waconia Church
209 East 2nd Street
Waconia, MN 55387
O: 952.442.2920
email: wmoravian@gmail.com
www.waconiamoravian.org

NEW JERSEY (NP, ED):
CINNAMINSON -
Palmyra Church
1921 Cinnaminson Avenue
Cinnaminson, NJ 08077
O: 856.829.2886
email: palmyramoravian@gmail.com
www.palmyramoravian.org

EGG HARBOR -
Egg Harbor City Church
245 Boston Avenue
Egg Harbor City, NJ 08215
O: 609.965.1920
www.moravianchurchehc.org

RIVERSIDE -
First Church
228 East Washington Street
Riverside, NJ 08075-3629
O: 856.461.0132
F: 856.764.7032
email: riversidemoravian@verizon.net
www.riversidemoravian.org

UNION -
Battle Hill Church
777 Liberty Avenue
Union, NJ 07083
O: 908.686.5262
F: 908.378.5866
email: bhmoravian@verizon.net

NEW YORK (NP, ED):
BRONX -
Tremont Terrace Church
1621 Pilgrim Avenue
Bronx, NY 10461
O: 718.829.2156
F: 718.829.0044
email: tremontterrace@verizon.net

BROOKLYN -
Fellowship Church (Meeting at Church of the Evangel U.C.C.)
1950 Bedford Avenue
Brooklyn, NY 11225
O: 718.287.7200

John Hus Church
153 Ocean Avenue
Brooklyn, NY 11225
O: 718.856.2200
F: 718.856.2201
email: johnhusmoravian@optonline.net
www.johnhusmoravianchurch.com

NEW YORK -
First Church
154 Lexington Avenue
New York, NY 10016
Mail: PO Box 1874
Murray Hill Station
New York, NY 10156-0609
O: 212.683.4219
F: 212.683.9734
email: firstmoravian@verizon.net

United Church
200 East 127th Street
New York, NY 10035
Mail: PO Box 90
New York, NY 10035-0090
O: 212.722.2109
F: 212.987.2818
email: unitedmoravian@gmail.com
www.unitedmoravian.org

QUEENS -
Grace Church
178-38 137th Avenue
Springfield Gardens
Queens, NY 11434
O: 718.723.2681
F: 718.723.4288
email: info@gracemoravianchurchny.org
www.gracemoravianchurchny.org

STATEN ISLAND -
Castleton Hill Church
1657 Victory Boulevard
Staten Island, NY 10314
O: 718.442.5215 or 718.442.5309
F: 718.442.5211
email: office@castletonhill.org
www.castletonhill.org

Great Kills Church
62 Hillside Terrace
Staten Island, NY 10308
O: 718.317.7788
F: 718.356.2826
email: office@greatkillsmoravian.org
www.greatkillsmoravian.org

New Dorp Church
2205 Richmond Road
Staten Island, NY 10306-2557
O: 718.351.0090
F: 718.351.0290
email:
ndmcthree.moravian@verizon.net
www.newdorpmoravian.org

Vanderbilt Avenue Church
285 Vanderbilt Avenue
Staten Island, NY 10304
O: 718.447.2966
email: office@vanderbiltmoravian.org
www.vanderbiltmoravian.org

NORTH CAROLINA (SP):
ADVANCE -
Macedonia Church
700 NC Highway 801 N
Advance, NC 27006
O: 336.998.4394
F: 336.940.5317
email: macedonia@yadtel.net
www.macedoniamoravian.org

BETHANIA -
Bethania Church
5545 Main Street
Bethania, NC 27010
Mail: PO Box 170
Bethania, NC 27010-0170
O: 336.922.1284
F: 336.922.1294
email:
bethaniamoravian@triad.twcbc.com
www.bethaniamoravian.org

CHARLOTTE -
Little Church on the Lane
522 Moravian Lane
Charlotte, NC 28207
O: 704.334.1381
F: 704.333.2281 (call first)
www.littlechurchonthelane.com

Peace Church
4418 Rea Road
Charlotte, NC 28226
O: 704.759.9939
F: 704.927.1688
email: general@peacemoravian.com
www.peacemoravian.com

CLEMMONS -
Clemmons Church
3535 Spangenberg Avenue
Clemmons, NC 27012
Mail: PO Box 730
Clemmons, NC 27012
O: 336.766.6273
F: 336.766.3794
email: Office@clemmonsmoravian.org
www.clemmonsmoravian.org

DURHAM -
Christ the King Church
4405 Hope Valley Road
Durham, NC 27707
O: 919.489.1711
F: 919.419.0032
email: office@ctkhome.org
www.ctkhome.org

EDEN -
Leaksville Church
712 McConnell Street
Eden, NC 27288
Mail: PO Box 35
Eden, NC 27289
O: 336.623.9440
email: leaksvillemoravian@gmail.com
www.leaksvillemoravianchurch.org

GREENSBORO -
First Church
304 South Elam Avenue
Greensboro, NC 27403
O: 336.272.2196
F: 336.275.7800
email: office@greensboromoravian.org
www.greensboromoravian.org

HUNTERSVILLE -
New Beginnings Church
203 Seagle Street
Huntersville, NC 28078
Mail: PO Box 2278
Huntersville, NC 28070-2278
O: 704.992.2003
F: 704.992.2002
email: newbeginnings100@bellsouth.net
www.newbeginningsmoravian.org

KERNERSVILLE -
Good Shepherd Church
PO Box 2377
Kernersville, NC 27284-2377
O: 336.993.6633
F: 336.993.6633 (call first)
email:
secretary@goodshepherdmoravian.com
www.goodshepherdmoravian.com

Kernersville Church
504 South Main Street
Kernersville, NC 27284
O: 336.993.3620
F: 336.993.7052
email: kmchurch@embarqmail.com
www.kernersvillemoravian.org

KING -
King Church
228 West Dalton Road
King, NC 27021
O: 336.283.5322
email: office@kingmoravianchurch.org
www.kingmoravianchurch.org

LEWISVILLE -
Unity Church
8300 Concord Church Road
Lewisville, NC 27023
O: 336.945.3801 or 336.945.3877
email: unitymc@windstream.net
www.unitymoravian.org

LEXINGTON -
Enterprise Church
2733 Enterprise Church Road
Lexington, NC 27295-9233
O: 336.764.1281
email: emcpastor@bellsouth.net

MAYODAN -
Mayodan Church
104 South 3rd Avenue
Mayodan, NC 27027
Mail: PO Box 245
Mayodan, NC 27027-0245
O: 336.548.2645
F: 336.548.2645 (call first)
email:
mayodanmoravian@triad.twcbc.com

MT. AIRY -
Grace Church
1401 North Main Street
Mt. Airy, NC 27030
O: 336.786.5627
F: 336.786.2896
email:
office@gracemoravianchurch.org
www.gracemoravianchurch.org

NEWTON -
New Hope Church
2897 Sandy Ford Road
Newton, NC 28658
O: 828.294.4802
F: 828.294.1237
email: newhopemoravian@gmail.com
www.newhopemoravian.org

OAK RIDGE -
Moravia Church
2920 Oak Ridge Road
Oak Ridge, NC 27310
O/F: 336.643.5166
email: moraviamoravian@att.net
www.moraviachurch.org

RALEIGH -
Raleigh Church
1816 Ridge Road
Raleigh, NC 27607
O: 919.787.4034
F: 919.787.4250
email: office@raleighmoravian.org
www.raleighmoravian.org

RURAL HALL -
Mizpah Church
3165 Mizpah Church Road
Rural Hall, NC 27045
O: 336.924.1661
email:
mizpahmoravianchurch@windstream.net
www.mizpahmoravianchurch.org

Rural Hall Church
7939 Broad Street
Rural Hall, NC 27045
Mail: PO Box 487
Rural Hall, NC 27045-0487
O: 336.969.9488
F: 336.450.1535
email: secretary@rhmc.org
www.rhmc.org

WALNUT COVE -
Fulp Church
1556 US 311 Highway South
Walnut Cove, NC 27052
O/F: 336.591.7940
email: fulpmoravian@embarqmail.com
www.fulpmoravian.org

WILMINGTON -
Covenant Church
4126 South College Road
Wilmington, NC 28412
O/F: 910.799.9256
email: office@covenantmoravian.org

WINSTON-SALEM -
Advent Church
1514 West Clemmonsville Road
Winston-Salem, NC 27127
O: 336.788.4951
F: 336.788.0739
email: amchurch@triad.rr.com
www.adventmoravian.org

Ardmore Church
2013 West Academy Street
Winston-Salem, NC 27103
O: 336.723.3444
F: 336.723.5710
email: office@ardmoremoravian.org
www.ardmoremoravian.org

Bethabara Church
2100 Bethabara Road
Winston-Salem, NC 27106
O/F: 336.924.8789
email: bethabaraoffice@windstream.net
www.bethabara.com

Bethesda Church
740 Bethesda Road
Winston-Salem, NC 27103
O: 336.765.1357
F: 336.768.6977

Calvary Church
600 Holly Avenue
Winston-Salem, NC 27101
O: 336.722.3703
F: 336.724.1956 (call first)
email: office@calvarymoravian.org
www.calvarymoravian.org

Christ Church
919 West Academy Street
Winston-Salem, NC 27101-5103
O: 336.722.2007
F: 336.724.1704
email: office@christmoravianchurch.org
www.christmoravianchurch.org

Fairview Church
6550 Silas Creek Parkway
Winston-Salem, NC 27106
O: 336.768.5629
F: 336.768.5637
email:
fmc@fairviewmoravianchurch.org
www.fairviewmoravianchurch.org

Friedberg Church
2178 Friedberg Church Road
Winston-Salem, NC 27127-9073
O: 336.764.1830
F: 336.764.4524
email: info@friedbergmoravian.org
www.friedbergmoravian.org

Friedland Church
2750 Friedland Church Road
Winston-Salem, NC 27107
O: 336.788.2652
F: 336.784.1534
email: lindalyons2@triad.rr.com

Fries Memorial Church
251 North Hawthorne Road NW
Winston-Salem, NC 27104
O: 336.722.2847
F: 336.722.2132
email: frieschurch@aol.com
www.frieschurch.org

Home Church
529 South Church Street
Winston-Salem, NC 27101
O: 336.722.6171
F: 336.723.5085
email: home1771@homemoravian.org
www.homemoravian.org

Hope Church
2759 Hope Church Road
Winston-Salem, NC 27127
O: 336.765.8017
email: hopemoraviannc@triad.rr.com
www.hopemoraviannc.org

Hopewell Church
701 Hopewell Church Road
Winston-Salem, NC 27127
O: 336.788.2289
email: hmc701@triad.twcbc.com
www.hopewellmoraviannc.org

Immanuel New Eden Church
3680 Old Lexington Road
Winston-Salem, NC 27127
O: 336.788.1561
email: immanuelneweden@bellsouth.net

Konnoak Hills Church
3401 Konnoak Drive
Winston-Salem, NC 27127
O: 336.788.9321
F: 336.785.0211
email: khmc3401@bellsouth.net
www.khmoravian.org

Messiah Church
1401 Peace Haven Road
Winston-Salem, NC 27104-1397
O: 336.765.5961
F: 336.659.6642
email: messiah1@clearwire.net
www.messiahmoravian.org

New Philadelphia Church
4440 Country Club Road
Winston-Salem, NC 27104
O: 336.765.2331
O: 336.768.5961
F: 336.765.5536
email: pastor@newphilly.org
www.newphilly.org

Oak Grove Church
120 Hammock Farm Road
Winston-Salem, NC 27105
O: 336.595.8167
email:
oakgrovemoravian@embarqmail.com

Olivet Church
2205 Olivet Church Road
Winston-Salem, NC 27106
O: 336.924.8063
F: 336.922.9005
email: olivet@windstream.net
www.olivetmoravian.org

Pine Chapel
324 Goldfloss Street
Winston-Salem, NC 27127
O: 336.723.7118
email: pinechapelmoravian@att.net

Providence Church
929 Old Hollow Road
Winston-Salem, NC 27105
O/F: 336.767.8234

St. Philips Church
3002 Bon Air Avenue
Winston-Salem, NC 27105
O: 336.770.5933
email: office@stphilipsmoravian.org
www.stphilipsmoravian.org

Trinity Church
220 East Sprague Street
Winston-Salem, NC 27127
O: 336.724.5541 or 336.724.5542
F: 336.724.1246
email: office@trinitymoravian.org
www.trinitymoravian.org

Union Cross Church
4295 High Point Road
Winston-Salem, NC 27107
O: 336.769.2411
email: ucmc@unioncrossmoravian.org
www.unioncrossmoravian.org

NORTH DAKOTA (NP, WD):
DAVENPORT -
Canaan Church
4465 159th Avenue SE
Davenport, ND 58021
O: 701.347.4730
www.moraviannd.com

DURBIN -
Goshen Church
4201 153rd Avenue SE
Durbin, ND 58059
Mail: PO Box 336
Leonard, ND 58052
O: 701.645.2466
www.bethelgoshen.com
email: pastor@bethelgoshen.com

FARGO -
Shepherd of the Prairie
6151 25th Street South
Fargo, ND 58104
O: 701.235.5711
email: office@shepherdfargo.org
www.shepherdfargo.org

LEONARD -
Bethel Church
State Highway 18
Leonard, ND 58052
Mail: PO Box 336
Leonard, ND 58052
O: 701.645.2466
www.bethelgoshen.com
email: pastor@bethelgoshen.com

OHIO (NP, ED):
DOVER -
First Church
319 North Walnut Street
Dover, OH 44622
O: 330.364.8831
F: 330.602.6711
email:
pastor@firstmoravianchurch.org
www.firstmoravianchurch.org

DUBLIN -
Church of the Redeemer
3883 Summitview Road
Dublin, OH 43016-8426
O: 614.766.5030
or 614.766.5032
email: info@redeemermoravian.org
www.redeemermoravian.org

GNADENHUTTEN -
Gnadenhutten Church
133 South Walnut Street
Gnadenhutten, OH 44629
Mail: PO Box 126
Gnadenhutten, OH 44629-0126
O: 740.254.4374
F: 740.254.4437
email: gnadenmor2@yahoo.com
http://web.tusco.net/gnadenmoravian

NEW PHILADELPHIA -
Fry's Valley Church
594 Fry's Valley Road SW
New Philadelphia, OH 44663-7830
O: 740.254.9373
email: frysvalleymc@yahoo.com

Schoenbrunn Community Church
2200 East High Avenue
New Philadelphia, OH 44663
O: 330.339.1940
email: pastor@scmchurch.org
www.scmchurch.org

Sharon Church
4776 Moravian Church Road SE
New Philadelphia, OH 44663
Mail: PO Box 385
Tuscarawas, OH 44682-0385
O: 740.922.5507
email: sharonsec@roadrunner.com
www.sharonmoravian.org

UHRICHSVILLE -
First Church
315 North Water Street
Uhrichsville, OH 44683
Mail: PO Box 249
Uhrichsville, OH 44683
O: 740.922.0887
email: uhrichsvillemoravian@gmail.com

ONTARIO, Canada (NP, ED):
TORONTO -
New Dawn Church
7 Glenora Avenue
Toronto, ON M6C 3Y2
Canada
O: 416.656.0473
email: newdawnmoravian@bellnet.ca

PENNSYLVANIA (NP, ED):
ALLENTOWN -
Calvary Church
948 North 21st Street
Allentown, PA 18104-3785
O: 610.435.6881
email: calvarym@ptd.net
www.calvarymoravian.net

BETHLEHEM -
Advent Church
3730 Jacksonville Road
Bethlehem, PA 18017
O: 610.866.1402 or 610.868.0477
F: 610.868.0507
email: adventmoravian@verizon.net
www.adventmoravianchurch.com

Central Church
73 West Church Street
Bethlehem, PA 18018-5821
O: 610.866.5661 or 610.866.0607
F: 610.866.7256
email:
office@centralmoravianchurch.org
www.centralmoravianchurch.org

College Hill Church
72 West Laurel Street
Bethlehem, PA 18018
O: 610.867.8291
F: 610.865.3067
email:
church@collegehillmoravian.org
www.collegehillmoravian.org

East Hills Church
1830 Butztown Road
Bethlehem, PA 18017
O: 610.868.6481
F: 610.868.6219
email: office@easthillsmc.org
www.easthillsmc.org

Edgeboro Church
645 Hamilton Avenue
Bethlehem, PA 18017
O: 610.866.8793
F: 610.866.8583
email:
churchoffice@edgeboromoravian.org
www.edgeboromoravian.org

West Side Church
402 Third Avenue
Bethlehem, PA 18018
O: 610.865.0256
email: mail@westsidemoravian.org
www.westsidemoravian.org

**Canadensis -
Canadensis Church**
4791 Route 447
Canadensis, PA 18325
Mail: PO Box 209
Canadensis, PA 18325-0209
O: 570.595.7114

**Coopersburg -
MorningStar Church**
234 South Main Street
Coopersburg, PA 18036
O/F: 610.282.1908
email: coopmoravian@aol.com

**Easton -
First Church**
225 North 10th Street
Easton, PA 18042
O: 610.258.6317
email: eastonmoravian@rcn.com
www.firstmoravianeaston.org

Palmer Township Church
2901 John Street
Easton, PA 18045-2544
O: 610.253.2510
F: 610.253.7401
email: pmc@palmermoravian.org
www.palmermoravian.org

**Emmaus -
Emmaus Church**
146 Main Street
Emmaus, PA 18049
O: 610.965.6067
F: 610.966.5420
email: pastor@emmausmoravian.org
www.emmausmoravian.org

**Hellertown -
Mountainview Church**
331 Constitution Avenue
Hellertown, PA 18055
O: 610.838.9344
F: 610.838.2807
email:
mountainviewmoravian@verizon.net
www.mountainviewmoravianchurch.com

**Lancaster -
Lancaster Church**
PO Box 5262
Lancaster, PA 17606
O: 717.397.9722
email: office@lancastermoravian.org
www.lancastermoravian.org

**Lebanon -
Lebanon Church**
1115 Birch Road
Lebanon, PA 17042-9123
O: 717.273.5864
F: 717.273.0255
email: lebmoravian@comcast.net
www.freewebs.com/lebanonmoravian

**Lititz -
Lititz Church**
8 Church Square
Lititz, PA 17543
O: 717.626.8515
F: 717.626.8258
email: office@lititzmoravian.org
www.lititzmoravian.org

NAZARETH -
Nazareth Church
4 South Main Street
Center Square
Nazareth, PA 18064
Mail: PO Box 315
Nazareth, PA 18064-0315
O: 610.759.3163
F: 610.759.3175
email: nazmoroffice@rcn.com
www.nazarethmoravian.org

Schoeneck Church
316 North Broad Street Extension
Nazareth, PA 18064
O: 610.759.0376
F: 610.759.9762
email:
schoeneck@schoeneckmoravian.org
www.schoeneckmoravian.org

NEWFOUNDLAND -
Newfoundland Church
Route 191
Newfoundland, PA 18445
Mail: PO Box 221
Newfoundland, PA 18445-0221
O: 570.676.8201

PHILADELPHIA -
Redeemer Church
2950 South 70th Street
Philadelphia, PA 19142
O: 215.365.6448
www.redeemermoravianphiladelphia.net

READING -
Reading Church
1116 Perry Street
Reading, PA 19604-2005
O: 610.374.0886
email:
readingmoravianpa@gmail.com
www.readingmoravian.org

YORK -
Covenant Church
901 Cape Horn Road
York, PA 17402
O: 717.755.3269
email: covenantyorkjeff@gmail.com
www.covenantyork.org

First Church
39 North Duke Street
York, PA 17401
O: 717.843.2239
email: yorkfirstmoravian@verizon.net
www.firstmoravianchurch.worthyofpraise.org

VIRGINIA (SP):
ARARAT -
Willow Hill Church
577 Willow Hill Road
Ararat, VA 24053
email: info@willowhillmoravian.org
www.willowhillmoravian.org

CANA -
Crooked Oak Church
3574 Bear Trail Road
Cana, VA 24317
email: ijeaster@ccpsd.k12.va.us

Mt. Bethel Church
127 Mt. Bethel Church Road
Cana, VA 24317
O: 276.755.4690
www.mountbethelmoravianchurch.com

WISCONSIN (NP, WD):
APPLETON -
Freedom Church
W3457 Center Valley Road
Appleton, WI 54913-8937
O: 920.734.1278
email: freedommoravian@gmail.com
www.freedommoravianchurch.com

CAMBRIDGE -
London Church
N5610 Hwy. O
Cambridge, WI 53523
Mail: PO Box 45
Cambridge, WI 53523-0045
O: 608.764.1482
email:
pastor@londonmoravianchurch.org

DEFOREST -
Christian Faith Church
805 East Holum Street
DeForest, WI 53532
O: 608.846.5876
email: cfmcoffice@gmail.com
www.cfmoravianchurch.org

EPHRAIM -
Ephraim Church
9970 Moravia Street
Ephraim, WI 54211
Mail: PO Box 73
Ephraim, WI 54211-0073
O: 920.854.2804
email: worship@ephraimmoravian.org
www.ephraimmoravian.org

GREEN BAY -
West Side Church
1707 South Oneida Street
Green Bay, WI 54304
O: 920.499.4433
F: 920.499.9966
email: office@wsmoraviangb.org
www.wsmoraviangb.org

LAKE MILLS -
Lake Mills Church
301 College Street
Lake Mills, WI 53551
O: 920.648.5412
F: 920.648.3669
email: lmmc3@frontier.com
www.lakemillsmoravianchurch.org

MADISON -
Glenwood Church
725 Gilmore Street
Madison, WI 53711
O: 608.233.8709
F: 608.233.2595
email: glenwoodmoravian@tds.net
www.glenwoodmoravian.org

Lakeview Church
3565 Tulane Avenue
Madison, WI 53714
O: 608.249.1973
email: lakeviewrev@sbcglobal.net
www.lakeviewmoravianchurch.org

PITTSVILE -
Veedum Church
County Road E
Pittsville, WI 54466
Mail: PO Box 244
Pittsville, WI 54466-0244
O: 715.884.6911

RUDOLPH -
Rudolph Church
1490 Main Street
Rudolph, WI 54475
Mail: PO Box 144
Rudolph, WI 54475-0144
O: 715.435.3333
email: rmchurch@solarus.net

SISTER BAY -
Sister Bay Church
10924 Old Stage Road
Sister Bay, WI 54234
O: 920.854.4080
email: sbmcoffice@dcwis.com
www.sisterbaymoravianchurch.org

STURGEON BAY -
Sturgeon Bay Church
323 South 5th Avenue
Sturgeon Bay, WI 54235
O: 920.743.6218
F: 920.743.0440
email: sbmc@sbmoravian.org
www.sbmoravian.org

WATERTOWN -
Ebenezer Church
N8095 High Road
Watertown, WI 53094
Mail: N8071 High Road
Watertown, WI 53094
O: 920.206.0222
email: emc1853@aol.com
www.ebenezermoravianchurch.org

Watertown Church
510 Cole Street
Watertown, WI 53094
O: 920.261.7494
F: 920.206.9030
email: info@watertownmoravianchurch.org
www.watertownmoravianchurch.org

WISCONSIN RAPIDS -
Kellner Church
Junction of County Hwys U and W
Wisconsin Rapids, WI 54494
Mail: 8016 County Road FF
Wisconsin Rapids, WI 54494
O: 715.423.2688

Saratoga Church
11131 52nd Street South
Wisconsin Rapids, WI 54494
O: 715.325.3081
email: smoravch@wctc.net

Wisconsin Rapids Church
310 First Avenue South
Wisconsin Rapids, WI 54495-4155
O: 715.423.0180
email: moravian@wctc.net
www.wrmoravian.org

NEW & EMERGING MINISTRIES

ALBERTA, CANADA:
Sherwood Park
The Connection
The Common Ground Alberta
Community Cafe
The Rev. Ian Edwards &
The Rev. Dr. Eileen Edwards
Church Planters
15 Davy Crescent
Sherwood Park, AB T8H 1P3
Canada
www.commongroundcommunitycafe.org

MINNESOTA:
St. Michael
Safe Harbor Church
The Rev. David Glasser
Church Planter
9702 41st Street NE
St. Michael, MN 55376

Meeting location:
10904 57th Street NE
Albertville, MN 55301
O: 763.497.9024
email: dave@safeharbor-church.net
www.safeharbor-church.net

NORTH CAROLINA:
Winston-Salem
Come and Worship
The Rev. Brad Bennett
395 Janet Ave.
Winston-Salem, NC 27104

Meeting location:
Atelier on Trade
533 N. Trade St.
Winston-Salem, NC
email: bsj3bennett@earthlink.net
sam@moravianantioch.org

Winston-Salem
Anthony's Plot
The Rev. Russ May
2323 Sunnyside Ave.
Winston-Salem, NC 27127

Meeting location:
Anthony's Plot Community
2323 Sunnyside Ave.
Winston-Salem, NC
336-306-3562
email: info@anthonysplot.org
russ@anthonysplot.org
volunteer@anthonysplot.org
www.anthonysplot.org

PENNSYLVANIA:
Lehigh Valley
Esperanza for Bethlehem
The Rev. Tracy Robinson
The Rev. Rhonda Robinson
Church Planters
1522 Crest Park Court
Bethlehem, PA 18015

Meeting location:
617 East 4th Street
Bethlehem, PA 18015
O: 610.504.9127
email: pastortracy@
esperanzaforbethlehem.org or
pastorrhonda@
esperanzaforbethlehem.org
www.esperanzaforbethlehem.org

MORAVIAN FELLOWSHIPS

CALIFORNIA:
Hope Fellowship
Gina Antonio
1147 Hollyburn Avenue
Menlo Park, CA 94025

Meeting Location:
1199 East Bay Shore Road
East Palo Alto, CA 94303

FLORIDA:
Margate Fellowship
The Rev. Joe Nicholas
1880 NW 183rd Street
Miami, FL 33056
O: 305.628.2061, F: 305.625.5365

Meeting Location:
Prince of Peace Lutheran Church
6012 NW 9 Court
Margate, FL 33063
email:
margatemoravian@gmail.com

New Covenant Fellowship
The Rev. Ofreciano Julias
1621 Quail Drive Bldg 203
West Palm Beach, FL 33409
H: 561.313.3651

Meeting Location:
West Palm Beach Moravian Church

Nueva Esperanza Fellowship
Illovis Gonzalez, *Provincial Acolyte*
c/o 6001 SW 127 Avenue
Miami, FL 33183

Meeting Location:
New Hope Moravian Church

Suriname Moravian
Fellowship
Armand Sabar, *Coordinator*
245 NE 191 Street Unit #3009
Miami, FL 33179
O: 305.401.5479

Meeting Location:
Prince of Peace Moravian Church

Rayaka Ingnika Fellowship
Jose Willis, *Coordinator*
3581 Schrock Street
Sarasota, FL 34239-3403
H: 941.536.6284
email: willis1011@verizon.net

Meeting Location:
Primera Iglesia Bautista
4445 South Lockwood Ridge Road
Sarasota, FL 34231

Tampa Fellowship
Federico Velasquez, *Coordinator*
6602 North 24th Street
Tampa, FL 33610-1310
O: 813.476.7969
C: 813.431.1917

Meeting Location:
St. Paul Lutheran Church
5103 North Central Avenue
Tampa, FL 33610

MORAVIAN FELLOWSHIPS CONTINUED

NORTH CAROLINA:
Morning Star Fellowship
Cliff Dodson, *Coordinator*
34 Baton Lane
Asheville, NC 28803
O: 828.778.2411
O: 828.253.0043 (Morning Star)
Mail: PO Box 8608
Asheville, NC 28814

Meeting Location:
St. Mark's Lutheran Church
10 North Liberty Street
Asheville, NC 28801

Community Fellowship
Jack Nance, *Coordinator*
3733 Konnoak Drive
Winston-Salem, NC 27127
H: 336.784.5252

Welcome-Arcadia Road
Welcome, NC 27374
O: 336.731.8265
Mail: PO Box 397
Welcome, NC 27374-0397

Mountain Laurel Fellowship
Julia Simmons, *Coordinator*
563 Rector Road
Ennice, NC 28623
H: 336.657.3032
email: julia@dialoguematters.org

Meeting Location:
Transou UMC
2nd and 4th Sundays at 11:00am
Laurel Springs, NC 28644

SOUTH CAROLINA:
Palmetto Fellowship
Martha Stocks, *Coordinator*
105 Pine Tree Circle
Spartanburg, SC 29307
O: 864.582.1442
email: palmettomoravian@aol.com
www.palmettomoravianfellowship.org

Meeting Location:
Central United Methodist Church
233 North Church Street
Spartanburg, SC 29307
O: 864.597.0200

WASHINGTON:
Northwest Fellowship
Joan Thomas
20904 3rd Avenue South
Des Moines, WA 98198
O: 206.824.6411
email: mimisgiftbooksjoan@gmail.com

WISCONSIN:
Mamre Fellowship
Don Wegner, *Coordinator*
W5884 Church Road
Johnson Creek, WI 53038-9736
H: 920.699.3272

Meeting Location:
N9015 County Highway Q
Watertown, WI 53094

MORAVIAN CHURCH IN NORTH AMERICA
PROVINCIAL & DISTRICT OFFICES

The Provincial Elders' Conference -
Northern Province

The Rev. Dr. Elizabeth D. Miller, President
Office: 1021 Center St., PO Box 1245, Bethlehem, PA 18016-1245
O: 610.867.7566, 800.732.0591, Ext. 19
email: betsy@mcnp.org
www.mcnp.org

Northern Province - District Executive Boards

Eastern District
The Rev. David E. Bennett, President
1021 Center St., PO Box 1245, Bethlehem, PA 18016-1245
O: 610.865.0302, 800.732.0591, F: 610.866.9223
email: edeb@mcnp.org
www.mcnp.org/easterndistrict

Western District
The Rev. James T. Hicks, President
PO Box 12677, Green Bay, WI 54307-2677
O: 920.883.2212
email: jamesthicks@aol.com
www.moravianwest.org

Canadian District
Bryan Peacock, President
600 Acadia Dr. SE, Calgary, Alberta T2J 0B8, Canada
O: 403.271.2700
email: bryan@mcnp.org
www.moravian.ca

The Provincial Elders' Conference -
Southern Province

The Rev. David B. Guthrie
459 S. Church St., Winston-Salem, NC 27101
O: 336.725.5811, 888.725.5811, F: 336.723.1029
email: dguthrie@mcsp.org
www.mcsp.org

CHURCH CAUSES
Northern Province

Members and friends of the Moravian Church can show continuing interest in its work by making the Church a beneficiary in their will or by making an outright monetary gift. For the address of any corporation listed below, please see pages immediately preceding. The programs of the Northern Province are administered by the following incorporated boards:

The Board of Elders of the Canadian District of the Moravian Church in Ameca, Northern Province

Board of World Mission of the Moravian Church

Canadian Moravian Foundation

The Executive Board of the Eastern District of the Moravian Church in America, Northern Province

The Executive Board of the Eastern District of the Moravian Church in America, Northern Province for the Foster Fund

The Executive Board of the Western District of the Moravian Church in America, Northern Province

Hope Conference and Renewal Center

Interprovincial Board of Communication

Linden Hall School for Girls at Lititz, Pennsylvania

Marquardt Memorial Manor, Inc.

Moravian Academy

The Moravian Archives

Moravian Care Ministries, Inc.

Moravian Church, Northern Province

Moravian College

Moravian Hall Square Historic District, Inc.

Moravian Hall Square Retirement Community, Inc.

Moravian Manors, Inc.

Moravian Music Foundation, Inc.

Moravian Open Door, Inc.

Moravian Theological Seminary

Mt. Morris Camp and Conference Center

The Provincial Women's Board

The Society for Promoting the Gospel

Sperling-Zimmerman Memorial Home

Trustees of the Moravian Larger Life Foundation

Van-Es Camp and Conference Centre

Southern Province

The programs of the Southern Province are administered by the following boards and agencies:

The Board of Cooperative Ministries*
Board of World Mission of the Moravian Church
Interprovincial Board of Communication
Laurel Ridge, Moravian Camp, Conference, & Retreat Center*
Mission Society of the Moravian Church, South, Inc.
Moravian Music Foundation, Inc.
Moravian Theological Seminary
The Provincial Elders' Conference
Provincial Support Services*
Provincial Women's Board*
Salem Academy and College
Salemtowne
Sunnyside Ministry*

Not incorporated. Bequests to these boards and agencies should be made for their use to the Moravian Church in America, Southern Province.

REMITTANCES
Contributions for provincial or general church causes should be sent to the provincial treasurer:

NORTHERN PROVINCE: Christina Giesler, Controller
1021 Center Street, PO Box 1245, Bethlehem, PA 18018-1245

SOUTHERN PROVINCE: Dennis Stanfield, Treasurer
459 South Church Street, Winston-Salem, NC 27101

PLANNED GIFTS AND BEQUESTS: For information about estate plans or information about charitable trusts, annuities and other forms of planned gifts to support one or more of the above ministries or your church, contact
Paul McLaughlin, President
Moravian Ministries Foundation
119 Brookstown Ave., Suite 305,
Winston-Salem, NC 27101
Phone: 1.888.722.7923

PRAYER DAYS AND SPECIAL EMPHASES

The following prayer days or special emphases have been authorized by the Northern Provincial Synod or by the Provincial Elders' Conferences of the Northern and Southern Provinces of the Moravian Church in North America:

Ecumenical Sunday: The last Sunday in January.

For Retired Ministers (optional): The last Sunday in January.

For Moravian Unity Work: The first Sunday in March.

Moravian Music Sunday: Fifth Sunday of Easter (fourth Sunday after Easter).

For Moravian Retirement Community (Southern Province):
The second Sunday in May.

For Outdoor Ministries (Northern Province): The Sunday after Trinity.

For Camps & Conferences (Southern Province): The Sunday after Trinity.

For World Peace and Nuclear Disarmament (Northern Province):
The first Sunday in August.

For Public Education and Moravian Educational Institutions
(Southern Province): The last Sunday in August.

For Public Education (Northern Province): The last Sunday in August.

For Christian Education: The second Sunday in September.

For Church Development (Northern Province): The third Sunday in September.

For the Church's Ministry to Older Adults (Northern Province):
The fourth Sunday in September.

For Older Adults (Southern Province): The fourth Sunday in September.

For Children: A Sunday in October.

For World Mission: The second Sunday in October.

For Peace with Justice and Freedom (Northern Province):
The third Sunday in October.

Moravian Women's Sunday (Northern Province):
The first Sunday in November (date optional).

For the Bible Society: The Sunday before Thanksgiving.

For Moravian College and Theological Seminary (Northern Province):
The Sunday on or immediately after November 20.

World AIDS Day: December 1.

THE UNITAS FRATRUM
(International Moravian Church)
for the year ending December 31, 2013 Provided by the Chair of the Unity Board

Province	C	O	M	COM	T
Alaska	22	2	10	---	1,900
America, North	93	6	104	17,044	20,947
America, South	56	11	60	13,102	15,703
Burundi***	---	---	45	---	40,000
Congo	80	---	---	---	21,600
Costa Rica	2	3	4	---	600
Cuba***	8	15	4	---	600
Czech Republic	28	---	46	---	5,211
Czech Mission Province**/*	9	7	11	---	650
Eastern West Indies	51	3	46	---	15,400
European Continental*	24	28	50	---	15,000
Garifuna***/*	---	---	---	---	9,000
Great Britain	30	---	22	---	1,500
Guyana**	8	---	3	---	1,026
Haiti	7	---	---	---	4,500
Honduras	125	---	30	---	25,000
Honduras Mission Province**/*	74	---	27	---	16,868
Jamaica & Cayman Islands	65	---	34	5,446	7,897
Kenya***	---	---	---	---	600
Labrador**/*	4	---	1	---	1,900
Malawi	10	11	5	---	5,190
Nicaragua	226	---	100	---	97,000
Peru***	---	5	4	---	50
Ruvuma & Njombe***	9	4	12	1,389	1,552
Rwanda***	---	---	5	---	5,000
Sierra Leone**	2	1	2	120	185
South Africa	87	176	67	32,672	42,000
South Asia*	5	---	3	---	385
Suriname	67	---	28	---	60,000
Tanzania, East**	56	10	58	10,431	23,683
Tanzania, Kigoma	30	---	43	---	30,204
Tanzania, Northern	25	3	34	---	3,905
Tanzania, Rukwa	51	405	---	33,832	60,037
Tanzania, Southern	164	---	153	109,544	180,124
Tanzania, South West	208	42	469	---	530,008
Tanzania, Western	61	270	85	---	110,000
Uganda***/*	5	3	---	---	102
Zambia**	17	49	13	---	7,884
Zanzibar***	1	4	1	---	155
Total, Dec, 31, 2013	**1,710**	**1,058**	**1,579**	**223,580**	**1,363,366**

C = Congregations
O = Outstations
M = Ordained Ministers
COM = Communicants
T = Total Membership

* no membership statistics received for 2013
** Mission Province
*** Mission Area

OFFICIAL HEADS OF FULL UNITY PROVINCES COMPRISING THE MORAVIAN UNITY

Phone numbers do not include international access code numbers. The international direct dial access code from U.S. phones is 011 except for calls to Labrador, Eastern West Indies, and Jamaica.

President of the Unity Board
The Rev. Robert Hopcroft
President, Great Britain and Ireland
Moravian Church House
5-7 Muswell Hill
London N10 3TJ United Kingdom
O: 44.208.883.3409
F: 44.208.365.3371
email:
Robert.Hopcroft@moravian.org.uk
www.unitasfratrum.org

Unity Business Administrator
The Rev. Dr. Jørgen Bøytler, Ph.D.
Lindegade 26
DK-6070 Christiansfeld
Denmark
O: 45.7456.1420
C: 45.4036.1420
email: boytler@ebu.de

Alaska
The Rev. Peter Green
PO Box 545
371 Third Avenue
Bethel, AK 99559-0545
O: 907.543.2478
F: 907.543.3942
email:
petergreen@alaskamoravianchurch.org
www.alaskamoravian.org

America (North)
The Rev. Dr. Elizabeth D. Miller
1021 Center Street
PO Box 1245
Bethlehem, PA 18016-1245
O: 610.865.3137
F: 610.866.9223
email: betsy@mcnp.org
www.mcnp.org

America (South)
The Rev. David Guthrie
459 South Church Street
Winston-Salem, NC 27101
O: 336.725.5811
F: 336.723.1029
email: dguthrie@mcsp.org
www.mcsp.org

D. R. Congo
The Rev. Moise M. Tshimanga
Eglise Morave au Congo
PO Box 126
Muene-Ditu, Congo
O: 24.381.603.0558
email: tshimangamoise@yahoo.fr

Costa Rica
Dr. Leopold Pixley, Ph.D.
Iglesia Morava en Costa Rica
Apartado Postal 2140-1002
Paseo de los Estudiantes
San José, Costa Rica
Central America
O/F: 506.227.1542
email: lpixley@costarricense.cr

Czech Republic
The Rev. Peter Krasny
Bozeny Nemcove 54/9
CZ 460 05 Liberec V
Czech Republic
O: 420.484.847916
email: krasny@jbcr.info
www.jbcr.info

Eastern West Indies
The Rev. Dr. Cortroy Jarvis
Cashew Hill
PO Box 504
St. John's Antigua, West Indies
O: 268.560.0185
F: 268.462.0643
email: cjarvis.ewip@gmail.com
www.moravians.net

European Continental
The Rev. Frieder Vollprecht
Badwasen 6
D-73087 Bad Boll, Germany
O: 49.7164.942130
F: 49.7164.942199
email: frieder.vollprecht@bb.ebu.de
www.ebu.de

Great Britain and Ireland
The Rev. Robert Hopcroft
Moravian Church House
5-7 Muswell Hill
London N10 3TJ United Kingdom
O: 44.208.883.3409
F: 44.208.365.3371
email:
Robert.Hopcroft@moravian.org.uk
or office@moravian.org.uk
www.moravian.org.uk

Honduras
The Rev. Isai Granwell
Iglesia Morava, Puerto Lempira
Depto. Gracias a Dios
Honduras, Central America
O: 504.9851.6850
F: 504.441.0627
email: hdmoravian1930@yahoo.com

Jamaica & the Cayman Islands
The Rev. Dr. Paul Gardner
The Moravian Church Office
PO Box 8369
3 Hector Street
Kingston CSO
Jamaica, West Indies
O: 876.928.1861
F: 876.928.8336
email: moravianchurch@cwjamaica.com
www.jamaicamoravian.org

Malawi
The Rev. Henry Mwakibinga
Moravian Church in Malawi
PO Box 119
Karonga, Malawi
email: moravian_cmm@yahoo.com

Nicaragua
The Rev. Cora Antonio
Iglesia Morava en Nicaragua
Puerto Cabezas RAAN Nicaragua
Central America
O/F: 505.792.2222
M: 505.835547
email: gonzalomoravo@gmail.com

South Africa
The Rev. Lennox Mcubusi
PO Box 24111
Lansdowne
7780 South Africa
O: 27.21.761.4030
F: 27.21.761.4046
email: mcsa@iafrica.com

Suriname
The Rev. Reynard Pansa
Evangelische Broeder Gemeente
PO Box 1811 Maagdenstraat 50
Paramaribo, Suriname
South America
O: 597.473073
F: 597.475794
email: ebgs@sr.net or
renoldpansa@yahoo.com
www.moravianchurch.sr

Tanzania, Kigoma
The Rev. Charles Katale
Lake Tanganyika Mission Province
PO Box 1267
Kigoma, Tanzania
email: revckatale@yahoo.com

Tanzania, Northern
The Rev. Peter Malema
PO Box 12320
Arusha, Tanzania
O/F: 255.27.250.7901
email: mcnt2007@yahoo.com

Tanzania (Rukwa)
The Rev. Nebort Kipeta Sikazwe
PO Box 378
Sumbawanga Rukwa
Tanzania, East Central Africa
O: 255.25.280.2714
F: 255.25.280.2079
email: sikazwenebort@yahoo.com

Tanzania (Southern)
The Rev. Clement Mwaitebele
Moravian Church in Tanzania
PO Box 32
Rungwe Tukuyu
Tanzania, East Central Africa
O: 255.25.255.2030
F: 255.25.255.2298
email: ctebele@yahoo.co.uk

Tanzania (Southwest)
The Rev. Nonsigwe Buya
PO Box 377
2643 Mbeya
Tanzania, East Central Africa
O: 255.25.250.2643
email: mctswp@hotmail.com

Tanzania (Western)
The Rev. Ezekiel Yona
PO Box 29
Tabora, Tanzania
East Central Africa
O/F: 255.26.260.4822
email: jitalazyo@yahoo.com

MISSION AREAS

*(Parenthesis indicate the supervising province -
correspondence should be directed to the supervising province)*

Moravian Church in Belize
(Honduras)

Moravian Church in Burundi
(Tanzania - Western)

Moravian Church in Cuba
(USA - Southern Province)

Moravian Church in Fr. Guiana
(Suriname)

Moravian Church in Garifuna
(Honduras)

Moravian Church in Haiti
(Jamaica)

Moravian Church in Kenya
(Tanzania - Western)

Moravian Church in Peru
(USA - Board of World Mission)

Moravian Church in Rwanda
(Tanzania - Western)

Moravian Church in Sierra Leone
(USA - Southern Province)

Moravian Church in South Asia
(Great Britain)

Moravian Church in Uganda
(Tanzania - Western)

Moravian Church in Zanzibar
(Tanzania - Eastern)

MISSION PROVINCES

Czech Republic
The Rev. Jiri Polma, *Chairman*
Komenskeho 603
CZ - 46822 Zelezny Brod
Czech Republic
O: 420.483.38923
email: jiri.polma@seznam.cz

Guyana
The Rev. Brinmore Phaul
The Moravian Church in Guyana
53 New Garden Street
Queenstown Georgetown
Guyana, South America
O: 592.226.2524
F: 592.227.4590
email: brinmorep@yahoo.com

Honduras
Rev. Salomon Ordonez
Ahuas, Honduras
email: ordonezsalomon@yahoo.com.mx

Labrador
Sarah Jensen
PO Box 220 Station B
Happy Valley-Goose Bay
Labrador A0P 1E0 Canada
O: 709.923.2262
email: moravianhv@hotmail.com
www.labradormoravian.blogspot.com

Tanzania, Eastern
(supervised by Tanzania, Southern)
The Rev. Clement D. Fumbo
Eastern Tanzania Mission Province
PO Box 16416
Dar Es Salaam, Tanzania
O: 255.715.391929
email: cfumbo@gmail.com or
moravian07@gmail.com

Zambia
(supervised by Tanzania, Southwest)
The Rev. Happy Crodwel Sikafunda
Moravian Church in Zambia
PO Box 38508
Lusaka, Zambia
O: 260.262.1215 or 260.976.051433
email: sikafunda2000@yahoo.com

UNITY UNDERTAKINGS
(Parenthesis indicate the supervising province)

**Star Mountain
Rehabilitation Center**
(European Continental Province)
Ms. Ghada Naser, *Director*
PO Box 199
Ramallah, Palestine
O: 972.2.296.2705
F: 972.2.296.2715
email: starmountaincenter@gmail.com
www.starmountain.org

**Unity Archive of the Moravian
Church**
Dr. Rüdiger Kröger, *Director*
PO Box 21
Zittauerstrasse 24
D-02745 Herrnhut
Germany
O: 49.358.734.8731
F: 49.358.734.8766
email: unitaetsarchiv@ebu.de

UNITY AGENCIES

Unity Women's Desk

459 South Church St., Winston-Salem, NC 27101
O: 1.336.725.6413, C: 336.416.2337
Rev. Patricia Garner, Coordinator
email: unitywomen2011@gmail.com
www.unitywomensdesk.org

Advisory Board:
Angelene Swart, *Africa Region*
email: angeleneswart@absamail.co.za

Sallie Greenfield, *American Region*
email: unitywomen2011@gmail.com

Muriel Held, *Caribbean Region*
email: muriheld@yahoo.com

Erdmute Frank, *European Region*
email: e.enkelmann@gmx.net

RELATED TO THE AMERICAN PROVINCES

Unity of the Brethren in Texas
James Marek, President of Synodical Committee
1304 TH Johnson Dr.
Taylor TX 76574

HISTORICAL NOTES

Organization dates of congregations in the United States and
Canada and dates of the worldwide Moravian Church:

JANUARY

1- 1815   Sharon, Tuscarawas, Ohio

    1858   Chaska, Minnesota

    1915   Waconia, Minnesota

    1968   United, New York, New York, merger of New York III and IV

    2010   MorningStar, Coopersburg, Pennsylvania, merger of Coopersburg
           and Grace

3- 1856   Ordination of John Andrew Buckley, the first Moravian minister
           of African descent, Antigua, West Indies

    1932   First service of confirmation of Moravians in Honduras

5- 1992   New Hope, Miami, Florida

12- 1757   The first Moravian convert baptized on Antigua, West Indies

19- 1964   Rio Terrace, Edmonton, Alberta, Canada

20- 1889   Wisconsin Rapids, Wisconsin

21- 1951   Konnoak Hills, Winston-Salem, North Carolina

28- 1996   Palm Beach, West Palm Beach, Florida

30- 1864   Sturgeon Bay, Wisconsin

31- 1971   St. Paul's, Upper Marlboro, Maryland

FEBRUARY

2- 1891   Bethel, Leonard, North Dakota

    1964   Trinity, New Carrollton, Maryland

3- 1957   Official organization of Morongo Moravian Church, Banning,
           California; result of Indian mission work begun in 1889

9- 1749   Warwick, now Lititz, Lititz, Pennsylvania

12- 1978   Covenant, Wilmington, North Carolina

    1989   Good Shepherd, Kernersville, North Carolina

13- 1870   Unionville, Michigan

    1983   New Hope, Newton, North Carolina

MARCH

1- 1457 Date observed in commemoration of the founding in Bohemia of the Unitas Fratrum, now known as the Moravian Church

5- 1939 Calvary, Allentown, Pennsylvania

14- 1849 Arrival of first Moravian missionaries in Bluefields, Nicaragua

1886 Great Kills, Staten Island, New York

1951 Mountainview, Hellertown, Pennsylvania

15- 1925 Grace, Mount Airy, North Carolina

21- 1993 King of Kings, Miami, Florida

23- 1975 First, Stone Mountain, Georgia

24- 1799 The first Moravian converts baptized on Tobago, West Indies

25- 1752 First, York, Pennsylvania

1995 Morning Star, Asheville, North Carolina

27- 1966 John Hus, Brooklyn, New York

28- 1954 Lakeview, Madison, Wisconsin

APRIL

1- 1756 Arrival on Antigua, West Indies, of Samuel Isles, the first Moravian missionary on that island

1888 First, Easton, Pennsylvania

3- 1896 Sister Bay, Wisconsin

4- 1773 Friedberg, Winston-Salem, North Carolina

6- 1851 Olivet, Winston-Salem, North Carolina

7- 1929 Glenwood, Madison, Wisconsin

9- 1917 Veedum, Pittsville, Wisconsin

10- 1949 Palmer Township, Easton, Pennsylvania

1988 Good News, Sherwood Park, Alberta, Canada

11- 1898 Enterprise, Arcadia, North Carolina

13- 1732 The first Easter sunrise service of the Moravians conducted in the Hutberg cemetery at Herrnhut, Germany

1760 Bethania, North Carolina

1859 Egg Harbor City, New Jersey

1885 Windsor, now Christian Faith, DeForest, Wisconsin

21-	1929	Leaksville, Eden, North Carolina
	1976	Our Savior's, Altura, Minnesota, merger of Bethany and Hebron
25-	1890	Arrival on Trinidad, West Indies, of Samuel Thaeler and John Holmes to organize Moravian work on that island
27-	1790	Arrival on Tobago, West Indies, of John and Mary Montgomery (parents of hymnwriter James Montgomery) to begin Moravian work on that island
	1852	New York II, now Tremont Terrace, Bronx, New York
	1969	Christ, Calgary, Alberta, Canada

MAY

3-	1728	Beginning of Losungen (Daily Texts) in Herrnhut, Germany
	1931	Rural Hall, North Carolina
5-	1822	St. Philip's, Winston-Salem, North Carolina
	1895	Fairview, Winston-Salem, North Carolina
6-	1860	West Side, Bethlehem, Pennsylvania
	1895	Bruderheim, Alberta, Canada
9-	1760	Count Zinzendorf dies. (b. May 26,1700)
12-	1727	Unanimous adoption of the first statutes, or Brotherly Agreement, by the settlers at Herrnhut, Germany, the first definite step toward reorganization of the Unitas Fratrum
17-	1863	Palmyra, Cinnaminson, New Jersey
18-	1902	Calgary, now Good Shepherd, Calgary, Alberta, Canada
19-	2002	New Beginnings, Huntersville, North Carolina
22-	1966	Redeemer, Philadelphia, Pennsylvania
	1983	Christ's Community Church, Maple Grove, Minnesota
24-	1856	Macedonia, Advance, North Carolina
	1878	Goshen, Durbin, North Dakota
25-	1844	West Salem, Illinois
	1986	Faith Church of the Nation's Capital, Washington, D.C.
26-	1853	Ephraim, Wisconsin
	1963	Acceptance of Saratoga Union, Wisconsin Rapids, Wisconsin, as a Moravian congregation

JUNE

1-	1895	Rudolph, Wisconsin
5-	1898	Willow Hill, Ararat, Virginia
6-	1954	Downey, California
9-	1957	East Hills, Bethlehem, Pennsylvania
11-	1857	Fry's Valley, New Philadelphia, Ohio
12-	1905	Edmonton, Alberta, Canada
	1943	Fargo, now Shepherd of the Prairie, Fargo, North Dakota
	1955	Battle Hill, Union, New Jersey, continuing the Elizabeth, New Jersey, congregation begun in 1866
14-	1777	Arrival of the first Moravian missionaries on St. Kitts, West Indies
17-	1722	Beginning of the building of Herrnhut, Germany, by the emigrants from Moravia
	1830	Hope, Indiana
	1853	Ebenezer, Watertown, Wisconsin
18-	1932	Hopewell, Winston-Salem, North Carolina
20-	1884	Arrival of first Moravian missionaries in Bethel, Alaska
21-	1621	The Day of Blood, so called because on that day 27 patriots, most of them members of the Brethren's Church, were executed at Prague, Bohemia
	1924	Advent, Winston-Salem, North Carolina
	1958	Grace, Westland, Michigan
25-	1742	Central, Bethlehem, Pennsylvania
	1747	Nazareth, Pennsylvania
	1876	Fries Memorial, Winston-Salem, North Carolina
26-	1988	Fellowship, Brooklyn, New York
27-	1895	Bruderfeld, now Millwoods, Edmonton, Alberta, Canada
29-	1924	Ardmore, Winston-Salem, North Carolina

JULY

6-	1415	Burning at the stake of John Hus, Bohemian martyr and forebear of the Unitas Fratrum
	1763	New Dorp, Staten Island, New York
	1800	Gnadenhutten, Ohio
14-	1912	Trinity, Winston-Salem, North Carolina
17-	1927	Crooked Oak, Cana, Virginia

26- 1846   New Philadelphia, Winston-Salem, North Carolina

    1896   Heimtal, South Edmonton, Alberta, Canada

30- 1747   Emmaus, Pennsylvania

31- 1752   Arrival of first Moravian missionaries in Labrador

AUGUST

13- 1727   Manifestation of the unity of the Spirit, at the Holy Communion service held in the Berthelsdorf, Germany, church; regarded as the spiritual birthday of the Renewed Moravian Church

    1837   Newfoundland, Pennsylvania

    1900   Clemmons, North Carolina

21- 1732   Departure of the first Moravian missionaries from Herrnhut for St. Thomas in the West Indies; the beginning of Moravian missions and of the modern missionary movement of the Protestant church

26- 1780   Hope, Winston-Salem, North Carolina

    2001   The Promise, Lewis Center, Ohio

27- 1727   Beginning of the Hourly Intercession

    1872   Formation of the Moravian Prayer Union

31- 1873   Castleton Hill, Staten Island, New York

SEPTEMBER

3- 1780   Friedland, Winston-Salem, North Carolina

5- 1869   Northfield, Minnesota

10- 1911   Daggett, Michigan

11- 1854   Watertown, Wisconsin

13- 1893   Union Cross, Winston-Salem, North Carolina

    1896   Mizpah, Rural Hall, North Carolina

16- 1741   Recognition and acceptance of Christ as the Chief Elder of the Moravian Church

    1858   Canadensis, Pennsylvania

    1984   New Dawn, Toronto, Ontario, Canada

18- 1768   Baptism of the first Moravian convert on Barbados, West Indies

25- 1887   Oak Grove, Winston-Salem, North Carolina

26- 1765   Arrival of John Wood and Andrew Rittsmansberger on Barbados, West Indies, from Herrnhut to begin Moravian work

OCTOBER

2- 1807   Beginning of the Moravian Theological Seminary at Nazareth, Pennsylvania, in 1858 transferred to Bethlehem

3- 1762   Schoeneck, Nazareth, Pennsylvania

    1896   Moravia, Summerfield, North Carolina

4- 1953   Raleigh, North Carolina

5- 1908   First, Greensboro, North Carolina

    1924   King, North Carolina

6- 1889   London, Cambridge, Wisconsin

7- 2002   Immanuel-New Eden, merger of Immanuel (1912) and New Eden (1923)

8- 1758   Graceham, Thurmont, Maryland

    1967   Rolling Hills, Longwood, Florida

10- 1885   Moving into the first house in Bethel, Alaska, by missionaries John Kilbuck and William Weinland

18- 1889   Stapleton, now Vanderbilt Avenue, Staten Island, New York

20- 1985   Church of the Redeemer, Dublin, Ohio

22- 1899   Bethesda, Winston-Salem, North Carolina

23- 1881   Canaan, Davenport, North Dakota

24- 1874   First, Uhrichsville, Ohio

25- 1896   Christ, Winston-Salem, North Carolina

    1914   Edgeboro, Bethlehem, Pennsylvania

31- 1858   Lake Auburn, Victoria, Minnesota

NOVEMBER

7- 1920   The Little Church on the Lane, Charlotte, North Carolina

9- 1980   Grace, Queens, New York

10- 1867   Kernersville, North Carolina

11- 1893   Fulp, Walnut Cove, North Carolina

12- 1909   Kellner, Wisconsin Rapids, Wisconsin

13- 1741 Formal announcement to the congregations of the Moravian Church of the immediate Headship of the Lord Jesus Christ in his church on earth

1771 Home, Winston-Salem, North Carolina

1893 Calvary, Winston-Salem, North Carolina

1965 Covenant, York, Pennsylvania, merger of Bethany and Olivet

14- 1779 Baptism of the first Moravian convert on St. Kitts, West Indies

16- 1924 Pine Chapel, Winston-Salem, North Carolina

1980 Unity, Lewisville, North Carolina

17- 1753 Arrival of the first Moravians from Bethlehem, Pennsylvania, on the Wachovia Tract in North Carolina to establish a settlement; observed as the anniversary of Bethabara, the first congregation of the Southern Province

1850 Fort Howard, now West Side, Green Bay, Wisconsin

18- 1930 Beginning of Moravian work in Honduras by George Heath in Cauquira

1951 Messiah, Winston-Salem, North Carolina

21- 1880 Providence, Winston-Salem, North Carolina

24- 1963 Park Road, Charlotte, North Carolina, name Peace adopted in 1999

1991 Christ the King, Durham, North Carolina

25- 1852 Mt. Bethel, Cana, Virginia

29- 1896 Mayodan, North Carolina

30- 1746 Lancaster, Pennsylvania

1986 Prince of Peace, Miami, Florida

DECEMBER

4- 1874 Berea, St. Charles, Minnesota

7- 1754 Missionaries arrived in Kingston, Jamaica.

11- 1887 College Hill, Bethlehem, Pennsylvania

13- 1732 Arrival of Leonard Dober and David Nitschmann, the first foreign missionaries of the Moravian Church, on St. Thomas, West Indies

DECEMBER (continued)

16- 1877   Fries Memorial, Winston-Salem, North Carolina

17- 1914   Reading, Pennsylvania

19- 1747   Lebanon, Pennsylvania

21- 1856   Lake Mills, Wisconsin

22- 1866   Freedom, Appleton, Wisconsin

25- 1862   First, South Bethlehem, Pennsylvania, now Advent, Bethlehem, Pennsylvania

27- 1748   First, New York, New York

    1842   First, Dover, Ohio

31- 1865   First, Riverside, New Jersey

    1947   Schoenbrunn, New Philadelphia, Ohio

To Order *Moravian Daily Texts* Contact:
Interprovincial Board Of Communication
Moravian Church In North America
PO Box 1245 • 1021 Center Street
Bethlehem, Pa 18016-1245
610.867.0593 Or 610.867.7566, Ext. 38
Or Order Online At:
store.moravian.org